W9-AZW-620

THE REAGAN PHENOMENON—

AND OTHER SPEECHES ON FOREIGN POLICY

THE REAGAN PHENOMENON—
AND OTHER SPEECHES ON FOREIGN POLICY

Jeane J. Kirkpatrick

American Enterprise Institute for Public Policy Research
Washington and London

Library of Congress Cataloging in Publication Data

Kirkpatrick, Jeane J.
  The Reagan phenomenon and other speeches on foreign policy.

  (AEI special)
  Includes index.
  1. United States—Foreign relations—1981–
—Addresses, essays, lectures. I. Title. II. Series.
E876.K57 1982   327.73   82–16434
ISBN 0–8447–1361–9

© 1983 by the American Enterprise Institute for Public Policy
Research, Washington, D.C., and London. All rights reserved.
No part of this publication may be used or reproduced in any manner
whatsoever without permission in writing from the American
Enterprise Institute except in the case of brief quotations embodied
in news articles, critical articles, or reviews. The views expressed
in the publications of the American Enterprise Institute are those of
the authors and do not necessarily reflect the views of the staff,
advisory panels, officers, or trustees of AEI.

"American Enterprise Institute" and (AEI) are registered service
marks of the American Enterprise Institute for Public Policy Research.

Printed in the United States of America

The American Enterprise Institute for Public Policy Research, established in 1943, is a publicly supported, nonpartisan, research and educational organization. Its purpose is to assist policy makers, scholars, businessmen, the press, and the public by providing objective analysis of national and international issues. Views expressed in the institute's publications are those of the authors and do not necessarily reflect the views of the staff, advisory panels, officers, or trustees of AEI.

Council of Academic Advisers

Paul W. McCracken, *Chairman, Edmund Ezra Day University Professor of Business Administration, University of Michigan*
*Kenneth W. Dam, *Harold J. and Marion F. Green Professor of Law, University of Chicago.*
Donald C. Hellmann, *Professor of Political Science and International Studies, University of Washington*
D. Gale Johnson, *Eliakim Hastings Moore Distinguished Service Professor of Economics and Chairman, Department of Economics, University of Chicago*
Robert A. Nisbet, *Adjunct Scholar, American Enterprise Institute*
Herbert Stein, *A. Willis Robertson Professor of Economics, University of Virginia*
James Q. Wilson, *Henry Lee Shattuck Professor of Government, Harvard University*
*On leave for government service.

Executive Committee

Richard B. Madden, *Chairman of the Board*
William J. Baroody, Jr., *President*
James G. Affleck

Willard C. Butcher
Paul F. Oreffice
Richard D. Wood

Tait Trussell,
  Vice President, Administration
Joseph J. Brady,
  Vice President, Development

Edward Styles, *Director of Publications*

Program Directors

Russell Chapin, *Legislative Analyses*

Thomas F. Johnson, *Economic Policy Studies*

Marvin Esch, *Seminars and Programs*

Marvin H. Kosters,
  Government Regulation Studies

Jack A. Meyer, *Health Policy Studies*

Rudolph G. Penner, *Fiscal Policy Studies*

Howard R. Penniman/Austin Ranney,
  Political and Social Processes

Robert J. Pranger, *International Programs*

Periodicals

AEI Economist, Herbert Stein,
  Editor

*AEI Foreign Policy and Defense
  Review,* Robert J. Pranger,
  Editor; James W. Abellera,
  Managing Editor

Public Opinion, Seymour Martin
  Lipset and Ben J. Wattenberg,
  Co-Editors; Karlyn H. Keene,
  Managing Editor

Regulation, Anne Brunsdale,
  Managing Editor

Contents

FOREWORD   xi
   Robert Nisbet

PREFACE   xv

PART ONE

THE REAGAN PHENOMENON

The Reagan Phenomenon and the Liberal Tradition   3
   Address to the Centro Studi per la Conciliazione
   Internazionale, Banco di Roma, Rome, Italy,
   May 28, 1981

Reagan Policies and Black American Goals for Africa   17
   Address to the National Urban League,
   Washington, D.C., July 20, 1981

The Reagan Reassertion of Western Values   28
   Address to the American Enterprise Institute's Public
   Policy Week, Washington, D.C., December 8, 1981

PART TWO

HUMAN RIGHTS AND POLITICS

Ideas and Institutions   39
   Address to the Council on Foreign Relations,
   New York City, March 10, 1981

Human Rights and Wrongs in the United Nations   46
   Statement before the Third Committee of the United
   Nations General Assembly, November 24, 1981

Human Rights in El Salvador   54
  Statement to the Third Committee on Item 12, Report
  of the Economic and Social Council, December 1, 1981
Human Rights in Nicaragua   62
  Statement before the Subcommittee on Western
  Hemisphere Affairs, Senate Foreign Relations
  Committee, United States Senate, Washington, D.C.,
  March 1, 1982
Human Rights in Afghanistan   70
  Statement in the General Assembly on Item 26, the
  situation in Afghanistan and its implications for
  international peace and security, November 18, 1981

PART THREE

THE UNITED STATES IN THE UNITED NATIONS

Standing Alone   79
  Address given at Arizona State University, Tempe,
  Arizona, October 23, 1981
The Problem of the United Nations   92
  Address to the Foreign Policy Association, New York
  City, January 26, 1982
The U.S. Role in the United Nations   99
  Address to the Heritage Foundation Conference on the
  U.S. Role in the United Nations, New York City,
  June 7, 1982

PART FOUR

ISRAEL: IN AND OUT OF THE UNITED NATIONS

Israel as Scapegoat   109
  Address to the Anti-Defamation League, Palm Beach,
  Florida, February 11, 1982
A Miserable Resolution   119
  Statement in the Emergency Special Session of the
  General Assembly in explanation of vote on the
  situation in the Golan Heights, February 5, 1982

Golan Again 124
Statement in the Security Council in explanation of
vote on the situation in the Golan Heights,
January 20, 1982

Delegitimizing Israel 126
Statement in the General Assembly at the Seventh
Emergency Special Session, April 23, 1982

Condemning Israel: The Iraqi Reactor 131
Statement in the Security Council on the complaint by
Iraq, June 19, 1981

Exacerbating Problems 135
Statement in the Security Council on the Dome of the
Rock Incident, April 20, 1982

Beyond Sadat 137
Address to the American Gas Association, Waldorf
Astoria, New York City, October 12, 1981

The Peace Process Continued 145
Address to the American Committee of the Weizmann
Institute of Science, Chicago, Illinois,
September 12, 1982

PART FIVE

SOME TROUBLESOME PROBLEMS OF FOREIGN POLICY

Southern Africa:
Namibia, the United Nations, and the United States 155
Address to the Overseas Press Club,
Waldorf Astoria, New York City, April 29, 1981

Fair Play for Namibia 163
Statement in the Security Council on the
situation in Namibia, April 21, 1981

Solving the Problem of Namibia 165
Statement in the Security Council on the
situation in Namibia, April 23, 1981

Fair Play for South Africa 167
Statement in the United Nations General
Assembly in explanation of vote on South
African credentials, March 2, 1981

Redefining Asian-American Ties   169
    Address to the Asia Society, New York City,
    April 14, 1981
Problems of the Alliance   174
    Address to the Committee for the Free World,
    Washington, D.C., January 23, 1982

Central America:
    Nicaragua and Her Neighbors   183
        Statement in the Security Council on the
        complaint by Nicaragua, March 25, 1982
    Sandino Betrayed I   194
        Statement in the Security Council in right of
        reply, March 26, 1982
    Sandino Betrayed II   198
        Statement in the Security Council on the
        complaint by Nicaragua, April 2, 1982

PART SIX

ON MANAGING FREEDOM

Managing Freedom   209
    Commencement Address, Georgetown University,
    Washington, D.C., May 24, 1981
Personal Virtues, Public Vices   213
    Address before the annual Ethics and Public Policy
    Dinner at which the writer received the
    Shelby Cullom Davis Award, Washington, D.C.,
    September 29, 1982

INDEX   221

Foreword

The papers brought together in this timely volume will be of great interest to all who are interested in the foreign policy of the United States during the presidency of Ronald Reagan. For, Jeane J. Kirkpatrick has from the beginning of the Reagan presidency played a significant role in the development and the application of the Reagan foreign policy. It is a well-known fact that Ronald Reagan's interest in Mrs. Kirkpatrick began when her now historic article, "Dictatorships and Double Standards," was brought to his attention. Ensuing personal conversations between the two only widened and strengthened the bond between them with respect to the proper place of the United States in the world of nations.

It thus came as no surprise when Jeane Kirkpatrick became one of President Reagan's very early appointments at high level in government. She was appointed to the vital post of United States Permanent Representative to the United Nations and also to the Cabinet and National Security Council. Inevitably, by the nature of all three roles, she found herself deeply involved in foreign affairs. It is fair to say that her lifelong academic-scholarly interest in political science was brought to a splendid practical fruition in her new ambassadorial status in New York and Washington.

It is in that light that the contents of this book take on unusual value. These public addresses—all of them prepared and presented after she assumed her ambassadorial post at the United Nations—not only reflect Mrs. Kirkpatrick's view of the world from her high American vantage point but also, it may be reasonably assumed, illuminate President Reagan's, for the evidence suggests accord between the two on the matters dealt with in this book.

The auspices of the addresses contained here are exceedingly diverse and far-flung. They include the Security Council and the General Assembly of the United Nations, the Senate Foreign Relations Committee, the Council on Foreign Relations, the Foreign Policy Association, the Asia Society, the National Urban League, the Anti-Defamation League, the Center for Studies in International Conciliation, in Rome, and the Uruguayan War College.

Almost equally diverse are the specific topics covered in the more than two dozen papers brought together here. Foremost perhaps is what she calls the "Reagan Phenomenon"— that is, the impact of this man's vision and aspirations for America upon the world. Her admiration for the president is very evidently deep. Ambassador Kirkpatrick deals also in one context or other with such important matters as Reagan's foreign policy in its relationship to Black American objectives for Africa, with the always complex situations in El Salvador, Nicaragua, Guatemala, and other Latin American countries, and with the Soviet occupation of Afghanistan. She deals thoughtfully and at length with the lonely position of the United States in the world, not least in the United Nations, where the formidable combination of Soviet bloc enmity and Third World resentment and envy of U.S. power and affluence leave our country with relatively few reliable allies even at best. Also contained in this book, along with a half-dozen other trenchant papers on Israel, is Ambassador Kirkpatrick's celebrated speech in opposition to what she referred to as the "miserable resolution" brought to the floor of the Emergency Special Session of the General Assembly on February 5, 1982. Every one of her speeches or papers on Israel is a very model of the statesmanship called for in our alliance with Israel. There is little in the world that is neglected. Africa, with special reference to Namibia, Asia, and the Middle East are all dealt with in one or other context and degree.

But just as there is variety and diversity, there is also unity in this important book. The unity springs of course from the author's long scholarly concern with national and international problems. But this unity is engendered also by Ambassador Kirkpatrick's extraordinary ability to fuse, to give creative union to, the moral on the one hand and the strategic on the other. She believes deeply in the kind of values which have lighted up so much of America's history for more than two centuries. She has a passionate regard for human rights everywhere in the world, and writes of these repeatedly in this book. She detests police states irrespective of ideological basis and seeks with every reasonable power to advance the cause of human rights even in those authoritarian nations with which the United States has and must have alliances or understandings of one kind or other. Ambassador Kirkpatrick is a pluralist in her view of the world, and knows full well that what we cherish politically in the United States is not now possible for all countries.

But both her regard for human rights and her pluralism are set in a profound understanding of the strategic objectives which must always govern American conduct of foreign policy. She knows far better than most of her predecessors in her high office that the Soviet Union and its minions represent a constant threat to the security of America; that behind every significant Soviet act in foreign affairs lies, however much veiled, an aggressiveness that rises from both ideological and geopolitical sources. She has a clear and unshakable realization that, while peace between the two great superpowers, America and the Soviet Union, is vital to the world, such peace can only be reasonably aspired to by a United States powerful in military resources and vigilant and shrewd in its political and military strategy in the world. Her perspective of democratic ideals and strategic reality is a luminous one. No one has spoken more eloquently than Ambassador Kirkpatrick in support of democratic ideals, of human rights in the world, but no one has seen more surely than she the crippling hypocrisy of so much of the liberal intellectual's advocacy of human rights: a stern, uncompromising insistence upon full human rights in nations we are obliged for strategic reasons to ally ourselves with, but, with this, an indifference that approaches sheer blindness to the frightful assaults upon human rights in the Soviet Union and in the growing number of countries which, spurred on by the Soviets, make the rhetoric of socialist humanitarianism camouflage for, not simply abuse, but obliteration of human rights.

In this book, Ambassador Jeane J. Kirkpatrick speaks out for America, both in the role of high official in the Reagan administration and in that of lifelong patriot and student of American values.

ROBERT NISBET

Preface

The speeches collected in this volume were selected from among those I have delivered during the twenty-one months that I have served as the United States Permanent Representative to the United Nations. Fewer than half were presented in the United Nations itself, but the focus of others was largely determined by the problems before that body, and also by my efforts to understand how the United Nations works, what shapes its agenda and outcomes, and why the United States was (and is) so lacking in influence in that global arena.

I wrote and am fully responsible for the speeches included here, but I had significant help from Rosemary Klas and from several colleagues at the U.S. Mission to the UN, notably from Carl Gershman, Charles Lichenstein, and Joseph Shattan. Naturally I desire to acknowledge my debt to them.

Statements made inside the United Nations are "official" in a sense that speeches delivered outside it are not. Both categories, however, reflect my personal views and interpretations and are, I believe, consistent with the Reagan administration's approach to foreign affairs.

I believe that the administration's foreign policy has been much more coherent, consistent, and successful than has been generally acknowledged.

JEANE J. KIRKPATRICK
Turtle Bay

PART ONE

The Reagan Phenomenon

The Reagan Phenomenon and the Liberal Tradition

It is a marvelous pleasure to be in Rome in the spring—a pleasure of many dimensions. For me the significance of this city lies not only in the beauty of its fountains and its squares, in the richness of its museums and its galleries or the majesty of its great public buildings, in its dazzling sun and its Mediterranean visage, but above all in its place in our shared history. It takes only a bit of poetic license to see Rome as the heart of Western civilization—our civilization. Capital of antiquity, capital of Christendom, home of the Renaissance and the modern mind, Rome for more than 2,000 years has reflected the essential aspects of the Western style of civilization—the rule of law, the mixed constitution, the idea of constitutionalism itself.

These and other key elements of the liberal democratic tradition are explicated in Italy's rich contributions to modern political philosophy. When I think of the Italian contribution to political philosophy, I think of Marsiglio, whom many consider the very founder of modern political thought. Marsiglio gave us the first modern version of a doctrine of social contract, with all that implies about the nature of government and political obligation.

I think of Machiavelli, who not only understood better than anyone before or since the tactics of winning and keeping power but also understood the spiritual aspects of society and politics, the dynamics of political change, and the inestimable advantages of republican government.

I think of Benedetto Croce, who so effectively illuminated aspects of freedom, nationality, and the modern temper.

Address to the Centro Studi per la Conciliazione Internazionale, Banco di Roma, Rome, Italy, May 28, 1981.

3

I think of Gaetano Mosca, whose analyses of the relations among social structure, culture, and politics made a major contribution to our understanding of social process and political change.

I think too of a contemporary political philosopher whom some of you doubtless know—Giovanni Sartori—whose writings, especially on democracy, are, I believe, the most profound since those of John Stuart Mill.

Without turning our meeting into a seminar, I want to underscore my strong personal appreciation of the Italian contribution to political philosophy. I value it not simply because it is part of our heritage but because it illuminates the essence of the Western, liberal political tradition.

Italian thinkers at least since Machiavelli have understood so well and depicted so clearly politics as a *human* activity, carried on by persons who have purposes, plans, skills, and visions of the public good. This interpretation of politics, sometimes called "hominocentric," is, finally, the only interpretation consistent with democracy, because democracy must conceive human beings as thinking beings capable of knowing their own interests, capable of acting on them, and not as blind automatons reflecting impersonal, superhuman "forces" of history.

When writers in the Italian tradition emphasize the human, purposive aspects of politics and the essential autonomy of the political sphere—as some of us in political science in the United States say, "the primacy of politics"—they tacitly place themselves on one side of the great ideological divide that in our time separates what we have come to call the "East," meaning the Soviet Union and associated subordinate states, from what we call the "Western" democracies, a category that includes Japan.

Because the Communist movement—within countries such as Italy and France and internationally—has quite deliberately sought to identify itself with the symbols of the liberal democratic tradition and to postulate a positive relationship to that tradition, there is confusion about the intellectual foundations and the moral commitments of the liberal democratic tradition on the one hand and the Marxist-Leninist, Communist movement on the other. This relationship is often presented as complementary, when it is in truth antithetical, and this fact—that the liberal democratic and the Marxist-Leninist traditions are antithetical in their conceptions of human life and politics as well as in their practices—has great practical importance for contemporary international relations.

The contrast between these approaches, the liberal democratic and the Marxist-Leninist, is not "merely" theoretical, as some nonacademic people like to believe. In Italy, I know, there is a larger appreciation generally among men of affairs of the importance of ideas to the domain of practical politics. There is doubtless more appreciation of the fact that the different intellectual approaches of the two movements dominant in our time have great practical consequences that may be clearly observed in the contest between the Soviet Union and those nations over which it maintains hegemony on the one hand and the alliance that links Italy, the United States, and the other Western democracies on the other.

The practical consequences of these alternative approaches may be observed in the attitudes and the practices of the two groups toward themselves, toward relations within their respective alliances, toward the rest of the world, toward the arms race, toward arms control negotiations. I propose to review briefly the essential differences between the liberal and the Marxist-Leninist approaches, what these differences mean to the administration of Ronald Reagan, and some of their implications for the conduct of international affairs in the contemporary world.

Basic Approaches

The liberal democratic tradition is inextricably bound up with the long struggle against arbitrary power and with notions of liberty, individual rights, consent, and representation. Its key beliefs and practices emerged and took shape in the eighteenth and early nineteenth centuries. At the same time, new doctrines of legitimacy arose in Italy as well as in Great Britain, France, and the United States. These new doctrines of legitimacy argued that just government depends on the consent of the governed and, furthermore, that just power flows *only* from the people. They were accompanied by doctrines of representation that claimed that each man is entitled to speak for himself about who should rule and to what broad ends. This notion that men (and women) are qualified to express opinions on the composition of government and its laws was considered an incredibly radical idea. In many parts of the world it is, of course, still considered a very radical idea. The same spirit of confidence in ordinary individuals is also manifest in doctrines of laissez faire expressed by Adam Smith and David Ricardo, who argued that men worked best and produced most wealth when they were left to work for themselves, to make their own decisions about what to work at and where to do it.

Alongside each of these doctrines arose institutional practices that embodied the concern for restraining power. Liberalism has always been concerned above all with restraining arbitrary power. And liberal statesmen in all the Western countries devised institutional restraints to limit the conditions under which people could seek, win, and exercise power and to limit how long rulers could legitimately hold power. Within the nations that shared the liberal democratic tradition, the institutional mechanisms devised for limiting the powers of government were and are still as various as the nations that adopted them. They include the separation of powers, limits on terms of office, bills of rights, written constitutions, the rule of law, provisions for bringing down cabinets. In economics, institutional mechanisms for limiting power featured the market system. In culture, they included institutional guarantees of free thought, free religion, a free press, free universities.

Because a free press, free speech, free assembly (in matters pertaining to politics, at least) are requisites to both liberalism and democracy, *all* democracy is liberal democracy. There is no meaningful sense in which one can talk about liberal democracy versus social democracy versus people's democracy versus any other kind of democracy. There is only one kind of government that features the characteristic institutions of democratic government, and that is liberal democracy, which simultaneously provides reliable limits on the power of rulers, representation of the governed in all decisions about who shall rule, and a rule of law. Without those elements there is no democracy. That is why all democracy is liberal democracy.

Marxism arose in opposition to liberalism. Liberalism sees the individual as the unit of action, believes each individual is best able to judge his own interest, defines the public good in terms of the interests of individuals, relies on individual initiative

6

and individual activity to maximize wealth and achieve the greatest good for the greatest number, and conceives of history as made by the purposes and actions of individuals. Marxism, of course, conceives not individuals but classes and other collectivities and supraindividual "forces" as the units of historical action. It believes that individuals are not the best judges of their own interests but that the revolutionary vanguard of the proletariat is the best judge of the interests of everyone. It sees the public good not as determined by people discussing among themselves their own views and values; it sees the public good as moving "forward" to the "next" stage of history. And, unlike the Italian political thinkers I cited, it does not see history as made by human beings acting to achieve their own purposes. Instead it conceives history as beyond human control, moving inexorably toward its predetermined end.

The greatest differences of all between these traditions concern their attitudes toward the freedom of persons and the concentration of power. The liberal democratic tradition believes that it is impossible to concentrate ultimate power—economic, political, social power—in any small group of persons without endangering or destroying the freedom of all of us. That is why liberal democrats have always been preoccupied with developing constraints on power.

Now, what has all this to do with contemporary American politics and foreign policy? The fact is, the philosophical differences between the liberal democratic and the Marxist-Leninist traditions are intimately related to contemporary American foreign policy and politics, first, because liberal beliefs and practices lie at the core of the Reagan administration's orientation toward politics, economics, and policy; and second, because the clashing approaches to society and politics can be seen today in most of the major aspects of East-West conflict.

An examination of the philosophical foundations of the liberal tradition is particularly relevant to a consideration of Ronald Reagan, his presidency, and his administration, because the president and many of his principal advisers see themselves as purveyors and defenders of the classical liberal tradition in politics, economics, and society. In this regard let me mention a fact about the Reagan administration that has generally escaped notice: it is how relatively many academics are present in that administration at relatively high policy-making levels. The

7

presence of intellectuals in politics almost always, I think, constitutes a signal that there is something more ideologically self-conscious going on than is usual in American politics. There are more people in the Reagan administration thinking about fundamental questions than our highly pragmatic political tradition usually features.

The Reagan Phenomenon

The first fact to emphasize in considering the Reagan administration is that the elections of 1980 were in no sense routine American elections. They were not a case of politics as usual. Instead they marked a turning point in American politics, similar to the election of Franklin D. Roosevelt in 1932 at the beginning of the Great Depression. It is often said that the election of Roosevelt was a realigning election, an election in which political forces converged in such a way that persons behaved differently than they had before, realigning our political parties and transforming partisan politics for a long time thereafter. Usually when such realigning or critical elections occur, they reflect trends that have been building for years, perhaps a decade, and are finally expressed in a single dramatic election.

I believe that the election of 1980 was such an election not merely because it resulted in a Republican president instead of a Democratic one. The mere rotation of parties, the replacement of a Democrat by a Republican, is not a dramatic or seminal event in the United States. The election of Ronald Reagan was only one manifestation of the changed electoral mood. Equally significant—cumulatively more significant—were the unanticipated Republican victories in the Congress that gave the Republican party control of the U.S. Senate for the first time in more than two decades. The defeat of many of the leading Democratic liberals in the Senate, furthermore, meant that the ideological complexion of the Senate had changed even more than its formal party composition suggested. Parallel changes in the composition of the House of Representatives also occurred; here too, the defeat of many incumbent Democrats, particularly leading liberal Democrats, brought about a shift in the ideological center of gravity. The most dramatic proof of that shift was, of course, the passage in the House of the key elements of the new administration's budget. The passage of the budget resolution not only required the defeat of the liberal coalition that had dominated American politics for the last twenty-five years, but also required the defeat of the ideas about economics and the relationships between government and economics that had been dominant in American politics for the last twenty-five years.

The changing public mood could also be seen at the state level in elections to the state legislatures and in the election of larger numbers of Republicans to the statehouses. The fact that Democrats, especially liberal Democrats, were voted out at so many levels of the political system proved that a good deal more was involved in that election than public rejection of an unpopular president. Jimmy Carter's lack of personal charisma could not explain the defeat of such senior senators as George McGovern, Frank Church, Birch Bayh, and John Culver, each of whom had a political base distinct from that of any presidential candidate.

Another way that we know that a greater than usual departure from the norm was occurring is by looking at the political composition of the Reagan coalition. Ronald Reagan is an interesting figure in American politics. In his two elections as governor of the state of California, Reagan was supported by coalitions which included large numbers of Democrats. He had to be, after all, since he was elected in a state where Democrats outnumbered Republicans by more than two to one. The coalition that swept Ronald Reagan to power in California included unusually large numbers of Democrats, blue-collar workers, minorities, especially Hispanics, who are very numerous in California, elderly persons living on pensions, who are also especially numerous in California—the kinds of people who do not often vote Republican. Reagan was elected and reelected by such a coalition.

Another clue to the fact that Ronald Reagan is an unconventional figure in American politics was his own race for the nomination of the Republican party. Remember that he made an unsuccessful race for that nomination in 1976 and then a successful race in 1980. In both cases he was opposed by the larger part of what we would call the Republican "establishment." Most of the entrenched leadership of the Republican party preferred one of Reagan's opponents in the race for the nomination: Gerald Ford in 1976, and George Bush or Gerald Ford in 1980. In both these instances, in running for the nomination Reagan assembled an unconventional coalition to support his candidacy. And in his election as president he also assembled an unconventional coalition, which swept him to a landslide victory. That unconventional coalition, once again, included unusually large numbers (for a Republican) of blue-collar workers, union families, Democrats, Hispanics, and certain other minorities, including Jewish voters.

Reagan demonstrated in each of these electoral contests that he both embodied and represented a realigning force. He demonstrated a gravitational pull that tugged some people away from their normal Democratic voting habits and toward him. In understanding the unconventional political style of Ronald Reagan, it is, I think, important to recall that the president himself began life as a Democrat and remained a Democrat through the period of Harry Truman's presidency. He has said more than once that he is the first union president ever to be elected president of the United States. He was six times reelected president of his union, which was the Hollywood Screen Actors Guild, one of the most politically important unions in the state of California. He also took the initiative in organizing for the state of California the Labor Committee for Truman in the 1948 election. Ronald Reagan was not simply a casual liberal Democrat, he was a working New Deal–Fair Deal Democrat. This is rather important, because it is sometimes said of Reagan that he was the first neoconservative, a breed defined by my friend Irving Kristol as a liberal who has been "mugged by reality." I don't know whether Ronald Reagan was the first neoconservative. But I do know that the fact that he embodies a good many of the major political trends of our times—a fact that clearly emerges from his own political biography—is a factor in his appeal to so many other Americans with similar political evolutions.

Public opinion data during the years between the election and defeat of Jimmy Carter, that is, between 1976 and 1980, provide more specific evidence of the kind of sea change in American attitudes which not only defeated a great many Democrats in 1980 but created a new consensus in both domestic and foreign affairs of which Ronald Reagan's election was the most dramatic manifestation.

As anyone who has dealt with politics understands very well, movements of public opinion are always more complicated than simple labels suggest. Nonetheless, with only a bit of over-

10

simplification, we can say that the elections of 1980 marked the end of the era of the New Deal in domestic affairs and the end of the Vietnam epoch in foreign affairs.

In the domestic, socioeconomic spheres the problems that most preoccupied the American electorate in 1980 were quite different from those that swept Herbert Hoover out of office in 1932. For several years before the 1980 election, public opinion polls repeatedly showed that large majorities of Americans believed that inflation was a more important economic problem confronting them than unemployment. Taxes also seemed to many unconscionably high. American attitudes toward taxes are a bit different and a bit more positive than those characteristic of Latin political systems. Americans don't always, necessarily, think taxes are too high; but it was quite clear that by 1980 a majority of Americans thought they were giving a great deal more than they were getting from their government. In the minds of many voters, moreover, government regulation had become an illness rather than a cure. In addition, two trademarks of American industrial success—innovation and productivity—had declined. Our economic growth rate had slowed, the dollar's value was down, and the real income of American workers had decreased. Ronald Reagan's promise to "get government off our backs" found a very responsive audience among Democrats as well as Republicans, among working-class Democrats as well as among middle-class businessmen.

In foreign affairs the change in public opinion was even more dramatic because it was more rapid. The United States went through a period of psychological isolationism after the Vietnam War, but, beginning some time not long after 1976, ordinary Americans began once again to take a much greater interest in world affairs. Successive public opinion polls conducted by the various organizations, including Gallup, Roper, and Yankelovich, showed that majorities of Americans understood that U.S. influence had declined. They understood that Soviet military strength had increased to equal ours and conceivably was on the verge of outstripping ours. And in one of the sharpest turnabouts of mass public opinion ever recorded, the American public began to strongly support the refurbishment of our military establishment.

They began to support increased defense spending even if that meant an increase in the taxes they already thought were too high. Even more significant was the fact that this turnabout

11

concerning military spending and military strength began *before* the Soviet Union invaded Afghanistan and *before* the Iranian militants captured the U.S. embassy in Tehran. The fact that the turnabout began before these traumatic occurrences is important, because it establishes that the change was not merely a reaction to a fleeting event but that it reflected more profound currents in the American body politic.

The elections of 1980 marked the end of a national identity crisis through which the United States had been passing for some ten or fifteen years. This was a period of great national self-doubt and self-denigration for Americans. Now there is a new national consensus in both our domestic and our foreign affairs, and that new consensus reflects a return of the nation's self-confidence—a returned confidence in the basic decency of Americans; a returned confidence in the legitimacy of American institutions; a returned confidence concerning the fundamental success of the American experience; and a returned confidence concerning the relevance of our nation's basic principles to the contemporary world.

More than once it has occurred to me that the elections of 1980 in the United States bear a certain resemblance to those of 1958 in France—that is, to the beginning of the Gaullist epoch in France. Why? Because the Gaullist epoch marked a resurgence of French identity and French self-confidence after a period of national doubt and denigration; second, because it marked a significant departure from the period just past; and third, because the new period of national unity and identity affected both the content and the style of French foreign and domestic policy, as the new American consensus is likely to affect both the content and the style of American foreign and domestic policy.

As President de Gaulle had a certain idea of France, I believe that the Reagan administration and the president himself are moved by a certain idea of the United States. That idea of the United States does not require that we be great or grand, but it does require that we be strong and free. And that certain idea of the United States includes a reaffirmation of the basic principles of the liberal democratic tradition. The principles reaffirmed in President Reagan's vision of the modern liberal democratic state are grounded in the conviction that the state should be subordinate to the society and not the society to the state, that the market system is the most successful economic approach to stimulating production and distributing goods, and that the free individual is the source of creativity in the economic, political, and cultural spheres.

It is no accident, as the Marxists like to say, that during precisely the same period that U.S. experience was leading progressively larger numbers of Americans to a reaffirmation of the fundamental principles of liberal economics, politics, and culture, the Soviet Union—that exemplar of the diametrically opposite approach to society, economics, and politics—was itself engaged in a period of unprecedented military buildup and political expansion. During the decade from 1970 to 1980, the Soviet Union expanded its sphere of control in Africa, Asia, the Middle East, and the Western Hemisphere. The evolution of Soviet policy internally and externally suggested that the policy of détente—that is, the policy of deliberately building networks of relations between the West and the Soviet bloc—had not produced the expected liberalization in the Soviet Union, nor had the deliberate deescalation of the Western side of the arms race (including some moves to unilateral disarmament by the United States) stimulated parallel reductions in Soviet military development.

The contrary seems to have been the case. The Western nations were the ones which became entangled in relations with the East that threatened their independence, and the Soviet Union took advantage of the Americans' "risks for peace," as Jimmy Carter called them, to dramatically improve their comparative position in the military sphere. During the past decade the Soviet Union not only has continued to encourage the establishment of friendly governments proclaiming Marxism-Leninism but, more important, has set about systematically to ensure that wherever a government friendly to it takes office, the loyalty and the tenure of that government are guaranteed by the presence of Soviet and proxy troops and military advisers. This, I think, is the significance of the Soviet, Cuban, East German, Vietnamese presence in Ethiopia, Angola, Yemen, Afghanistan, Nicaragua, Kampuchea, and Laos. It is even the basic significance of the Soviet brigade in Cuba. The purpose of the troops is to ensure the "irreversibility of the revolution" and the implementation, therefore, of the Brezhnev Doctrine. The result of these unanticipated and unwelcome developments was, of course, the "changed correlation of forces" that the Soviets note with such gratification.

The return of American confidence in the nation's fundamental principles and approach, and the determination to defend these principles in the world, coincide with a period of unprecedented Soviet expansionism and power. They also coincide with dramatic new evidence from Poland concerning the ultimate vulnerability of the Marxist-Leninist one-party state, and the vulnerability of the Soviet empire, to precisely those human inclinations to freedom and self-determination that are enshrined in the Western liberal democratic tradition.

What does this coincidence of the new American consensus and of Soviet expansionism and internal vulnerability portend for East-West relations? Two consequences of the Reagan landslide for foreign affairs are already plain. One is the set of measures aimed at restoring the American economy. The other is the drive to rebuild American military strength. These two policies, clearly evident in the budget of the Reagan administration, have been endorsed already by both houses of the Congress. Although years will be required before the full impact of these changes is felt, the attitudes and intentions of the Reagan administration have already begun to have, I believe, discernible effects in the world. At a minimum, the new policies should communicate to the Soviet Union and the rest of the world the determination of the American president and the American Congress to defend the legitimate interests of the United States and its allies. The fact that giant increases in defense spending have been undertaken by a president bent on economy should make the message all the clearer.

Moreover, the rebuilding of the U.S. arsenals by a government committed to reaffirming the basic values of the American tradition means that the new U.S. leaders see a connection between American power and the preservation of freedom. *The restoration of the conviction that American power is necessary for the survival of liberal democracy in the modern world is the most important development in U.S. foreign policy in the past decade.* It is the event which marks the end of the Vietnam era, when certainty about the link between American power and the survival of liberal democratic societies was lost.

Obviously the restoration of American confidence and the rebuilding of U.S. strength do not solve the problems of East-

West relations or resolve the tensions within the Western alliance. They do importantly affect the conditions under which East-West relations will be conducted, however.

As regards the Soviet Union, the new administration shares with all previous American administrations a conviction that free societies and governments are superior to dictatorships—by whatever name those dictatorships are called. The Reagan administration, however, is less optimistic than recent American governments about the evolution of Soviet society and government and less pessimistic about the evolution of our own society. The president and his advisers do not believe that all modern societies are "converging" into ever more similar bureaucratic regimes. Neither do they believe the Soviet leadership can be seduced through progressive entanglement with consumer societies. But this assessment does not mean that the Reagan administration sees the Soviet Union and its clients states as immovable. On the contrary, President Reagan, Secretary Haig, and other administration leaders talk and act on the assumption that greater clarity and firmness of purpose on the American side can lead to successful relations with the Soviets.

They understand, as we all understand, that relations between the two blocs will inevitably be affected by the different relations of the governments of each to their own citizens and to each other. The fact that the Western states are democracies means that the policies of the Western states require the consent of their citizens—and that means that Western leaders always make policy under greater constraints and limitations than do Soviet leaders. The fact that the Western alliance comprises sovereign states independent of one another enhances the possibilities for disagreement and disunity among them. Under these circumstances it is necessarily more difficult to achieve common positions.

However, the emergence of Solidarity and pluralism in Poland demonstrates to the rest of the world and perhaps to the Soviet Union the vulnerability of governments that cannot count on the loyalty of their own citizens because they do not rest on consent—and also the vulnerability of alliances with governments that cannot count on the loyalty of their own citizens.

It is more difficult by far to achieve consensus within a democratic society or among democratic nations than it is to give commands. But an alliance based on consensus is the only kind possible for independent nations and the only kind possible for nations that are democratic. That means inevitably that discussions about weapons development and deployment, about contributions to alliances, about troop levels, about economic policies, about negotiations will be more difficult. Negotiations about negotiations are inevitable, in an alliance of free peoples. That is the way it is in our alliance, and that is the way it will be. What is important is that such discussions and disagreements not be taken by us or by anyone else as signs of weakness; they should instead be understood as dialogues among partners.

The Reagan administration understands the terms and conditions of alliance with equal partners. It is also prepared to treat nations outside the Western alliance as friends and equals and, where it seems mutually desirable, as allies. It is willing to help in promoting development and securing self-determination. It is willing to respect neutrality and nonalignment and to deal with nations outside the framework of East-West relations. The Soviet Union's efforts to incorporate nations on all continents into its network of subversion and alliance inevitably sucks some other nations into the vortex of East-West rivalries. But in Namibia, for example, and elsewhere in Africa, Asia, and the Middle East, the Reagan administration stands ready to deal with nonaligned nations on their own terms, outside the East-West framework—wherever Soviet expansion has not made those nations a part of the East-West balance of forces.

In the past decade the chief Soviet challenges to us and to our societies, to the spirit and institutions associated with free individuals, have occurred outside Europe in such areas as the Horn of Africa, southern Africa, the Persian Gulf, the Indian Ocean, Central America, and the Caribbean. In the past decade the Soviets have played an expansionist game on a global chessboard. Our freedom is still the principal stake.

The biggest difference between the East and the West is that we in the Western alliance are—all of us—fundamentally reluctant players in this global chess game. As free peoples, we have many other, more enjoyable private purposes to occupy our lives. Nonetheless, disinclination for competition must not be permitted to distract us from protecting that vision of the free society that is the distinctive glory of our civilization and, of course, of Rome.

Reagan Policies and
Black American Goals
for Africa

As a political scientist I know that about nine out of ten American Blacks are Democrats and that during the last election, when voters of the most diverse kinds were deserting Jimmy Carter in droves, most Black voters remained loyal. I also know that politically active persons tend to have especially strong, tenacious political views. I assume, then, that I am speaking this evening to an audience most of whose members are confirmed Democrats who were not exactly pleased by the outcome of last November's elections and who are not predisposed to be enthusiastic about the policies and plans of the Reagan administration.

To persuade you of the virtues of the Reagan administration's foreign policy is probably impossible; so I propose instead a more modest goal: to convince you that our foreign policy is not as bad as you think it is.

First, however, I want to say that I am delighted to be here this evening and to have the opportunity to address this forum. I have long admired the work of the National Urban League, and I have admired also the wise leadership that has been provided by your distinguished president, Vernon Jordan. Since virtually the beginning of this century, your organization has been a leading force in the effort to eliminate racial discrimination from our society. By your efforts you have made an extraordinary contribution not only to the well-being of American Blacks but also to the strength of our society as a whole.

Address to the National Urban League, Washington, D.C., July 20, 1981.

If we are a more united and cohesive society today than we were a generation ago, this is due in no small measure to your continuing dedication to achieving racial equality in the context of a democratic society.

Since it is relevant on this occasion, I might add that your efforts have also contributed—indirectly and directly—to American foreign policy. The civil rights movement has helped keep our attention focused on this nation's fundamental commitments. Moreover, fighting Jim Crow at home has enhanced the stature of the United States in the eyes of the international community and strengthened our just claim to speak on behalf of freedom.

The civil rights movement also affected American foreign policy in a more direct way. It is surely no coincidence that this movement arose and flourished during the very period when the peoples of Africa and Asia were gaining their independence from colonialism. These movements reinforced each other. Martin Luther King, Jr., borrowed the philosophy of nonviolent struggle from Mahatma Gandhi, the great leader of the Indian independence movement. Dr. King, whose picture hangs in the office of Zambian President Kenneth Kaunda, in turn inspired the leaders of independence movements in Africa. The civil rights and independence movements alike reflected growing egalitarianism and a changing world order in which both second-class citizenship for American Blacks and colonialist subjugation of the peoples of Africa and Asia could no longer be tolerated.

I think it is fair to say that the civil rights movement, which as Gunnar Myrdal understood was rooted in the deepest principles of the American creed, also reinforced the aspects of our political culture that made us more sensitive to the concerns of the newly emerging nations. As a former colony and a new multiethnic nation, we had special reason to understand nationalism and nation building. Moreover, the enhanced political influence of American Blacks and their growing preoccupation in the post–civil rights era with international questions had an inevitable impact on the conduct of our foreign policy. It heightened our concern with Africa. The mere fact that 26 million Americans trace their ancestral roots to Africa—and that the rich influences of Africa are fixed in our national fabric—further guaranteed that we would take more than routine notice of developments on that continent.

It is also true, however, that beginning in the late 1960s and continuing into the next decade, the United States and many of the countries in the developing world became increasingly divided from one another. In an important sense, this clash was the inescapable consequence of expectations created during the independence struggle—expectations that were not, and probably could not be, quickly fulfilled. It was expected that political independence would lead quickly to economic and social development and the equalization of living standards between the developing world and the advanced industrial states. But of course it did not and could not work out that way. Here, too, there is a parallel with the experience of American Blacks, who were disappointed to find that social and economic equality did not follow automatically or easily upon the achievement of political and legal rights any more than they had followed on the achievement of national independence. That many people have become impatient, frustrated, and resentful during this period should not surprise us in the least. This new challenge is more complicated than the old.

In the United States we have entered a new period whose chief challenge for women, and for Blacks and other minorities, is to use the newly available legal and political rights to win larger shares of wealth, power, skills, status, and the other good things society has to offer. In the developing world we have entered a new period in which the less-developed nations, now freed of the last vestiges of the old colonialism, confront the task of using their independence to achieve the greatest good for the greatest number of their citizens.

I believe this new period offers the prospect of a closer and more cooperative relationship between the United States and many of the nations of what has come to be called the third world. Such a relationship is now possible because attitudes toward development are changing, and there is a new appreciation in both the industrialized countries and the developing world of their mutual interest in economic cooperation.

I believe that the orientation and policies of the Reagan administration are peculiarly well suited to this new phase in our relations with less-developed nations. My theme for the evening is that the Urban League's concerns and commitments on foreign policy are not significantly different from those of the Reagan administration. Once the thicket of misunderstanding

19

has been cleared away, I think you will find that our goals are entirely compatible with yours and our methods acceptable to you. My basic message is that you are going to like our policies better than you think you do.

First, however, it is necessary to dispel three misconceptions about the administration's foreign policy that have taken root and flourished in the past six months: one is the myth that the United States does not care about human rights; another is the myth that the United States does not care about the less-developed countries and does not intend to help them; and a third is the myth that the United States government views the world exclusively from the perspective of East-West conflict. These myths misrepresent the goals, perspectives, and plans of the Reagan administration. They create distrust, disapproval, and embarrassment among Americans and inhibit our capacity to be effective in the world.

First, the question of human rights: I desire to say simply that protecting, expanding, and enhancing human freedom, democracy, and the rule of law is a central commitment of this administration in foreign policy. We believe it is inextricably bound to our national interest. All of us involved in making, securing, and implementing the administration's foreign policy believe that human rights can be, should be, must be, will be taken into account by U.S. foreign policy.

How there came to be such confusion on this point is another complex story rooted in our criticisms of Carter foreign policy. My own experience is a case in point. Greatly to my surprise, I heard it said that I thought human rights should have no important role in foreign policy. The basis of this utterly mistaken view was my criticism of the specifics of the Carter human rights policy—its failure to *achieve* its goals in foreign affairs. Those goals were moderation and democracy. The results were Khomeini in Iran and the Ortega brothers in Nicaragua.

It is not useful to continue the stale debate about the past administration's policies. What is important now is what this administration proposes. I can assure you that I speak for this administration when I say that we are firmly opposed to arbitrary arrest and detention, torture, restraints on free speech, press, religion. We believe democratic government based on free, periodic, competitive elections is the best government. We

20

plan to encourage democracy and the rule of law wherever we have the opportunity to act in a way that will leave peoples more free and governments more lawful. That goes for Africa, South America, the Middle East, Asia, wherever.

The second myth that undermines our foreign policy is that we do not care about the less-developed countries or mean to help. The notion is abroad that we in this administration don't really care about the less-developed nations because we are traumatized by East-West relations or overcome by a new isolationism and concerned only with our own national security, narrowly conceived, or because relative affluence has rendered us indifferent to the hardship of others. But, of course, none of these propositions is true.

We care about the development of the less-developed nations for both rational and moral reasons: we care because our economic, social, and political well-being are inextricably bound together with theirs; and we care because, as in the past, the American people respond with empathy and concern for the hardships of others.

The reason the theme of interdependence has increasingly come to dominate discussions in the United States of the world economy and of America's role in it is that the U.S. economy today is more than ever before intertwined with the economies of other nations. Since 1960 the combined annual export-import trade of the United States has expanded from $35 billion to $473 billion, making us the world's largest trading nation. Millions of American jobs depend on our exports to the rest of the world.

Moreover, our trade with the less-developed nations has expanded most rapidly of all—to the point where these exports now account for over 35 percent of the U.S. total. Today we sell as many manufactured goods to the less-developed countries as we do to Europe, Japan, and the Communist countries combined. Conversely, the importance to the United States of imports from developing countries—of oil and other vital raw materials and of manufactured goods as well—hardly needs restating.

In 1979, 45 percent of total U.S. imports, with a value of $95 billion, came from less-developed countries, and less than half this total reflected energy costs. I do not desire to bore you with figures, but it is significant in thinking about our relations with the developing countries that during the last five years the less-developed countries have consistently provided more than 30 percent of U.S. food imports. It is significant, too, that the United States is and has been a major source of capital for the developing countries.

Interdependence, then, is a fact of the contemporary world. So are continuing poverty, malnutrition, disease, illiteracy, and inefficiency in many societies that we call "developing." Neither the characteristic optimism of the age, nor the rising expectations of those who live there, nor public, private, or multilateral assistance has altered the fact that some twenty-nine of the world's countries still have average annual incomes of about $150 per capita, still have populations that grow faster than resources, and still remain utterly vulnerable to every natural or social disaster. More people than we can bear to think about live at the raw edge of subsistence, in societies that feature low social and geographical mobility, primitive technology, and rigid social and economic structures. And things are not necessarily getting better. The less-developed countries now expend 27 percent of their export earnings for oil; and in 1980 one-half of the developing countries grew less than 1 percent in real per capita terms.

In many societies, life is not necessarily getting easier, and it is not necessarily getting safer. Despite the widespread assumption that democracy was rapidly replacing autocracy everywhere, dictatorships of one kind or another flourish on most continents; and despite the persistent belief that modernity would somehow render people more rational and more peaceable, fanaticism, tyranny, aggression, and violence remain the everyday reality in many parts of the world, in developing and developed countries alike, not only producing a high toll of human misery but also augmenting the steady stream of refugees that is a hallmark of the turbulent half-century just past.

The interaction and interdependence of the United States and the developing countries are not only economic. Refugees from war, revolution, population pressures, natural disasters, and just plain poverty produce their impact also on our country and our government.

Self-interest and empathy alike guarantee that we are and will remain deeply concerned with the nations of southern Africa, of the Horn of Africa and its northern tier, of the Middle

East, of Southwest Asia, East Asia, Latin America, and the Caribbean—indeed, the world.

The new United States government not only cares about the less-developed areas; we are ready to help. First, we are giving direct aid, bilaterally, regionally, and through the many multilateral institutions. As I am sure you know, although the administration is seriously committed to controlling inflation, cutting expenditures, and balancing the budget, we have recommended to the Congress support for most United Nations agencies at approximately current levels. In our budget, our contributions to the United Nations system were exempt from the cuts to which most parts of the budget were subjected.

We also think we can expedite trade with the less-developed countries by opening markets and eschewing economic protectionism. This administration can and will open markets, provide access to capital markets, and otherwise work to stimulate trade and development opportunities.

We believe, moreover, that the Reagan administration is singularly well suited to help the developing countries develop— not just by giving them emergency handouts but also by providing the kind of advice and help that will culminate in self-sustaining growth. It can help make the case for a new, more realistic ideology of development, which takes account of the experience of actual countries.

The old development ideology maintained that underdevelopment was the result of exploitive policies pursued by the industrialized countries, particularly the United States. The strategy for development, therefore, centered on the need for a political struggle against the so-called neocolonialist West, which was called upon to transfer massive amounts of resources to the third world. Development was also thought to require command economies in which an all-powerful state bureaucracy would impose sacrifices upon the population. Freedom, it was held, was a luxury that the poor could not afford. It would have to be denied, at least for the present, in order to achieve equality.

Whatever one may think of this view from a political or a moral standpoint, the fact is that it did not work as a method of development and was probably counterproductive. The countries taking this course—generally speaking, countries that are part of the Soviet bloc or that practice radical socialism—stagnated economically. Moreover, their failure could not be attributed to the absence of resource transfers from the West since during this very period the developing countries accumulated debts to the West, above and beyond the help they received in the form of grant aid, totaling some $500 billion.

At the same time, there were a number of success stories. South Korea, Taiwan, Singapore, and Hong Kong progressed so rapidly that they began to compete effectively with the economies of the West. Other countries, such as Malaysia and Brazil, followed a similar upward course. In Black Africa, the Ivory Coast, Kenya, and Malawi achieved significant growth in contrast to the poor performance of some of their neighbors.

The important point about these successes is that they were accomplished in defiance of the conventional wisdom about development. Instead of fighting against the industrialized West, these countries sought a partnership based on close cooperation and mutual advantage. Rather than impose command economies on captive peoples, they emphasized market forces, free trade, and individual initiative. Where others had sought to make the state the motor of economic development, they encouraged the private sector through tax concessions to both corporations and individuals.

The case of Sri Lanka is particularly interesting in this regard because here we have a country that abruptly altered its policies four years ago, substituting as the main force for growth the incentives of the market for the coercion of the state. In the first three years under this new approach, unemployment dropped by five percentage points, and the real rate of economic growth more than doubled—despite a number of natural disasters and the escalating price of oil.

Such models of development are a source of hope, not just because they demonstrate that success *is* possible, but also because they reaffirm the importance of freedom—the very freedom that the civil rights movement struggled to achieve and which is the core value of our nation. It is especially encouraging to note the growing awareness in the world that economic liberty, far from being an obstacle to material well-being, is a precondition for it. As the experience of the Western democracies and the newly industrialized countries has shown, wealth is a consequence of freedom. It is created by innovation and experiment, by human intellect and effort; by the activity, in other words, of free, creative individuals. Freedom is not a luxury for the rich, therefore, but a necessity above all for the poor.

Interdependence and the growing trend toward market-oriented development among the poorer nations provide a particularly solid basis for a new relationship between our country and the less-developed world. Meanwhile, the lessons of experience with development and the core convictions of President Ronald Reagan and his administration coincide almost perfectly, for just as President Reagan's vision of politics features the free individual, his approach to economics features the free individual as the source of creativity, energy, and production—the source of the wealth of nations.

This brings me to the third myth that causes many people to think ill of this administration's foreign policy: the myth that we see all other countries through the lens of East-West relations. Once again, it is surely not so, least of all in Africa.

The United States government wants in Africa precisely what Africans want for themselves—a continent composed of strong, stable, independent states that are able to articulate their own interests and promote the well-being of their populations. Our interests are entirely consistent with the hopes and aspirations expressed in the charter of the Organization of African Unity.

We are, moreover, fully committed to working to achieve peace, stability, self-determination, and democracy for all the nations of Africa. We will work for these goals in all available arenas—in our bilateral relations, through cooperation with the Organization of African Unity, and in the United Nations.

The high priority that the Reagan administration gives to its relations with the nations of Africa is reflected in our commitment of resources as well as high-level attention. In the relatively brief period since President Reagan assumed office, five very senior officials of African countries—all at the ministerial level or higher—have come to Washington for talks, and we have sent a number of key advisers to Africa on fact-finding missions. I myself have spoken with the foreign ministers of at least a dozen African countries and ambassadors from two dozen others.

With regard to the independence of Namibia, when we took office on January 20, we found a situation in which all movement toward a solution of this longstanding problem had stopped. If a free, independent, democratic Namibia was to be born, a new initiative was necessary. This we have now begun.

As a necessary step to reinvigorate the search for an internationally accepted settlement in Namibia, the administration has held discussions with front-line and other African states, with the Western Contact Group, and with the South African government. In these discussions we have stressed our commitment to work for a settlement that will promote peace, security, and stability in southern Africa and self-determination and independence for the people of Namibia. To the government of South Africa in particular, we have made clear that while this problem remains unresolved, it will be a major obstacle between our two countries.

I do not know if these new initiatives are going to succeed. The problem has lasted more than twenty-five years, and we have been in office only six months. But it is evident that the old policies of confrontation have not brought the people of Namibia closer to the independence and freedom that are their due. It's time to try something new.

Need I add that there can be no doubt about where this administration stands on the question of apartheid? We have said, and I repeat here, that we find South Africa's policies of racial separation repugnant. It is our profound hope that there will be steady progress in South Africa toward eliminating it. We have not gone through a revolution in race relations in our own country only to acquiesce in a system of racial separation practiced by others. Together with the National Urban League, we support measures designed to improve the lot of Black and Colored workers in South Africa. Such measures exemplify the policy of constructive engagement that we believe will best promote evolutionary change in that country.

We are also working on what we consider very practical ways to bring progress and justice to other parts of the African continent. For example, we have pledged $225 million over three years in special economic assistance to the new nation of Zimbabwe. This is concrete evidence of our willingness to work with governments in Africa to achieve their own goals. We want to see Zimbabwe succeed, and we will play our full part in helping it to do so.

There is also the heart-rending problem of refugees. In East Africa alone, there are more than a million refugees. I am proud to say that at an international conference held in Geneva last April on the plight of African refugees, we pledged $285 million to help feed, clothe, and resettle, in some cases in the United States, these destitute victims of famine, war, and revolution. Our pledge amounted to more than half the total amount pledged by all nations.

We are also committed to the peaceful resolution of other conflicts in Africa. We welcome, for example, the recent call by King Hassan of Morocco for a cease-fire and a referendum to settle the conflicts in the western Sahara. We share the profound distress, expressed publicly and privately by African leaders, over Libya's invasion of Chad and hope that the Organization of African Unity will be able to act decisively to end the Libyan occupation and restore Chad's sovereignty.

Not least, we will continue to insist upon the withdrawal of Cuban, Soviet, and East German military forces from Africa. We are concerned with East-West issues in Africa only where Soviet-sponsored violence and military adventures force them into the forefront of our attention.

The United States was never a colonial power. But just as we opposed the old colonialism, we cannot look with equanimity upon the imposition of a new colonialism, albeit one that hides its real purposes behind revolutionary slogans. We hope that the time is near when all foreign troops will be withdrawn from Africa, and we will pursue that goal.

Under the Reagan administration, American foreign policy has recovered from a period of self-doubt. Throughout the world countries recognize that America has regained its confidence and is now prepared to exercise its power with a firm and steady hand. Power, however, is not an end in itself, but is an instrument that must be used toward an end. For the United States—a great pluralist democracy—the end we seek is a world of peace, freedom, and diversity.

In order to succeed in our policies, we need the understanding, support, and participation of organizations like your own, which have helped make America internally strong and which represent values that America must stand for abroad as well as at home. Our own experience and advantages as a nation give us a special responsibility to help others achieve a better life in peace. We welcome that responsibility as well as the prospect of working with you to achieve our common goals.

The Reagan Reassertion
of Western Values

The election of Ronald Reagan was a watershed event in American politics, which signaled the end of one major postwar period and the beginning of a new one.

This new period may be understood best, I think, as the third period of the postwar era. The first, which spanned two decades, began with the Soviet takeover of Eastern Europe and the subsequent creation of NATO and ended at some point in the late 1960s—probably at that moment in early 1968 when the establishment that had guided American foreign policy throughout the postwar era turned against our involvement in Vietnam. This first period has been called, for want of a better term, the period of the cold war.

Some critics of American foreign policy look back with dread and regret on the "dark years of the cold war" and express a morbid fear lest we reenter such a period. I must say that I have reservations about this view. In the context of the twentieth century, a century filled with horrors on a scale quite literally unprecedented in human history, the years of the cold war were a relatively happy respite during which free societies and democratic institutions were unusually secure. The West was united, strong, and self-assured. The United States and the democratic ethos we espoused were ascendant everywhere in the world, if not everywhere triumphant.

The circumstances in which we found ourselves during those years encouraged the expression of our national penchant for optimism, vision, and leadership. We were strong, we were

Address to the American Enterprise Institute's Public Policy Week, Washington, D.C., December 8, 1981.

prosperous. No country or group of countries could compete on equal terms with us economically or could successfully challenge our military power. Moreover, the major trends also seemed hopeful. With our help, our wartime allies and our adversaries had recovered swiftly from the war and had firmly established themselves as stable and prosperous industrial democracies. In Africa and Asia, one country after another attained independence and looked forward to the prospect of democratic development in close cooperation with the West. And in the Soviet bloc itself a series of political crises in Eastern Europe—in Hungary, in Czechoslovakia—coupled with an ideological crisis brought on by Khrushchev's denunciation of Stalin's terror gave substance to the hope that communism might indeed mellow if only we showed sufficient patience and fortitude. While we felt under no compulsion to delude ourselves about the inherently antagonistic nature of communism, we were confident that that free world—which was not at that time bracketed in derogatory quotation marks—would ultimately prevail.

All things change, or seem to. The conditions on which rested American confidence and the Western alliance seemed to many to be undermined by their own success. This sense that solutions to the problems of the postwar period were being overtaken by events clearly is present in Arthur Schlesinger's comment on the alliance in his book *The Kennedy Years:*

> By 1960 the economic dependence on the United States had largely disappeared. Western Europe had been growing twice as fast as America for a decade; it had been drawing gold reserves from America; it had been outproducing America in coal. Americans were flocking across the Atlantic to learn the secrets of the economic miracle. And, at the same time, the military dependence had taken new and perplexing forms. If the prospect of a Soviet invasion of Western Europe had ever been real, few Europeans believed it any longer. Moreover, the Soviet nuclear achievement, putting the United States for the first time in its history under the threat of devastating attack, had devalued the American deterrent in European eyes. These developments meant that the conditions which had given rise to the Marshall Plan and NATO were substantially

gone. The new Europe would not be content to remain an economic or military satellite of America. The problem now was to work out the next phase in the Atlantic relationship.

The hopes and expectations of the postwar period, as we now remember, were finally destroyed by the protracted and bitterly disillusioning conflict in Vietnam and by a sequence of political, economic, and cultural shocks that polarized our society and shattered the confidence of our ruling elites. It is not necessary to review in detail this second period in the postwar era, which began with the full emergence of the New Left in the late 1960s and ended with the defeat of Jimmy Carter and the victory of Ronald Reagan in the last election. Let us simply recall the major points.

This period, which has euphemistically been called the era of détente, was marked by the relentless expansion of Soviet military and political power and a corresponding contraction of American military and political power. It was marked as well by the rise, in what came to be called the third world, of dictators espousing anti-American and anti-Western ideologies and by the rise in Western Europe of tendencies favoring a neutralist position in world affairs. Not least, this same period saw the emergence of OPEC as a major economic power whose monopoly pricing introduced inflationary shocks throughout the world economy—most disastrously in the very "third world" countries that were presumably linked by experience and ideology with the fraternal oil-producing states.

Within the United States, an attitude of defeatism, self-doubt, self-denigration, and self-delusion—an attitude that Solzhenitsyn called "the spirit of Munich"—displaced what had been a distinctly American optimism about the world and our prospects as a nation. For a time the proponents of defeatism cultivated an air of superior optimism. We had, so it was said, liberated ourselves from the fear of communism and were therefore free to identify with the "forces of change" that were sweeping the world. According to this point of view, it was futile to try to resist these forces, and it was reckless to do so as well since the effort to hold back the tides of change would bring the wrath of the world down upon our heads. Far better, it was said, to adopt an attitude of equanimity toward what only appeared to be the decline of American power but was in fact, in this view, a process of mature adjustment to reality. Such an attitude, in the words of a top official of the last administration, was really "a sign of growing American maturity in a complex world."

The seizure of the hostages in Iran and the Soviet invasion of Afghanistan destroyed this attitude of determined equanimity as completely as the events of the late 1960s had destroyed the hopes of the first postwar period. Looked at from this perspective, the election of Ronald Reagan was a victory for those who rejected the idea of the inevitability of America's decline. In this respect, President Reagan's election was a watershed that marked the end to a period of retreat. Similarly, the president's inauguration—endowed with unique significance by the simultaneous release of our hostages, which closed out the most humiliating episode in our history—signaled a new beginning for America.

The new period we have now entered is, I believe, an exceedingly dangerous one—perhaps the most dangerous we have faced—and its outcome is far from clear. It is not only conceivable that an affluent and technologically advanced democratic civilization may succumb to one that is distinctly inferior in the wealth and well-being of its people. This has occurred more than once in history. The decisive factor in the rise and fall of nations is what Machiavelli called *virtu*, meaning vitality and a capacity for collective action. In the battle with totalitarianism, a free society has enormous advantages of which we are all well aware. But without the political will not merely to survive but to prevail, these advantages count for naught.

We have now entered a period when the moral and political will of our nation will be tested as never before. If I am hopeful that we can meet this test, it is because of the new situation that exists as a result of Ronald Reagan's victory in the last election, as well as because of the effective causes of that victory, and because certain changes in the world have created new opportunities for our country and its allies. Still, the challenges we must face are awesome, and it is by no means a foregone conclusion that we will prevail in the tests that lie ahead.

Probably no administration in American history faced problems of foreign policy as serious, as far-flung, and as difficult as those that confronted the government of Ronald Reagan when it assumed office last January. What are euphemistically termed East-West problems had spread and intensified, and so had those called (with equal oversimplification) North-South. Further, most of the intellectual tools we had used to approach world problems had proved inadequate and had to be discarded. The massive, unprecedented, unflagging Soviet military buildup had created what Soviet theoreticians describe as a "new world correlation of forces"—which, if it does not feature Soviet military superiority, unquestionably is characterized by rough parity. It is characterized, that is, by the end of U.S. and Western military superiority.

The meaning and significance of this new correlation of forces are found not in the painstaking estimates of missiles, throw weights, tanks, and MIRVs, but in an equally unprecedented Soviet foreign policy—more menacing to the independence and peace of others than at any time since Stalin moved to swallow neighboring states in the period of the Nazi-Soviet pact. We and our friends have been reluctant to acknowledge the extent, intensity, and violence of this Soviet challenge—doubtless because it is so very unpleasant to think about and poses problems so very difficult to manage, much less to resolve.

Northern and southern and central Africa, the Middle East and Asia, Central and South America and the Caribbean, have all in the past decade become targets of Soviet-sponsored efforts at destabilization and takeover. The functional scope of Soviet expansion has enlarged alongside its expanding geographical focus: sea lanes, strategic minerals, space, and culture have become operational objects of Soviet ambition.

Menacing as they have been, Soviet strength and aggressiveness are by no means the only important problems confronting the Reagan administration—though critics often accuse us of thinking so. North-South relations have also become more troubled.

In some of the less-developed countries, separatism and fundamentalism exacerbate the problems of nation building, making it more difficult to develop national identifications and political institutions, more difficult to maintain civic peace, stable boundaries, and regional order. In many of these countries low growth or no growth, soaring energy costs, and proliferating trade barriers frustrate dreams and plans, leaving bitterness in their wake.

It has been several decades since the expectation of progress was juxtaposed to the facts of stagnation and poverty. Resignation has given way to rage. The result is new demands, new reproaches, new rights claimed, new duties assigned, creating little growth but many hard feelings. The fact that a "right" to development has been promulgated during the past year at the United Nations creates no new economic growth; it does, however, lay the foundation for newly felt entitlements and resentments.

Bad as they are, the problems of Soviet expansion and the problems of instability and poverty in what even I have come at the United Nations to call the third world are at least familiar, and both have been made more difficult still by the decline of American power. But what *really* complicates the policy problems of the Reagan administration is the obsolescence of the familiar theories that have been relied on to deal with the problems.

Just as the cold war and the accompanying doctrine of limited war succumbed to the Vietnam experience, several popular theories about Soviet goals and policies were similarly disproved by the Soviet invasion of Afghanistan—among them, the two doctrinal cornerstones of détente.

The first of these cornerstones was the expectation that the proliferation of economic and cultural ties and rewards would function as incentives to restrain Soviet expansion. The main concept behind détente was the "linkage" of the military, the economic, and the political. The idea, as explained by Henry Kissinger, was "to move forward on a very broad front on many issues" in order to create many "vested interests" on both sides. That was the theory. Under that theory, unprecedented incentives were developed; yet unprecedented aggression nonetheless occurred.

A second conceptual casualty of the Carter period was the theory that "weaker is stronger"—according to which U.S. military superiority constitutes a provocation, which stimulates countermeasures and overreaction by the Soviets, leading them to ever greater arms efforts. It followed, then, according to this argument, that U.S. "restraint" in military buildup would quiet Soviet suspicions and produce reciprocal restraint. One version of this theory—that arms, being provocative, cannot produce security—is still heard. But the basic argument that U.S. restraint in military buildup would be matched by Soviet restraint has been stilled, at least for the present, by the weight of recent experience.

A third, related popular theory—the stimulus-response, frustration-aggression theory—also has fallen victim to Soviet expansionism. According to this theory, the Soviet Union behaved aggressively because it was frustrated by a sense of insecurity deriving from its relative weakness, much as an adolescent may be provoked to rebellion by frustration deriving from a sense of impotence. The solution to aggressive behavior, then, this theory argued, lay in creating a feeling of security by eliminating the impotence.

These theories are all examples of the mirror image approach to international relations, which assumes that all "superpowers," indeed all powers, are alike in fundamental respects, that their basic motives are peaceable and decent, and that undesirable or "bad" behavior is simply a reaction to some prior condition. Thus Soviet leaders desire not superiority but parity, not conquest but security, not power but safety.

This approach is nearly irresistible to an age and to a society like ours, which regularly deny the existence of evil and explain away its manifestations as a response of the weak to the strong. As there are no bad boys, so there are no bad governments. It is only necessary, the theory argues, to change the environment in order to alter the behavior. These theories not only rest on erroneous assumptions, but also nourish a spurious sense that it is possible to control one's adversary merely by altering one's own behavior.

Because their key assumptions are rooted in popular conceptions of human psychology and behavior, these theories have widespread appeal. A massive Soviet buildup and expansionist policies on a global scale were required to break their power —even temporarily.

The intellectual situation vis-à-vis problems of development closely parallels that concerning East-West relations. The problems of the less-developed nations persist and have grown worse, but it was clear by 1980 that the theories that have guided U.S. policies were utterly inadequate to cope with those problems.

Since World War II, when most of the new nations came into being, things have not, generally speaking, moved onward and upward, fulfilling dreams of inevitable historical progress. Polities have not become stronger and more democratic, nor economies more productive, nor societies more egalitarian and participatory. Moreover, the methods that had been widely relied on failed to produce the expected or desired results. National ownership, central planning, altruistic social incentives were all once believed to be better suited to the communal spirit of the third world. But they produced bureaucracy, stagnation, and decay instead of the anticipated economic development. Determinism, socialism, and utopianism have proved no better guides to development policy than the grand theories concerning "superpower" behavior proved in dealing with the Soviet Union. One important, I believe fundamental, reason that the foreign policy of the Reagan administration seems to many to lack a comprehensive doctrine is that this administration's policy is not postulated on these conventional assumptions. We have not postulated our policy on these conventional assumptions and theories because they have become depleted and been discarded. But if we have rejected those theories, where does that leave us? Where does it leave those of us who must devise policies and make decisions?

The answer, I believe, is that both our methods and our policies must be more respectful of historical experience and more pragmatic—while never confusing historical method with historicism or pragmatism with lack of principle.

In dealing with development, for example, respect for history means taking care to note what kinds of policies have actually promoted development, growth, and increased affluence in real societies, what kinds of policies have been associated with stagnation and chaos. In dealing with Soviet and Cuban behavior, we should also begin with the facts: facts of 85,000 Soviet troops in Afghanistan, of more than 35,000 Cuban troops in Africa, of Cuban arms, advisers, and ambitions in the Middle East and Central America, the fact of SS-20s in Europe, the fact that Soviet and Cuban armies function today in Ethiopia, Angola, Yemen, and elsewhere much like the Roman legions, which maintained the rule of a distant imperial power.

Finally, a new foreign policy must begin from the equally important, irreducible fact that the Soviet empire is decaying at its center, challenged above all by Poland's insistent demands for greater freedom and autonomy, and from the fact of the exhaustion of Marxism as an ideology capable of motivating men and women. Above all, perhaps, a new foreign policy must begin from the irreducible fact that the United States has non-negotiable goals and nonnegotiable moral commitments—and that these require our support for self-determination and for national independence, for the nurturing of regional order, for the protection of freedom wherever it exists and, within the limits of our power, skill, and opportunities, its promotion where it does not yet exist.

That being the case—that is, this being where we begin—how do we proceed? The answer must be, I think, very carefully—remembering always that we are an open society and must honor the imperatives of that society. Speaking to this point in a discussion of the United States and the West, the distinguished historian Herbert Muller offered this advice:

> It is, above all, an open society: open politically because of its democratic processes; open intellectually because nothing—no faith whatever—is immune to inquiry and criticism; open spiritually because it is never resigned, always resolved to keep working for a better future (even if by futile efforts to restore a mythical past); open, like all modern societies, because of the very technology that is tending to regiment and standardize its life, since this also assures continuous change; and open, therefore (lest I sound too cheerful), to horrors as well as wonders such as men hardly dreamed of before our century. A sober conclusion is that every person had better keep his eyes and ears open, and his mind closed only on the essential principles of his freedom, dignity, and responsibility.

And that, I believe, is precisely what we are trying to do in the construction and administration of this nation's foreign policy.

PART
TWO

Human Rights and Politics

Ideas and Institutions

Somewhat to my surprise, after an article of mine appeared in *Commentary* in November 1979—the article the president read—I began to find myself described as a leading critic of Carter's human rights policy. The surprise was that I didn't know that I had written an article about human rights policy. Such had not been my intention. The words "human rights" never appear in the article.

From my point of view that article was about the failure of a policy to produce its expected goals. The goals, I thought, were moderation and democracy; and the results, I thought, were Khomeini and the Ortega brothers. The decisive instrument of the failure, I thought and still do, was a mistaken conception of how democracy is established and preserved. It was only after other people began to describe this as an article about human rights policy that I began to do some serious reading about our human rights policy and discovered that, indeed, human rights policy had become for the Carter administration—and I guess in the minds of a great many other people—coterminous with the promotion of democratic government and of all good things in the world. Once I really began to look into it, I decided, yes, I *was* a critic of *that* human rights policy—and I've been visibly being that ever since.

Now, however, that I and a good many people with whom I share certain orientations find ourselves in office, we have an obligation—obviously—not just to think about where other people's policies went wrong but about what will make our policy work better. It seems to me that there are four distinctions that are crucial to thinking about human rights and human rights

Address to the Council on Foreign Relations, New York City, March 10, 1981.

policy—distinctions often overlooked in our time. The first is the distinction between ideas and institutions. The second is the distinction between rights and goals. The third is between intentions and consequences. And the fourth, finally, is the distinction between private and public morality.

First the distinction between ideas and institutions. It is terribly important to bear in mind at all times, I think, that ideas and words are far more manipulable than are institutions. Ideas have only to be conceived in order to exist. The idea of a right is very easy to conceive; and we can claim any right that we can think of.

Ideas are the product of the mind. Many ideas can probably never be realized. Not everything that can be conceived can be created. One can, for example, conceive a unicorn, describe it, destroy whole forests in a determined effort to find one, and still fail. One of the characteristics of ideas, of words, is that they are highly susceptible to change. We can drop one set of ideas, or one set of rights we claim, and we can emphasize other ideas. And we can do it more or less at will. We are in charge when we talk about ideas. Those of us who are specialists in the manipulation of ideas are in charge.

Institutions on the other hand are stabilized patterns of human behavior. Institutions involve millions of other real, living, flesh-and-blood people. Institutions involve the subjectivities of other people. They rest on the expectations of other people. They are shaped by the experience of other people. They are made up of habits and internalized values and beliefs. From time to time, of course, they rest also on coercion. These internalized expectations become inextricably bound up with the identity of the people who hold them; they are reinforced with habit and are extremely resistant to change. This is one of the reasons why revolutionaries are frequently prepared to write off a generation when they seek genuine change: they know the internalized expectations of mature people will prove so resistant to change that such people will never acquire the new identifications and expectations necessary to consummate the revolution.

Rights, then, are easy to claim and extremely difficult to translate into reality. Edmund Burke addressed the distinction between ideas and institutions. On one occasion he said of the French Revolution:

> I should therefore suspend my congratulations on the
> liberty of France until I was informed as to how it had

been combined with government, with public force, with discipline, with obedience of armies, with the collection and the effectiveness of a well distributed revenue, with morality and religion, with solidity and property, with peace and order, with civil and social manners. All these are good things, too. Without them liberty is of no benefit whilst it lasts and is not likely long to continue.

That is, he said he would not congratulate the French on their revolution until he knew that the idea of liberty had been translated through institutions into the reality of the daily lives of the people of France.

Now the failure to distinguish between the domains of rhetoric and politics is the very essence of rationalism. Rationalism encourages us to believe that anything that can be conceived can be brought into being. Rationalism not only encourages utopianism; utopianism is a form of rationalism. Utopianism shares the characteristic features of rationalism, including a disregard for experience, a disregard for the concrete, for probability in favor of reason, abstraction, and possibility.

Robert Owen—who was both rationalist and utopian, a man with marvelously good intentions—proposed once that there should be organized a world convention to "emancipate the human race from ignorance, poverty, division, sin, and misery." In our time, if we had such a world convention, it would propose a universal declaration of rights; and we would say that people had a right to live free of ignorance and poverty, division and sin and misery. And we would attempt then to hold other nations responsible, I think, for the eradication of these ills. Disregarding the distinction between ideas and institutions leads to the expectation that declarations give rights existential reality and that they constitute valid, practical programs of action.

The second distinction I want to emphasize is the distinction between rights and goals. In our time, as everybody knows, rights proliferate at an extraordinary rate. To the familiar old eighteenth-century rights of life, liberty, security of persons, and property have been added the right to nationality, the right to privacy, equal rights in marriage, the right to education, the right to culture, the right to leisure, the right to the full development of one's personality and powers, the right to self-determination, self-government, to adequate standards of living. As a matter of fact, recently in Geneva, where the Human Rights

41

Commission is meeting, there has been affirmed a right to development which carries with it its own concomitants, including the right to a new economic order, the right to peace, and the right to an end to the arms race.

Such declarations of human rights take on the character, as one critic said, of a letter to Santa Claus. And the same commentator noted that such rights can multiply indefinitely because "no clear standard informs them and no great reflection produces them." For every goal toward which human beings have worked there is, in our time, a right. Neither nature nor experience nor probability informs these lists of entitlements. The fact that they are without any possibility of realization, however, does not mean that they are without consequences. There are important consequences.

Treating goals as rights is, I think, grossly misleading about the way in which real goals are achieved in real life. Rights are vested in persons or groups, but goals are achieved by human effort. The language of rights subtly vests the responsibility for achievement in some "other"—some other person, some other group, some other entity. If the people of the world do not enjoy their full economic rights, it must be because someone —the monopoly capitalists, say, or the Zionists or Communists or male chauvinists or someone—is depriving them of their rightful due.

Utopian expectations concerning the human condition, which are grounded in that failure to distinguish between ideas and institutions, are compounded then by a vague sense that Utopia is one's due, one's right. When the belief that one has a right to develop coincides with the facts of primitive psychology, of caste systems, social hierarchies, societies based on ascription, on dictatorship—and those are, of course, the characteristics of many societies in the world that claim the right to development—then the tendency to blame someone is almost overwhelming.

The third distinction that I think has special relevance to human rights and foreign policy is the distinction between intention and consequence. In political philosophy, as in ethics, there are theories that emphasize motives and there are theories that emphasize consequences. There are the ethics of motives and the ethics of consequences. Preoccupation with motives is a well-known characteristic of the political purist.

Political purists have multiplied in our time, almost as rapidly as rights. Their distinguishing characteristic is, above all, an emphasis on internal criteria for action, on conforming behavior to what one feels is right. Doing what one knows is right becomes more important than producing any given desirable result. In human rights and foreign policy the tendency to prefer an ethic of motives to an ethic of consequences leads to an overweening concern with the purity of the intentions as embodied in our policies. When our motives are viewed as more important than the consequences of our actions, then whether our policies have in fact contributed to the creation of a new form of tyranny in a place like Iran seems to matter less than whether our intentions were good. The principal function of a human rights policy that emphasizes motives rather than consequences is, I believe, to make us feel good about ourselves. It feels good to feel good, to be sure. But one wonders about that as a goal of foreign policy.

The fourth distinction important to thinking about human rights and foreign policy is the distinction between personal morality and political morality. Personal morality derives from the characteristics of individuals and depends on the cultivation of personal virtues like faith, hope, charity, discipline, and reliability. Political morality, on the other hand, depends not on the personal morality of individuals but on the juxtaposition and interrelation of the parts of a society.

This is a fact that is well known in political philosophy and has been at least since Plato, who defined justice in terms of the relationship among the parts of a society. It was just as clear to the Founding Fathers of this country. Justice, democracy, liberty are all the products of an arrangement of offices, a distribution of power, embodied in a constitution. Constitutions produce political goods by respecting and harmonizing the diverse parts of the political community. All the important political goods—democracy, due process, protection of rights to free speech, assembly—are, as the Founding Fathers understood, the consequence of a wisely structured constitution.

The Founding Fathers did a marvelously creative job of applying these principles and designing a government that would in fact ensure the rights they cherished. It is very significant in this regard that the Founding Fathers proposed to ensure these rights by the arrangement of offices they set down in the Constitution, not by the Bill of Rights. Herein lies the real significance of the noninclusion of the Bill of Rights: the Founding Fathers thought it was unnecessary; they were convinced, I think quite rightly, that the arrangement of offices in their well-constructed Constitution would itself provide protection of those rights. Rights, they believed and I believe, are embodied in institutions, not in rhetoric. They are the consequences of wise judgments, not of good motives. Their protection and their realization are always the consequence of complex arrangements; they always rest on patterns of social and political life, rather than on individual virtues.

If these distinctions are important and must be taken into account by a sound foreign policy, where does this leave us in relation to human rights? It seems to me, first of all, that it does not at all diminish the importance of human rights as a factor in our foreign policy. Human rights can be, should be, must be, will be taken into account by U.S. foreign policy. The end of a foreign policy that takes account of human rights will be, and should be, to enhance the lives of others. The end of a foreign policy should be to produce positive consequences for the actor and potential beneficiary. Such a policy will, I think, take careful account of context as well as motives. It will calculate the means available and appropriate for achieving the desired end. It will assess the interrelations between means and ends, remembering always that human society is as complex as human nature itself. We have had enough of rationalism in our foreign policy, enough of purism, and of purely private virtues in public policies. It is my hope that in its approach to human rights and foreign policy, this administration will take the cure of history.

The cure of history is nothing more or less than the cure of reality. If we take the cure of history, I think, we will discover something about the very essence of freedom and of human rights. We will discover that the freedom of the American people is based not on the inspiring slogans of a Thomas Paine but on the careful web of restraints, permissions, interests, traditions woven by the Founding Fathers into the Constitution and explained in the *Federalist* papers. And rooted, of course, in our concrete rights as Englishmen. Similarly we will find, if we take the cure of history, that the freedoms of modern France are built not on the stirring declarations of the French Revolution but on the long arduous struggles of the French people to give reality to the rights they proclaimed—a reality that exists in the constitutional structure, in the conventions, in the institutions of French society and French politics.

If we take the cure of history, I think we will also find that in the real world force is sometimes necessary to defend human rights and that American power is necessary to protect and expand the frontiers of human rights in our time. In this administration, we believe we have a more adequate perception of the relationship among force, freedom, morality, and power. We have, we believe, a more adequate conception of the relationship between abstract rights and concrete societies, between blueprints and institutions. We think that by attempting less sweeping programs we can produce more progress in human rights. Time, of course, will tell whether our more modest expectations will prove more productive in human freedom and well-being.

Human Rights and Wrongs
in the United Nations

The government of the United States was founded squarely and explicitly on the belief that the most basic function of government is to protect the rights of its citizens. Our Declaration of Independence states, "We hold these truths to be self-evident: that all men are created equal, that they are endowed by their creator with certain inalienable rights, that among these are life, liberty and the pursuit of happiness." It adds, "To protect these rights, governments are instituted among men, deriving their just powers from the consent of the governed."

These notions—that the individual has rights which are prior to government, that protection of these rights is the purpose of the very existence of government, that the just powers of government depend on the consent of the governed—are the core of the American creed. That being the case, we naturally believe that the United Nations has no more important charge than the protection and expansion of the rights of persons. The charter commits the United Nations as a whole to this task; several bodies in the United Nations are explicitly devoted to it. My government stands always ready to join other nations in any serious effort that will expand the perimeters of liberty, law, and opportunity. We believe that the rights of individuals are most effectively promoted and expanded by and through democratic political institutions—where governments are chosen in periodic competitive elections, elections that feature freedom to criticize government, to publish criticisms, to organize opposition and compete for power. Human rights violations may

Statement before the Third Committee of the United Nations General Assembly, November 24, 1981.

occur even in such systems, but they are relatively few and readily corrected. The reason that popular governments protect human rights best is that people do not impose tyrants upon themselves. Tyrants impose themselves upon people.

There would be no serious human rights abuses if all peoples enjoyed self-government and democracy. The dynamics of freedom and political competition could be relied upon to work to protect minorities, dissenters, and critics against the arbitrary use of governments' powers against them. But, unfortunately, many, perhaps even most, people do not live in democracies, but live instead under rulers whom they have not chosen and who cannot be counted upon to respect their rights.

Governments, moreover, are not the only source of oppression and tyranny. Serious political philosophers such as Thomas Hobbes, John Locke, Baron Montesquieu, Rousseau, and their medieval predecessors understood that human rights exist independently of government and that human rights violations exist independently of government as well; that human rights can be and are violated by private violence as well as by public coercion. A government of laws protects and expands rights because it protects individuals against private violence.

Because human rights can be violated by individuals and groups as well as by governments, the protection of human rights should necessarily have a double focus. It should take account of all major sources of abuse: violations by government and violations by private violence, including organized private violence. Tyranny and anarchy are alike incompatible with freedom, security, and the enjoyment of opportunity.

It is, of course, not enough for the partisans of freedom to define the character and identify the sources of human rights violations. A serious commitment to human rights by this or any group also requires that one's judgment be fair and reasonable. Fair judgment of human rights practices would judge all by the same moral standards. A reasonable judgment requires that all nations be judged with reference to their specific character and situation. Thus it is not fair to judge one nation or group by the Sermon on the Mount and all other nations on the curve. It is not reasonable to expect weak governments in strife-torn societies to maintain order and administer justice as well as long-established governments in countries with stable institutions. And it is neither fair nor reasonable to single out for harsh criticism the human rights violations of some nations while ignoring entirely the gross abuses of others.

My point is that fair, reasonable judgments of human rights problems depend on both *standards* and *contexts*. All infringements of the rights of citizens must be judged by the same standard, and the concrete circumstances in which they occur must always be taken into account. This is an accepted principle in our law, which always defines murder as a crime but distinguishes between first, second, and third degree murder in penalizing it.

Although these principles would appear to be almost self-evident, some curious practices have grown up in recent years around the banner of human rights, as some persons and some governments have attempted to use human rights less as a goal than as a political weapon; less to expand the domains of freedom and law than to expand the scope of their hegemony.

To bring about this transformation of function, an effort has been mounted to deprive the concept of human rights of specific meaning by pretending that all objects of human desire are "rights" which can be had, if not for the asking, then at least for the demanding. The proliferation of "rights"—to a happy childhood, to self-fulfillment, to development—has proceeded at the same time that the application of human rights standards has grown more distorted and more cynical.

No aspect of United Nations affairs has been more perverted by the politicization of the last decade than have its human rights activities. In Geneva and in New York, human rights has become a bludgeon to be wielded by the strong against the weak, by the majority against the isolated, by the blocs against the unorganized. South Africa, Israel, and the non-Communist nations of South America have been the principal targets of United Nations human rights condemnation—South Africa on grounds of apartheid, Israel on grounds of alleged practices in the West Bank and in the territories occupied in the 1967 war, and assorted non-Communist Latin American countries because, in addition to being nondemocratic, they have been unorganized and unprotected in this body in which, from time to time, moral outrage is distributed much like violence in a protection racket.

My government believes that apartheid is a morally re-pugnant system which violates the rights of the black and colored peoples who live under it. It is a system through which the inhabitants of one country are denied equal access to free-dom, economic opportunity, and equal protection of the laws. It is a system by which one ruling minority refuses to share power, and profits from its possession of monopoly power. As such it is reprehensible. It cannot be condoned by governments and people who believe in government based on the consent of the governed, freely expressed in competitive elections in which all citizens are permitted to participate.

But let us be clear. Apartheid is not the only system for denying people the enjoyment of freedom, the right to choose and criticize their rulers, the rule of law, the opportunity for a good job, a good education, a good life. There are other grounds on which other regimes in the last decade have denied their citizens dignity, freedom, equal protection of the law, material well-being, and even life; other regimes that have more cruelly and more brutally repressed and slaughtered their citizens.

In my government's view, it is entirely appropriate that the agencies of the United Nations should condemn the spirit and the practice of apartheid and deplore its human consequences, providing, of course, that the same bodies of the United Nations demonstrate a serious moral concern for freedom, equality, and law. But the record of human rights in the United Nations belies the claim to moral seriousness that would fully justify its judgments.

The human rights agencies of the United Nations were silent while 3 million Cambodians died in Pol Pot's murderous Utopia. The human rights agencies of the United Nations were silent while a quarter of a million Ugandans died at the hands of Idi Amin. The human rights organizations of the United Nations have been silent about the thousands of Soviet citizens denied equal rights, equal protection of the law, denied the right to think, write, publish, work freely, or to emigrate to some place of their own choosing. As we meet here, Andrei Sakharov, one of the world's most distinguished physicists and bravest men, who has been confined to exile in Gorky, has entered upon a hunger strike to protest the refusal of the Soviet government to allow his daughter-in-law to emigrate.

But the United Nations is silent.

The activities of the United Nations with respect to Latin America offer a particularly egregious example of moral hypocrisy. Four countries of Latin America were condemned for one or another human rights violation during the last General Assembly: resolutions condemning El Salvador, Guatemala, Chile, and Bolivia were voted last winter in Geneva during the sessions of the Human Rights Commission. Doubtless, some of these countries, some of these governments, are guilty as charged. But the moral standing of their judges is undermined by their studious unconcern with the much larger violations of human liberty elsewhere in Latin America, by the government of Cuba. That government has driven over 1 million of its citizens into exile. It has incarcerated more political prisoners than any other Latin American nation. It has repressed freedom, denied equality, and, incidentally, deprived its citizens of what is termed here the right to development—a talent for which Cubans had demonstrated a large capacity prior to Fidel Castro's "liberating" revolution.

Consider what has happened to Cuba's poets. Virtually all of them are in exile or in jail. Exiles include Heberto Padilla, winner of the UNEAC prize for poetry in 1968; Reinaldo Arenas, author of the novel *Hallucinations*, which was a best seller in Europe; Rogelio Llopis, whose short stories have been translated into English, German, Polish, and Hungarian; Edmundo Desnoes, author of *Memorias del subdesarrollo*; Antonio Benitez Rojo, whose stories won a UNEAC prize in 1968 and who, until he sought asylum in Paris in mid-1980, was the director of publications for Casa de las Americas; and José Triana, recipient of a Casa award for his play *La noche de los asesinos*.

Among the imprisoned is Angel Cuadra, an internationally celebrated poet whose works have been translated into English, German, and Russian. Carlos Ripoll, writing in *Partisan Review*, tells his story:

> He was arrested and charged with conduct "against the security of the State" after unsuccessfully seeking permission to emigrate from Cuba in 1967. Having served two-thirds of a fifteen-year sentence, he was paroled in 1976, but then an anthology of his elegiac, apolitical poetry, entitled *Impromptus*, was published in the

United States and, as a result, his parole was revoked. From prison, he wrote to the exiled poet Juana Rosa Pita in May 1979, "there was no legal basis for this new reprisal against me. Only that I am a poet; that the world speaks my name; that I do not renounce my song. I do not put it on bended knees, nor do I use it for other, political or partisan ends, but only literary, universal, timeless ones." After participating in prison "rehabilitation programs," Cuadra was to be released again in July 1979. However, when the authorities learned that he had managed to smuggle out the manuscript of a new collection of his poetry which appeared in English translation under the title *A Correspondence of Poems*, they transferred him to Boniato prison instead of releasing him. . . . Under a constitutional provision giving retroactive effect to penal laws favoring prisoners, Cuadra is entitled [by Cuba's own laws] to be set free; according to that constitutional norm, he has served his sentence. His attempts to secure a court order for release have, however, failed.

Cuban poet Armando Valladares's sufferings are also documented. His case was described by Ripoll, Amnesty International, PEN, and at length in *Le Monde* of November 13, 1981. At the time of his arrest in 1960, Mr. Valladares was twenty-three years old. He was already writing poetry and painting, but at this young age, he was not as yet published. After his incarceration, he continued to write and to draw, wherever possible. His poetry has been published in several languages in two volumes, the first entitled *From My Wheelchair*, the second, *The Heart with Which I Live*. His book, *Prisoner of Castro*, was published in both Spanish and French. In recognition of Mr. Valladares's writing and his talent as a poet, the French PEN Club invited Mr. Valladares to become a member in 1979 and in the following year, 1980, awarded Mr. Valladares its Liberty Prize. As a reprisal for the publication of these works, in 1979 Mr. Valladares was moved to the remote prison of Boniato, deprived of his possessions, including all his books and his Bible. He is currently confined at Combinado des Este prison. As further reprisals for having written his book and poetry, his elderly parents and sister, having received permission to emigrate, were told that they would be allowed to leave only if Valladares were to write a letter to the foreign press denouncing the publication of his work. In a letter sent to PEN in 1980, Valladares wrote that such a letter would be the equivalent to "committing moral and spiritual suicide." He refused to write it.

Mr. Valladares has never had specific charges brought against him. He has not violated any of Cuba's laws or regulations. He did not participate in any terrorist activities; no munitions, arms, or explosives were ever found in his home or in his possession. The sole reason for his twenty years of imprisonment is that he did not share the Cuban government's ideology and refused to submit to its rehabilitation programs. In August 1974, the prison director ordered that no food be given to Mr. Valladares, and after forty-nine days of such imprisonment and punishment, he was left a total invalid. This is, of course, a direct violation of Article 5 of the Universal Declaration, regarding cruel punishment. Armando Valladares has been officially adopted by Amnesty International as a prisoner of conscience and Amnesty International has submitted numerous appeals on his behalf. The International PEN Club has also appealed for his release as well as the London-based Writers and Scholars International and many other human rights organizations all over the world. On November 12, 1980, the French PEN Club wrote to the Cuban ambassador in Paris but received no reply. The Venezuelan government has repeatedly asked for the release of Mr. Valladares. In 1979, a Venezuelan official met with Carlos Rafael Rodriguez, vice prime minister of Cuba, to ask for Valladares's release. During the Non-Aligned Conference held in Havana during the fall of 1979, the same official met with Fidel Castro and pleaded again for Valladares's release on humanitarian grounds. Since then, the president of Venezuela, Luis Herrera Campíns, has also explored the possibility of gaining Valladares's release through various Cuban government channels. But all attempts have failed.

What are we to think of defenders of human rights who ignore the victims of major tyrants and vent all their ferocity on the victims of minor tyrants? Mr. Chairman, nothing is more necessary with respect to the treatment of human rights questions in the United Nations than to affirm and to adhere to a single standard. For if we do not have a single standard, then our resolutions and recommendations are merely tendentious political statements without moral content. Either we consistently uphold the right of all people to be free regardless of the kind of system they live under, or we do not, ourselves, have the right to talk about human rights and to make recommendations that we expect others will follow.

In a word, nothing less than the moral integrity of the United Nations is at issue in our deliberations here. Nothing less than the commitment of this organization to its own reason for being is at stake.

Human Rights in El Salvador

Mr. Chairman, the United States shares with the sponsors of this resolution a deep concern with the freedom and well-being of the people of El Salvador. We share with them also an intense desire to see peace restored to that suffering land and a new democracy constructed out of the ruins of oligarchy and dictatorship. We do not believe the resolution before us contributes to that end.

It is said that the resolution before this committee is born of concern with human rights in El Salvador, and there are present among its articles expressions of concern for the suffering, intimidation, and oppression of the people of El Salvador. But, Mr. Chairman, two articles in this resolution give the whole a tendentious, partisan political aspect. Present here, under the guise of purely humanitarian concerns for human rights in El Salvador, is a bold effort to intervene in El Salvador's bitter internal strife on the side of the insurgents, and to help those insurgents gain, through international pressure, status and power which they are incapable of winning on the battlefield or through competitive elections.

The resolution before us today, then, has less to do with human rights than with politics. It does not express an evenhanded concern for violence in El Salvador or for grave violations of human rights, nor an evenhanded concern with the life, security, and tranquillity of the civilian population, as would a resolution concerned with the suffering and oppression of the El Salvadoran people. Instead, it "regrets, in particular" the depredations of "*governmental* paramilitary organizations." It does not offer support for the government's effort to hold elections and establish a government based on the will of the

Statement in the third committee on Item 12, Report of the Economic and Social Council, December 1, 1981.

people. Instead, it calls for a "negotiated political solution" as a precondition for democratic elections. Under the guise of human rights, this resolution seeks endorsement for the program of the Farabundi Marti National Liberation and Democratic Revolutionary Fronts (FMLN/FDR), a program which has recently been presented in capitals around the world and was advocated only last week here in New York by a leading spokesman for the Frente.

Three fundamental questions should be considered by any nation seriously considering support for this resolution:

Is the government of El Salvador guilty of the gross human rights abuses indicated in this resolution?

Is the FMLN/FDR worthy of the support of governments and persons genuinely concerned about respect for freedom, law, democracy, and development?

Is this proposed resolution a serious, morally and politically justifiable intervention in the politics of a member nation?

My government believes that all three questions should be answered negatively. I desire to discuss each briefly.

Is the government of El Salvador guilty of gross abuses of human rights, such that it deserves to be singled out for such attention by this body?

Mr. Chairman, the moral quality of the government of El Salvador is attested, first, by the willingness of its leaders to submit themselves to the judgment of its people in competitive elections that feature freedom to criticize the government, campaign against it, and offer alternative rulers. Foreign observers are invited to witness all phases of these elections.

It should hardly be necessary to point out that power-hungry dictators do not submit themselves to such tests of popular consent. Democrats, who believe government should rest on the consent of the governed, do. The government of El Salvador is made up of democrats who respect the right of the El Salvadoran people to choose their rulers and their capacity to do so. President José Napoleón Duarte and his cabinet do not believe they have the right to rule by force, or that their citizens have been too intimidated or brainwashed to make judgments concerning their own good. Like democrats everywhere, they are ready to let the people decide.

A second indicator of the character of this government and of its vision for its people is its land-reform program—the most radical in the Western Hemisphere. That program replaces large landholders with cooperatives, tenant farming with a land-to-the-tillers program, and testifies to all the world that this government is no continuation of the "oligarchy" of absentee landlords and landless peasants. It is a government committed to reform and social justice.

A third indicator of the character of the government is its solid support by virtually all the democracies of Latin America. Most of the leaders of these democracies know personally and respect José Napoleón Duarte and his cabinet, knew his predecessors, and understand the problem of trying to break with the history of traditional military rule and simultaneously stave off a determined, externally supported insurgency.

But what of the violence? If the government of El Salvador is filled with good men—with democrats and reformers—why is there continuing violence from the government side? The answer is, first, that the insurgency has penetrated the population and attempts to hide itself within it—so that fighting violent insurgents spills over into the society; and, second, that the government is not strong enough to claim effectively a monopoly on the use of coercion. A government with imperfect control of its security forces confronts a violent enemy bent on provocation and destruction.

As the long history of military coups and attempted coups demonstrates, strong government is not a normal part of El Salvador's political scene. Strong governments are not overthrown by *golpe de estados*—weak governments with imperfect authority over other aspects of society are so threatened. In El Salvador's history, such threats are a routine part of political life. The present government of El Salvador, which came into being when a group of reform-minded officers overthrew the regime of General Romero, is no exception. That government has incomplete power. Like most of its predecessors, it does not control all sources of force and violence in the polity. It lacks the power and authority to do so. The fact that it is confronted with a violent, well-armed adversary has enormously complicated the full consolidation of power by the government. Mr. Chairman, violence not only begets violence, it undermines the effort to teach and to practice restraint in the use of power. The result is that, in El Salvador, murderous traditionalists confront murderous revolutionaries—with *only* the government working to end this mutual murder and attempting to pacify adversaries.

There are societies and political conflicts which feature only would-be dictators and oppressors. But no such choice is offered in El Salvador. Political leaders exist there who are worthy of the support of democrats everywhere.

What of the moral quality of their adversaries? Do they have an equal claim to the support of persons and governments concerned about freedom, law, democracy, and development?

Mr. Chairman, the United States believes that the methods utilized by the FMLN provide all the evidence needed by reasonable men concerning the moral quality of the movement and the kind of regime it seeks to establish in El Salvador.

Lacking the popular support that could paralyze the economy with strikes or bring down the government with demonstrations or elections, the FMLN has sought to create a revolutionary situation by the systematic use of violence against the civilian population and the nation's economy. The FMLN is not a broad front of any kind. It is a band of armed men who rely on violence to achieve power.

The leadership of the FMLN claimed some 6,000 El Salvadorans killed in 1980 alone. The men of the FMLN have assassinated ordinary citizens, imposed bloody reprisals against villagers unwilling to assist them, and decimated peasant cooperatives in their determined efforts to sabotage the land-reform program. They have bombed restaurants, buses, theatres, factories, food-storage facilities, marketplaces, public utilities, bridges, and public buildings. They have occupied eight foreign embassies, kidnapped and killed diplomats, executed hundreds of presumed "informers," and until quite recently—when their "peace offensive" dictated a change in tactics—have taken no prisoners. They have sought and invited reaction from the extreme right in the hope that it will ultimately lead to a revolution from the extreme left, and have deliberately set off a chain reaction of violence and counterviolence which imperils the freedom, security, and well-being of every El Salvadoran. In short, they have behaved not as chivalrous Robin Hoods emerging from a Central American Sherwood Forest to comfort the oppressed, but as well-armed political freebooters inspired by an antidemocratic ideology, a consuming will to power and no inhibitions about the use of violence.

The international propaganda machine, from which the FMLN profits, keeps attention continually focused on the government's depredations.

I, therefore, desire to call this committee's attention to only a small sample of the kinds of atrocities committed on a regular basis by the radical armed insurgents against the civilian population of El Salvador:

1. On January 10, 1980, representatives of the Farabundi Marti National Liberation Front executed seven villagers in the department of Chalatenango.

2. On March 30, 1980, the FMLN fired into the crowd gathered at the funeral of Archbishop Romero in San Salvador, killing twenty-seven people.

3. During the week of June 11, 1980, nine Christian Democrats were assassinated by the FMLN.

4. On September 9, 1980, sixty peasants were executed in San Pedro Perulapan, "shot by guerrillas," according to an Agence-France Presse report, "who had held summary trials after charging the peasants with being collaborators of the government."

5. On October 21, 1980, near Armenia (Sonsonate) three men were found dead with notices attached to their bodies asserting that they had been executed for treason by the FMLN.

6. On November 16, 1980, Col. Carlos Choto, his wife, and two children were burned to death inside their house in San Salvador after the FMLN terrorists attacked their house with weapons, fire, and incendiary bombs.

7. On May 1, 1981, seven persons who had refused to join the FMLN were killed and four more were injured by a bomb explosion on the road linking Cinquera and Suchitoto.

8. In mid-August 1981, an FMLN attack on a bus in the Usultan department claimed twenty lives.

9. On September 11, 1981, over forty relatives of National Guard members living in Jucuapa and San Jose de las Flores cantons were shot to death by FMLN terrorists.

Mr. Chairman, violent men engage in random and indiscriminate killing as a matter of deliberate policy. The essence of their strategy is provocation: through persistent attacks which disrupt society and make ordinary life impossible, such revolutionaries challenge authority and force repressive countermeasures in the expectation that such repression will alienate parts of the population, polarize the society, undermine the legitimacy of the regime, and create the "objective" conditions needed to bring themselves to power.

Naturally, these tactics have not endeared the FMLN/FDR to the El Salvadorans, a people whose long experience with violence has taught the value of order. Had the FMLN succeeded in winning acceptance as a lesser evil, it would easily have come to power during the so-called final offensive of the 1980 Christmas season, a point at which the guerrillas enjoyed a large advantage in weapons and ammunition. But no popular response was forthcoming—and the offensive died for lack of roots.

In a statement of September 4, 1981, in response to another effort to intervene in El Salvador's affairs, the bishops of El Salvador commented:

> We are witnesses that in our country only a small sector of the population sympathizes with the FMLN and the FDR, which have lost popular support and which are now dedicated to sowing terror among the population. They are damaging the economy of the nation by destroying the property and services of the population in order to obtain a political/military advantage and to create the conditions necessary for taking power and imposing a Marxist-Leninist dictatorship.

During this period of the offensive, when vast quantities of arms from Soviet-bloc countries had made the FMLN the best-armed insurgent movement ever in Central America, FMLN leaders anticipated imminent military victory. They reiterated their disdain for a negotiated settlement, stating clearly a determination to impose a military solution. Only after the offensive failed and the government was resupplied, did the same leadership begin to evince interest in a political solution. But not, let us be clear, in a political solution that would permit the people to decide their future.

Partisans of nondemocratic politics have no trouble finding reasons why the people of El Salvador—or any other country— should not be permitted to choose their rulers and hold them accountable through competitive elections. The people have been brainwashed, say the brainwashers, and do not know their own minds. The people are intimidated, say the intimidators, and will not dare to express their true views.

We heard these claims in Rome as Mussolini deprived Italians of the right to choose their government; in Moscow when Lenin decided elections were not a proper instrument of revolution; in Germany as Hitler decided German "voting cattle," as he called them, were too corrupt to choose their rulers; in Venezuela when violent insurgents sought to keep the people from the polls; and more recently in Nicaragua as Sandinista leaders decided the people could not be trusted to know their own minds. We hear it now of El Salvador—whose brave, stolid people are said to be too frightened and confused to understand their own best interest.

Always, Mr. Chairman, those who seek power without the consent of the people find reasons why their rule should not be subjected to the discipline of popular election.

Obviously, it would be vastly preferable if all elections could be held where there is mutual trust and civic peace. But governments come into being even where these do not exist. Someone decides who shall rule. Can any democrat seriously argue that the decision is better made by a small minority operating under unstable conditions than by a larger majority operating under those same conditions?

Would it have been better in Zimbabwe?

Would it be better in Namibia?

It is a good thing to take the context of events into account when one passes judgment; to give thought to the effects of a climate of violence on government policies and our people's behavior; to take cognizance of probable effects of the historical experience and of expectations on government and people; to be sensitive to the broader international context surrounding particular events and choices.

When the context of the struggle in El Salvador is taken into account, it is, I believe, clear that the government of that beleaguered people is doing an honest job under extraordinarily difficult circumstances. It is clear also that the democracies in the region believe that the government and its leaders are the best available for El Salvador.

Finally, Mr. Chairman, as in all political choices, it is necessary to ask: who profits from the alternative courses?

To put that question is to answer it.

Actions that weaken the government of El Salvador today strengthen those who all over the world undermine peace, democracy, national independence, and the self-determination of peoples.

Surely this body should not make the task of El Salvador's democrats more difficult. Surely it does not desire to strengthen the fascism of the left. Surely it does not wish to intervene lopsidedly on the side of repression—ignoring the call of El Salvador's people as articulated by their bishops in that same statement of September 4: "We the bishops of El Salvador defend the right of self-determination of our nation and condemn at the same time any kind of intervention in the internal affairs of our country."

The bishops of El Salvador were right to defend the self-determination of their nation; this body would be right to heed their call and to reject this resolution.

Human Rights in Nicaragua

I have been asked to discuss today the extent to which the practices of the government of Nicaragua do and do not respect the human rights of Nicaragua's citizens. Such a discussion requires a minimal understanding of what human rights a government may be reasonably expected to respect as well as reliable and accurate knowledge of a government's policies and practices.

Mr. Chairman, I have argued elsewhere that rights should not be confused with wishes, or goals, that the list of human rights cannot be indefinitely lengthened like a shopping list in a global supermarket. I believe political and legal rights such as free speech, press, religion, freedom of assembly, freedom from arbitrary arrest, and the right to due process are the fundamental *rights:* they are the prerequisites to other social and economic goods. These basic political and legal rights share several important characteristics. Above all, they depend on *restraint* in the use of power. To observe the rule of law, to permit citizens to meet together and speak freely, it is not necessary that an economy be industrialized, a standard of living high, a people literate or urban. It is only necessary that this government *not* use its coercive power to ban newspapers, break up meetings, arrest opponents. Governments, we should be clear, do not—and should not—control all kinds of power in a society. They cannot, therefore, be held responsible for all the ways power is

Statement before the Subcommittee on Western Hemisphere Affairs, Senate Foreign Relations Committee, U.S. Senate, Washington, D.C., March 1, 1982.

exercised. But governments are responsible for their own decisions and policies. It is not reasonable, therefore, to hold a government responsible for the level of industrialization or for the rate of economic growth or productivity in a society (unless, of course, the government has claimed the exclusive right to manage the economy). It is entirely reasonable to hold a government responsible for its own decisions concerning arrest, trial, detention; for its own policies concerning elections and opposition; for its own practices vis-à-vis other sectors of the society.

Unfortunately, for the people of Nicaragua the policies and practices of that government demonstrate a pattern of systematic repression which began soon after the Sandinista triumph in July 1979 and has intensified with the progressive consolidation of power by Nicaragua's one-party dictatorship.

This is neither the time nor the place to review the events and policies that culminated in July 1979 in the defeat and resignation of Anastasio Somoza, the collapse soon thereafter of the transitional government headed by President Urcuyo, and the accession to power of the Sandinista directorate—though I believe there remain important lessons to be learned from these events. We are concerned here with the consequences of Sandinista rule for the freedom, security, and well-being of Nicaraguans.

In the past two and one-half years, Nicaraguans' hopes for greater freedom, democracy, and security from government tyranny have very nearly died as the new rulers moved expertly first to establish and then, progressively, to exercise control over the various sectors and institutions of Nicaraguan society. The pattern is familiar to all students of total power. The revolution has been conducted according to plan. The extension and consolidation of power follows the pattern of "coup d'état by installments" (Konrad Heiden's description of the Nazi seizure of near total power in German society).

One step at a time the Sandinista directorate moved against the fainthearted "bourgeois" democrats in their ranks—Robelo, Chomorro, Pastora, Cruz—waiting while they resigned in frustration and disappointment. One sector at a time they have moved against Nicaraguan society—now seizing radio, television stations, newspapers, now nationalizing new industries, now tightening control of the economy, now moving against the independent trade unions, now banning a bishop from access to

63

television, now organizing and reinforcing the Sandinista Defense Committees that bring the revolution, with rewards, demands, and surveillance into every neighborhood.

Alongside it all came a dramatic, extraordinary expansion of Nicaragua's army, National Guard, and international role. Today's National Guard is many times the size and strength of the one that reinforced Somoza's regime. It reinforces a political machine many times more sophisticated than Somoza's.

A political scientist describing the Nazis' consolidation of power in a single German town noted, concerning that process of destruction of society and politicization of human relations: "Hardly anyone in Thalburg in those days grasped what was happening. There was no real comprehension of what the town would experience if Hitler came to power, no real understanding of what Naziism was" (William Sheridan Allen, *The Nazi Seizure of Power: The Experience of a Single German Town*, p. 281). It is no easier to understand what is happening to Nicaragua.

Mr. Chairman, there are serious obstacles to a clear assessment of the practices relevant to human rights in Nicaragua. We are confronted in Nicaragua with the familiar patterns of doublespeak with which would-be totalitarian rulers of our times assault reality in the attempt to persuade us and, doubtless, themselves that making war is seeking peace, that repression is liberation, that a free press is a carefully controlled one. Thus on February 19, 1982, Daniel Ortega solemnly assured the opening session of an international conference (COPPAL) that the forced transfer of and violence against Miskito Indians was carried out only to protect their human rights:

> We have had to transfer them from the Rio Coco river banks, on the border of Honduras, to our country's interior investing efforts and resources that cost blood to the Nicaraguan people. True, there have been some dead in the north, in Nicaragua's Atlantic zone.
>
> We have had to resort to drastic measures to protect the rights of those Nicaraguans.

The world misunderstood the systematic destruction of the homes, villages, and economies of the Miskito Indians. The government was only protecting them against counterrevolutionaries. Furthermore, Radio Sandino explained (February 15, 1982):

Those communities located on the banks of the Coco River lived in neglected conditions since it is practically impossible to build roads in the area due to the swampy land. Also the soil is not very fertile for agriculture and cattle raising. The situation is worsened by the constant floods which produce very low crop yields that are not even enough for the communities' subsistence. As a result of this situation, all the advantages that they can now be given in the new settlements could not be offered to them.

Freedom from floods, freedom from bad soil and low crop yields, freedom from counterrevolutionaries, freedom from responsibility for their own lives: these are the human rights cited by Nicaragua's government to justify its claims to decide by force where the Miskitos should live, when they move, in what language their children should be educated, which dangers they should confront.

Thus the dialectic of revolution unfolds: Marxist-style liberation has already produced its antithesis in Sandinista Nicaragua. Old familiar arguments are invoked to justify new, more effective repressions.

Interior Minister Tomas Borge made a very long speech recently (January 27) attacking the only newspaper in Nicaragua which is not yet wholly controlled by the government. Borge's speech provides a useful compendium of contemporary versions of classic arguments against a free press.

First, he postulates a struggle and invokes foreign enemies against whom it is necessary to struggle. Then Borge identifies the "most important instrument of all enemies of Nicaragua and the revolution: the newspaper *La Prensa*." The offending newspaper is thus defined as an expression not of Nicaraguan opinion but of the enemies of Nicaragua.

Second, Borge explains that even though *La Prensa* undeniably is the most widely read newspaper in Nicaragua, its "circulation is not a demonstration of the people's support." "The fact that people buy cigarettes doesn't mean that cigarettes are good for their health." "That they buy drugs does not mean drugs are good." The appeal of *La Prensa*, he argues, is like that of pornography—"political pornography."

Still, *La Prensa* functions. Its voice, which daily condemned the arbitrary use of power by the Somozistas, remains the symbol of independence and continuing hope for a democratic

Nicaragua. But the campaign of intimidation is unremitting: government edicts, divine mobs, repeatedly forced temporary suspensions—on July 10, July 29, August 20, and intermittently through the fall. On January 13, 1982, combined actions of the military and the divine mobs closed *La Prensa* for three days after editorial offices were attacked and the homes of its editors, Pedro Joaquin Chomorro and Jaime Chomorro Barrios, were defaced.

By 1981 the foundations of Sandinista control over the symbolic environment had been established. The government controlled radio, television, and newspapers other than *La Prensa*. Moreover, laws were in place making it a crime to criticize the government without its authorization, to organize or promote candidates for the elections which had, by now, been "postponed" until 1985.

Nineteen eighty-one marked new levels of oppression in other spheres as well. Intimidation and control of the economy were extended; various private sector leaders were arrested, deported, or imprisoned, culminating in October in the sentencing of three chief private sector leaders guilty of criticizing the government's management of the economy. Proving they were hostile to all institutions autonomous of the state, the Sandinistas moved against labor as well as business, fiercely attacking Nicaragua's independent trade union movement (CUS), which responded by also withdrawing from the Council of State.

The most important development in repression against the various sectors of Nicaraguan society in 1981 was the progressive reliance on vigilante mobs to intimidate and punish persons and institutions who resisted conformity to the new orthodoxy. The MDN and the Social Democrats, two of Nicaragua's principal opposition parties, repeatedly were the victims of semi-official mob violence. MDN leader Alfonso Robelo's home was also attacked by the citizen groups who could count on understanding and support from the government.

Concentrating on new human and institutional targets did not mean Nicaragua's revolutionary government had lost interest in its old adversaries. No one knows the precise number of Somoza's National Guardsmen who still languish in Nicaragua's prisons. Five thousand is a conservative estimate of former National Guardsmen who, convicted by special tribunals, remain in prison. Many observers believe closer to 14,000 Somozistas remain overcrowded and underfed in Nicaragua's prisons.

When in September the government declared a one-year state of social and economic emergency and declared a number of broadly defined acts to be crimes, the government's power for moving "legally" against its critics was greatly expanded.

By the end of 1981, Nicaragua's one-party dictatorship had both expanded and consolidated power over diverse sectors of Nicaraguan life. Totalitarian control had not yet been established, but the process of eliminating and intimidating opponents was far advanced. So was the parallel establishment of new institutions that could penetrate and saturate the society with the teachings of the revolution.

The most dramatic and violent manifestation of the Sandinista effort to eliminate diversity, eradicate autonomous social groups, and bring the whole society under central control was the campaign against the people, the institutions, and the communities of the Miskito, Sumo, and Rama Indians of Nicaragua's Atlantic coast. The first moves against these largely autonomous, self-governing Indian communities took place in July 1979, when an effort was made to replace the 256 Indian communities' Council of Elders with Sandinista Defense Committees. Prohibition of lumbering, a major economic activity, arrest of a Miskito leader, expropriation of Indian lands, the imposition of Spanish in schools, and various other initiatives against the cultural and economic survival of the coastal Indians followed. All this proved to be a preface, however.

In the last months the Nicaraguan government has carried out a campaign of systematic violence against the Miskito Indians, burning their villages, destroying their institutions, forcing their evacuation and resettlement, killing those who resist, driving thousands into exile in Honduras. Of this campaign, Freedom House declared, "Circumstantial evidence clearly suggests that the central government has embarked on a policy to eradicate the indigenous peoples of the coastal area."

The Indian communities against whom these brutal measures have been directed have a long history of peaceful, cordial relations with Nicaragua's previous governments, who granted them semiautonomous status—that is, the right to preserve their way of life in their own communities.

The Sandinistas' violent offensive not only spelled tragedy for the Miskitos. It also symbolized the Sandinistas' hostility to any group which showed a capacity and a determinination to resist the transformation and incorporation into the all-new revolutionary society, culture, economy, and state.

Sandinista efforts to justify their policy as good for the Indians constitute a forceful contemporary reminder of the human costs of revolutionary elites ready to sacrifice untold thousands (millions) of men, women, and children to a fantasy concerning what is good for mankind.

In a statement of February 18, 1982, Nicaragua's bishops have graphically described the tragedy of the Atlantic coast Indians. Their statement provides a succinct, moving commentary of this massive violation of human rights:

Our thoughts on these events:

We recognize the governing authorities' right to undertake necessary measures to guarantee the defense and the integrity of the territory of the nation. We also recognize the autonomy of the state and its right to determine the implementation of emergency military measures in all or part of national territory in order to defend the country. Nevertheless, we wish to remind everyone that there are inalienable rights that under no circumstances can be violated, and we must state, with painful surprise, that in certain concrete cases there have been grave violations of the human rights of individuals, families, and entire populations of peoples. These include:

• relocations of individuals by military operations without warning and without conscientious dialogue
• forced marches, carried out without sufficient consideration for the weak, aged, women, and children
• charges or accusations of collaboration with the counterrevolution against all residents of certain towns
• the destruction of houses, belongings, and domestic animals
• the deaths of individuals in circumstances that, to our great sorrow, remind us of the drama of other peoples of the region

Such are the facts that compel us to denounce vigorously such attitudes of those who have the power and

force because they must be the first to guarantee ob-
servance of these human rights. And we urge the com-
petent authorities to take the necessary disciplinary
measures to prevent a repetition of such events in the
future.

On the other hand, we must remember that it is good
to maintain the national integrity and that it is a right
and historical duty of all Nicaragua to protect the
nation's territorial integrity. We must also remember
that it is a right and duty to preserve the legitimate
possession and use of the riches of the natural, traditional, and cultural patrimony of the indigenous people
of the Atlantic coast. In these we encounter and recognize with pride, not only the ancestry of our race, but
also the identity of our ancient, pre-Hispanic nation-
alities.

As we know, Mr. Chairman, the tragedy of Nicaragua's
Indians is by no means unique in our deeply troubled times.
Governments with totalitarian aspirations to control and transform the whole of society, and remake human nature, cannot
bear peoples with strong convictions and settled communities.
Jehovah's Witnesses, gypsies, Hmong, Bahais, Afghans—these
and other groups have run afoul of one or more of our century's
would-be totalitarians.

Unfortunately the whole pattern of repression that has
developed in Nicaragua is all too familiar in our times—revolutionary plans, violent overthrow of a preceding government,
"postponed" elections, controlled press, arrested opponents,
accelerated military buildup, surveillance, intimidation, economic
failure, politico-military expansion. This sad scenario describes
the spread of tyranny in this age.

It should no longer surprise us that the tyranny calls itself
liberation. We have all had plenty of opportunity to learn that
in our times, tyranny is always clothed in lies. As Solzhenitsyn
noted: "Violence does not and cannot exist by itself. . . . It is
invariably intertwined with *the lie*" since it must hide behind
"the sugary words of falsehood."

Human Rights in Afghanistan

The Soviet invasion of Afghanistan, launched on Christmas Eve nearly two years ago, was a momentous event that altered the climate and, indeed, the course of world politics. The invasion was a grave violation of the United Nations Charter, which enjoins all members to "refrain in their international relations from the threat or use of force against the territorial integrity or political independence of any state." As such, the Soviet invasion of Afghanistan shook the very foundations of world order.

The far-reaching consequences of this event should by now be apparent to all of us. It had a shattering effect upon the prospects for the continued stability of South Asia and the Persian Gulf, deepening anxieties throughout this vital region and raising the specter of a wider conflict. It also severely aggravated tensions between East and West. More than any single event in recent years, the Soviet invasion impelled a widespread reassessment of the world situation based upon a new and more sober appreciation of the danger that the policies of the Soviet Union now pose to global stability and world peace. The invasion thus marked a watershed in the postwar era, bringing to a definitive conclusion a period of optimism concerning the evolution of Soviet policy and intentions.

Nowhere, of course, have the consequences been more immediately or harshly felt than in Afghanistan itself. No sector

Statement in the General Assembly on Item 26, the situation in Afghanistan and its implications for international peace and security, November 18, 1981.

of Afghan society has been spared the consequences of the Soviet occupation and the ruthless effort to impose upon the Afghan people a Communist totalitarian system—an effort that began in 1978 with the initial Communist coup overthrowing the Daoud government. Almost 3 million people, about one-fifth of the entire Afghan population, have been forced to flee their country and now constitute the largest single refugee group in the world. Tens of thousands of people have been killed. Afghanistan's educated class has been decimated. Whole villages have been destroyed, their inhabitants killed or forced to flee. Mosques have been desecrated and religious leaders jailed or murdered. Schools have been turned into centers of political indoctrination. The country's economic and social infrastructure of roads, power and communication networks, hospitals, and educational institutions has been badly damaged and in many instances completely destroyed.

It is rarely noted that Afghanistan made significant economic and social progress during the decade of democratic freedoms and representative government brought about by the 1964 constitution. All this—and more—has now been undone.

There have been many attempts in the past to conquer Afghanistan. But nothing in the country's long history—with the possible exception of the devastating attacks more than 750 years ago by Genghis Khan—resembles the destruction wreaked in Afghanistan since 1978.

The Soviet Union and the Kabul regime have tried to conceal this destruction by sealing the country off from journalists and other foreign observers, and from humanitarian organizations such as the International Red Cross. Nevertheless, the truth about the situation there and about the terrible human suffering is becoming known to the world.

How far the Soviets are willing to go in their war against Afghanistan is indicated by the kind of weapons they have used there, including little booby-trap mines which the Soviets scatter by the thousands along the paths used by refugees and other civilians. These mines are frequently disguised as ordinary household items or toys. Children, naturally the least wary, are the ones most likely to pick them up. If they do, they risk being killed or having their limbs blown off.

On April 10 of this year, the Soviet Union signed an international convention prohibiting the use of such weapons. At the

71

time, its permanent representative to the United Nations called the convention "an illustrative example of the possibility of reaching agreements on measures aimed at curbing the arms race." The real "illustrative example," however, is contained in the Soviets' continued use in Afghanistan of the kind of anti-personnel weapons prohibited in the treaty. It is an example that illustrates both the character of the Soviet Union's involvement in Afghanistan and its attitude—in this instance, at least—toward a treaty obligation. In this connection, there are many reports from refugees and other victims of the Soviet invasion that lethal and incapacitating chemical weapons are being used in Afghanistan, in violation of both the Geneva Protocol of 1925 and the Biological Weapons Convention of 1972.

It is not possible to justify the Soviet actions in Afghanistan according to any meaningful interpretation of international law. The sole exception to the proscription against the use of force in international relations is provided for in Article 51 of the charter, which affirms "the inherent right of individual or collective self-defense if an armed attack occurs against a Member of the United Nations." But not even the Soviet Union itself has suggested that it has been the victim of an armed attack.

Moreover, it is hard to imagine how Afghanistan might conceivably have posed a threat to the Soviet Union. For decades the Soviet Union had proclaimed to the whole world, repeatedly, that its relations with Afghanistan were a model of peaceful coexistence, a prime example of neighborly relations between a small country and a big country, each with different systems of government and social structures, but living together in peace without interference. Since 1921 the two countries had signed numerous treaties, affirming and reaffirming Moscow's respect for Afghanistan's independence and territorial integrity and promising noninterference in Afghan affairs. It should not be forgotten, furthermore, that Afghanistan was a member of the Non-Aligned Movement and was not involved in any relationships that Moscow might look upon with concern.

How, then, could it have posed a threat? The argument is advanced that the Soviet Union felt threatened by the turmoil inside Afghanistan. But aside from student riots fomented by Babrak Karmal and his followers in 1965 and a brief period of unrest following the bloodless Daoud coup in 1973, there was no turmoil at all in Afghanistan before April 27, 1978—before, that is to say, the Communists violently seized power in Kabul and, with the help of growing numbers of Soviet "advisers," began forcibly to impose upon the people of Afghanistan a foreign ideology and a totalitarian system.

It is also suggested by apologists for the invasion that the Soviet Union feared that a tide of Islamic fundamentalism might sweep from Afghanistan into its Central Asian provinces. But even if this were true, it would hardly justify the Soviet invasion. In fact, the Afghans are a devout people, but they have not tried to impose their beliefs on others and historically they have allowed minority faiths to live peacefully within their midst. This attitude of tolerance is characteristic of the Afghans except when their faith itself is attacked, as it now is by communism. They are *not* tolerant, nor should they be, of an attack upon their freedom, independence, and identity, of which their religion is an important part. But there should be no doubt whatsoever that the threat in this instance is *to*—not from—the people of Afghanistan.

The Soviet Union also claims, of course, that its forces were invited in by the Kabul regime, which invoked *its* right to self-defense under Article 51. But so far, neither the Soviet Union nor the Kabul regime has produced a shred of evidence to prove that such an invitation was ever issued. It is hard to imagine what kind of evidence they *could* produce since, as we know, the invasion *preceded* the installation of Babrak Karmal, who wasn't even in Afghanistan at the time his predecessor was overthrown and killed by invading Soviet troops. Of late, Babrak Karmal has taken the line that the invitation was issued by the Afghan Communist Party. This, of course, is actually an admission that the invitation was not issued by any government.

The Kabul regime, moreover, has no legitimacy whatsoever in the eyes of the Afghan people. It exists only by virtue of Soviet actions and is, in fact, merely an appendage of Moscow. Soviet personnel direct virtually all aspects of its administration, including the Ministries of Foreign Affairs, Defense, Interior, Information and Culture, Justice, and Economic Planning. Since 1979, Soviet personnel have also commanded the Afghan army down to the brigade level and sometimes down to the company level. The Soviets even control Afghanistan's natural resources, in particular natural gas, which are extracted in a one-sided barter arrangement in exchange for goods used to sustain the Kabul regime.

Suspicions have been raised that the Kabul regime may also have acceded, in a treaty signed earlier this year, to the annexation by the Soviet Union of at least a part of the Wakhan corridor, the narrow strip of land that joins Afghanistan with China. A de facto annexation has already taken place since the area—from which the indigenous Kirghiz tribes have been forced to flee—is now under the control of the Soviet army.

Given the Kabul regime's utter subservience to Moscow, it is hardly surprising that it should have no base of support among the Afghan people. It is propped up by 85,000 Soviet troops. Yet the freedom fighters—poorly armed and trained, and virtually defenseless against some of the most sophisticated weapons in the Soviet arsenal—have been able to deny the Soviets control of perhaps 90 percent of the countryside and have made them contest many of the most important cities. In a desperate attempt to stem the disintegration of the Afghan army, the regime has offered many times normal pay to former enlisted men. Yet still they do not turn up, while draft-age men continue to slip out of the cities to join the resistance and whole units of the army desert en masse. The regime has repeatedly offered an amnesty to refugees who would return to Afghanistan from exile. Yet every week the refugee centers in Pakistan and Iran swell by the thousands.

What is clear today was clear in 1979. Then, as now, the Kabul regime was not threatened by an outside power, justifying defense under Article 51, but was in fact threatened by a popular uprising, a *spontaneous* popular uprising, of the nation—of the people in whom nationhood inheres and *solely* inheres in the absence of a legitimate government. It was an uprising against a regime that had slaughtered its own people, destroyed their homes, sent almost half a million people fleeing into exile, and delivered the country to an alien force—an uprising that continues to this very day against the present regime and its Soviet masters.

It is this uprising, and this uprising alone, that is justified to invoke the right of self-defense, for it is defending the independence and very existence of the Afghan nation against a foreign and brutal domination.

Small wonder, then, that the Soviet Union is doing whatever it can to obscure the truth about Afghanistan. There is no other way to understand the charge—repeated by the Soviet foreign minister before this body in September—that the real source of the conflict in Afghanistan is foreign interference by the United States and China. This charge is ludicrous but also revealing, for it shows the lengths to which the Soviet Union is forced to go to conceal the real nature of its policy.

There are only two realities in Afghanistan today: the Soviet occupation and the Afghan nation, and neither is compatible with the other. The Soviet Union can conquer Afghanistan only by eliminating the Afghan nation. This the world must not permit to happen, for if Afghanistan is vanquished, no independent nation will be safe.

The draft resolution now before us, like its predecessors, seeks an end to the occupation of Afghanistan. It calls for:

- immediate withdrawal of all foreign troops
- restoration of the sovereignty, territorial integrity, and non-alignment of Afghanistan
- restoration of the right of the Afghan people to choose their own form of government and economic and social system, free from outside intervention, coercion, or restraint, and
- return of the refugees to their homeland

My government is firmly committed to these terms.

The struggle of the Afghan nation for survival is consistent with the basic and most cherished purposes of the United Nations, which are to protect national independence and to maintain world peace.

It is only fitting, therefore, that the United Nations should affirm the basic and most cherished purpose of the Afghan nation, which is to regain its ancient homeland so that it may once again be independent and live at peace.

PART
THREE

The United States in the United Nations

Standing Alone

When I went to the United Nations nine months ago, I had very few considered views about the organization I was entering. As a result, the last nine months have been one of the most intensive learning experiences of my life. In the last nine months I and those of my colleagues who were also newcomers have been initiated into a new social and political culture—two of them, in fact, one at the Department of State and the other at the United Nations. Each of these is a complex system with its own patterns of recruitment, communication, organization, decision making, and feedback. Each has also its own penalties.

The penalties are incurred for violating the conventions and mores that dominate the system. If you look at this week's *Time* magazine, you will find that my team at the United Nations is called "inexperienced and inept." Being so categorized in a national magazine is one of the penalties for violating the conventions of the United Nations system.

There are others. Being isolated inside the United Nations and outvoted on issue after issue is another of the penalties the United States has been suffering for years. Last week the United States was outvoted 134 to 1 on one issue, but the experience is not really that unusual. We stood alone on three votes in the Human Rights Commission last spring—41 to 1, 30 to 1, 41 to 1; on one vote in the World Health Organization, 118 to 1; and on three votes in the Economic and Social Council,

Address given at Arizona State University, Tempe, Arizona, October 23, 1981.

including a 150-to-1 vote, which we cast against the Right to Development, which I will come back to later. Lest anyone imagine that this situation was created by universal revulsion against a pigheaded Reagan administration, I hasten to point out that the U.S. position at the United Nations, at least as measured by votes, has been deteriorating for years.

At least since 1960, the U.S. influence at the United Nations has been on a downward trend: 1960 was in fact a watershed year, one in which seventeen formerly colonial territories, sixteen of them African, were admitted to the United Nations. History is filled with ironies, as Hegel and Marx and many others have understood, and there is no greater irony in our time than that the decolonization process and the proliferation of former colonies as members of the United Nations should have been associated with the decline of U.S. influence. Obviously, as a former colony, the United States has always supported decolonization. Nineteen sixty was a watershed year for another reason if we think about our decline because it was a year in which the Soviet Union, for the first time, successfully attempted to seize for itself the decolonization issue, and it produced that year—1960—a decolonization declaration which was adopted in the United Nations by a vote of 89 to 1, with, yes, that's right, us as the "1." There were, as there often are in these votes, several abstentions.

In 1975, another political scientist and a predecessor of mine at the United Nations, Daniel Patrick Moynihan, wrote: "In the past year we were frequently reduced to voting in a bloc which, with variations, consisted of ourselves, Chile and the Dominican Republic." Since then we have lost Chile and the Dominican Republic. I would like to be clear that I have not enjoyed the experience of voting (on instruction) alone, or nearly alone, in the United Nations. It is not pleasant to lose, first of all. It is also not pleasant to provoke the disapproval of almost everyone. It is not agreeable to decline the good offices of colleagues eager to work out compromises on any issue, any principle. Voting alone is, in fact, especially unpleasant for people who take seriously the Founding Fathers' admonition that we should have a decent regard for the opinions of mankind; and mankind is precisely whom the many ambassadors gathered at Turtle Bay purport to represent. I, furthermore, have always suspected that anyone involved in regularly opposing large majorities is probably arrogant, sectarian, and at least eccentric—almost surely guilty of purist politics.

Are we at the United States Mission to the United Nations, I ask myself, arrogant and unduly sectarian purists? And, if we are not, then why in the world are we and the government we represent in such a minority in an organization that was largely fashioned by our leaders to reflect our ideals? Why are we so out of step with the world, or at least with the world as it expresses itself at the United Nations? Why do we so often disagree inside the United Nations with nations with whom we enjoy good relations outside the United Nations? Why in the United Nations do we find ourselves on different sides of questions from even our best friends? What is the matter with us?

In the nine months since arriving at the United Nations last January I have reflected a good deal on these questions in an effort to understand the basis of our estrangement from so much that takes place in this organization, to which we contribute nearly $1 billion of the taxpayers' money every year. I propose this afternoon to share with you some of my reflections about why and how we end up outnumbered 134 to 1, what this tells us about the United States, about our position in the world, and about the organization in which I spend so much time these days.

I should like to begin by making three preliminary observations. First, although the United States is usually outvoted and frequently isolated in the United Nations, it is not without friends; we are not pariahs. So far, at least, our isolation, when it occurs, is self-imposed. Other nations would be pleased to have us join them; they are pleased when we do join them. And we are not always alone. Last week we voted with a majority of some 100 nations in favor of the Kampuchea resolution.

The second fact I would like to note is that our relative isolation inside the United Nations stands in very sharp contrast to the position of the Soviet Union, which, though it often behaves like an international outlaw, violating basic provisions of the United Nations Charter, is invariably supported by its own client states and a certain number of fellow travelers. It never stands alone in the United Nations. More often than not, in fact, the Soviet Union votes with the majority. It was not always so. In the early days the United States shared the position of the majority; later we at least had reliable company in our dissents. Only since 1960 have we more and more frequently found ourselves severely outnumbered.

The third preliminary observation I should like to make is simply that relative isolation in a body like the United Nations *is* a sign of impotence. Losing votes by large majorities means that we cannot persuade other nations to vote with us. This is another way of saying that, except for the negative power of our veto, we have little influence inside the United Nations. This is a condition which seems anomalous for one of the two most powerful nations in the world and for the largest single contributor to the United Nations and its many affiliated agencies. It is anomalous.

There must be something about the arena itself that makes us so much less influential there than we are in the outside world. I find myself thinking often about the world inside the United Nations and the world outside the United Nations. What is the nature of this arena in which we find ourselves so powerless and alone? How does it differ from the world outside, on which it is wholly dependent? Like the world outside, the United Nations consists mainly of states that are not economically developed, not affluent, and not powerful. In the United Nations, these un-large, un-powerful, un-affluent states have banded together in groups, and through the groups small countries secure the election of their nationals to UN bodies and protect themselves from attack. Through the groups they determine the agenda and dominate the activities of the United Nations. The United Nations is *their* place.

In many ways, the United Nations resembles the legislature in the parliamentary system, with the General Assembly serving as the whole house and the Security Council as an executive or steering committee. As in a legislature, discussion and politics are the major occupations, and decisions are made by voting. As in a legislature, individual nations have banded together into blocs, whose combined strength is many times that of their individual members. The blocs offer influence, security, and fellowship. They function in the United Nations very much as political parties function in a legislature: they caucus, debate, take common positions. Much as political parties came into being to compete in the early parliaments, blocs at the United Nations came into being to compete more effectively in the General Assembly and the other bodies of the United Nations. Like political parties in a legislature, the blocs at the United Nations control the agenda, control the debate, and, finally, control the decisions that are made there.

In the United Nations the blocs are geographical, ethnic, and political in character. There is the Organization of African Unity, which unites all African nations except South Africa. There is the Latin American group, in which are gathered the nations of Latin America and the Caribbean; the Group of 77, or the G-77, which consists of some 120 less-developed countries who gather together to try to promote economic development. There is the European Community, or "the 10," as the nations of the EC usually call themselves. There's the Islamic Conference, the ASEAN group, and, of course, there's the Soviet bloc, into which category fall the nations of Eastern Europe and all the Soviet satellites, acknowledged and unacknowledged.

Overarching and overlapping all these groups is the most important bloc of all—important because of both its size and effectiveness: the Non-Aligned Movement. Founded twenty years ago on the initiative of Tito, Nehru, and Nasser at a time when the United Nations agenda tended to be dominated by East-West rivalries, this has become the most powerful bloc in the United Nations. The Non-Aligned group has grown to include 93 of the 156 nations in the United Nations. It contains all of the African and Arab, most of the Asian, and a few of the Latin American states.

The Non-Aligned bloc constitutes the automatic majority about which a good deal, but not nearly enough, has been written. Support from the Non-Aligned Movement guarantees the success of any resolution in the General Assembly or in any of the committees or organizations of the United Nations that operate on the principle of one country, one vote. The opposition of the Non-Aligned Movement—which is usually called the NAM around the United Nations—guarantees defeat, even inside the Security Council, where the Non-Aligned constitute a caucus of six votes, giving them virtually complete power to block an action and virtually ensuring that no policy can be adopted in the Security Council without their acquiescence.

Now, the power of the blocs depends, of course, on their cohesion as well as on their size, and the blocs are not equally cohesive. The Latin American group suffers from the same tendency toward schism that characterizes the politics of most

Latin American nations. The Latin American group is almost never able to agree on a common position. That is not just because of national character, it is also because Cuba, Guyana, and Nicaragua, usually joined by Mexico and Panama, block consensus. The OAU, the African group, on the other hand, operates with notable sophistication and discipline and is usually able to reach a common position and maintain it. So does the EC. On the other hand, deep divisions inside the Arab world prevent the Islamic Conference from acting on most issues except those involving Israel.

The Non-Aligned, with its approximately ninety-three members, is heterogeneous and cannot agree on many issues. But despite this heterogeneity, the NAM is sufficiently cohesive to have real clout in all arenas in the United Nations.

The United States, in the multiparty political system that the UN General Assembly constitutes, is a splinter party, sometimes able to work out a single-issue alliance with some other individual countries or group, usually the European 10 or the ASEAN nations or some Latin American countries, but basically alone. Because it is without reliable allies, because it belongs to no group, the United States lacks the influence on processes and decisions groups can exercise.

The simplest and most clear-cut reason, then, that the United States finds itself standing alone in the various bodies of the United Nations is that we have no party. It is ironic that a nation famed for its associational and organizational skills, as we are famed and memorialized by de Tocqueville, should find itself a country without a party at the United Nations.

Why and how that happened is another story. The important point for our purposes is that it did happen and that the result has been to leave us isolated among the blocs. We are, of course, not the only nation that is without a bloc. Japan, the European countries who are not members of the EC, Canada, Australia, and New Zealand are in somewhat analogous situations; so, because of the internal splits, are many Latin American countries; and, of course, so are the two pariah nations at the United Nations, Israel and South Africa.

Since the major parties—the big blocs—control the focus of attention and dominate the agenda at the United Nations, the overwhelming numerical superiority and organizational clout of the NAM and the G-77 mean that the United Nations focuses on issues of interest to *them*. More specifically, it focuses on issues on which it is possible to develop a consensus inside those blocs—inside the NAM and the G-77.

What is the NAM concerned with? Well, these days the NAM is concerned above all with Namibia, the PLO, South Africa, Israel, and Global Negotiations. I sometimes find myself thinking about an old joke about national character, according to which a group of international scholars at a conference were each asked to write a book on the elephant and to report back in six months with their manuscripts. The German came in with six volumes entitled the *Prolegomenon to the Elephant*, and the French specialist came in with a slim, elegantly bound volume entitled *The Love Life of the Elephant*, and the Americans came in with a thicker book called *Communism and the Elephant*. Well, if we were to project that today to the United Nations, we can be sure that the NAM's contribution would be *How Israel Destroyed the Palestinian Elephants*.

It is a dismal comment on human nature that in the NAM, as in most organizations, it is easier to build consensus about opposing than supporting something. The negative positions on which the NAM has its greatest consensus are Israel and South Africa (and occasionally the United States). Some of the purplest prose delivered concerns the alliance between Zionism and racism backed by the American imperialists—painted as the worst of all possible human coalitions.

I do not exaggerate. The NAM is a very large organization, and a good many of its members are not active at all. Saudi Arabia, for example, has not attended a meeting since Cuba was elected president of the NAM. Several other NAM members do not attend meetings regularly out of protest over its recent policies. And within the NAM there are a good many counter-currents and some very lively debates. Nonetheless, it is fair to say that the dominant ideologies inside the NAM are explicitly hostile to the United States.

This is easily established by a perusal, for example, of the Non-Aligned Movement's communiqué of September 25 and 28, 1981, which contained a strong, comprehensive indictment of the United States. The communiqué identifies the United States as a principal obstacle to the achievement of such universally shared goals as global negotiations, a law of the sea treaty, and disarmament and as guilty of causing an arms race, committing aggression against Libya, supporting Zionism, threatening the sovereignty, integrity, and independence of the Palestinian people, destabilizing the governments of Grenada, Nicaragua, and Cuba, and continuing colonial rule in Puerto Rico. The manifestly anti-U.S. ideological content of the NAM communiqué is underscored by its failure to mention the Soviet Union in a year in which the Soviet Union's occupation of Afghanistan continues, as does its support for the Vietnamese invasion of Kampuchea, its support for the Libyan invasion of Chad, and its support of Ethiopia's attacks on Somalia. In 1981 there was, in fact, not even a façade of ideological balance or neutrality as between the superpowers. There was simply an attack on U.S. policies and the U.S. role.

The NAM did not start this way, and it is interesting to reflect on how it developed this orientation. The NAM, as I already indicated, was founded by Nehru, Tito, and Nasser to oppose the division of the world into blocs of East and West and to promote détente between them. In the beginning it had a pacifist bent. The heritage of Mahatma Gandhi was very strongly felt inside the NAM.

All things change, and so did the NAM. Nehru died, India lost a war to China and suffered a great decline in international prestige. The influence of the pacifist trend diminished. African nations proliferated and came to dominate the NAM. By 1960, the principal preoccupation of the NAM had shifted from peace to decolonization. By 1966, decolonization meant basically South Africa and its handling of the South West Territories, which today we call Namibia. By 1966, the Non-Aligned Movement had made South Africa an outcast inside the United Nations. By 1967, the effort was under way to make Israel a pariah. By 1970, development had joined decolonization as a principal focus of the NAM's concern, but it is important to understand that development, when it is talked about inside the Non-Aligned Movement, frequently is a negative concept, more anti-Western, anti-industrialized nations than it is pro–economic development.

The dominant development theory, as initially enunciated inside the NAM, saw the world and the nations of the world as organized into a kind of global class struggle, with the many poor nations bound in ineluctable hostility to the few rich nations. And by the early 1970s the goal of development had been identified inside the NAM and in the United Nations with the Soviet Union. The Indian permanent representative to the United Nations commented in 1974: "The activities of the Soviet delegation at this session showed once again that the Soviet Union deeply understands and shares the aspirations of the Third World for development." Inferentially, the United States and the West did not, in spite of the fact that the United States annually gave far more development assistance to less-developed countries than, needless to say, did the Soviet Union.

There is really no room for question about the NAM's attitude toward the United States. I'm not talking about all the nations inside the Non-Aligned Movement but about the dominant attitude, which determines how the organization as such speaks. There is a very large question, however, about the appropriateness of the U.S. response to a NAM attack. It is a first principle of the political culture of the United Nations that no major Western power, least of all the United States, should answer an attack with an attack or should even answer an attack with a defense. It is believed that such an answer might be intimidating. Another axiom of United Nations political culture is that relations inside the United Nations should under no circumstances have consequences for bilateral relations with the United States.

Senator Moynihan noted the existence of a powerful tendency among associates of his and mine at the United Nations, and some of his State Department colleagues as well, to associate the dignity of a great power with masochism and to associate liberalism with passivity in the face of insult, as though the liberal response to an insult is to say nothing. Announcing his determination to answer attacks and acknowledging his understanding that he would thereby violate the prevailing rules of decorum, Moynihan quoted a French couplet that says:

> Cet animal est très méchant,
> Quand on l'attaque, il se défend.

It means, That is a very bad animal: when it is attacked, it defends itself. The practice of responding to attacks rather than suffering them stoically won for Moynihan the reputation for being confrontational and strident: last week an amiable European colleague accused me of "Libyan rhetoric."

The political culture of the United Nations, which is shared by most of the delegations and by most Americans, frowns on self-defense or counterattack by the United States. Superpowers, it asserts, should not demean themselves by responding to the provocations of lesser nations. As one colleague put it to me, "A dog does not fight with a chicken." I asked him what the dog did if ninety-six chickens were pecking at it. Superpowers have a special obligation, it is said, to be humble. To bear the slurs and slander of the less powerful is a kind of perpetual penance for their power. No one really expects that the Soviet Union will remain silent in the face of attacks. But then it is explained that no one expects much of the Soviet Union and no one measures its behavior by high standards. So it emerges that the political culture of the United Nations does not really require passive resignation and silence of all superpowers, only of one.

The Europeans have long since accepted their prescribed role, have grown accustomed to being "it" in a global game of dunk the clown, and have opted to "understand" the point of view of their third world accusers. Doubtless, collective guilt for the sins of their imperial past encourages acquiescence in this role. Doubtless, too, the fact that we were never a colonial power makes us less ready to accept blame for the problems of nations with whom we have, in fact, few relations. Perhaps, also, our European friends' role is made more comfortable and more tenable by their conviction that even if *they* do not defend the basic interests of the industrialized nations, the United States can be counted upon to do so. Moreover, as long as only the United States resists, it appears that only we are attacked.

Taking harsh criticism while lacking the moral right of reply is one way of being "it" at the United Nations; there are others. Accepting the responsibility for most of the world's misery is the most important example. This notion that the industrialized West is responsible for most of the world's misery is an integral if sometimes tacit part of the dominant theory of development at the United Nations. It is embodied, of course, in the United Nations' New International Economic Order, which was adopted by the General Assembly in May 1974.

The chief elements of the ideology of development embodied in that New International Economic Order are assertions that Western industrial powers are largely responsible for the poverty and the economic backwardness of the less-developed nations and, therefore, that they have a *unique* moral responsibility to solve the problem. The Soviet Union takes the view that since it was not a colonial nation, it has no responsibility for solving the problem of underdevelopment. As a result, it is, at this moment, not at Cancún, and it is not really encountering much criticism from the less-developed countries. For somewhat mystical reasons, even though we did not have a colonial past, we are seen as the inheritors of the colonial mantle and as sharing the unique responsibility of the European colonial powers.

The guilt of the Western nations is believed to be proved by their affluence. A kind of zero-sum economic universe is postulated in which property, if not actually theft, is something very much like it, so that one nation's wealth is a kind of living evidence that it has exploited another nation and created its pauperization. The dominant doctrine of development embodied in the New International Economic Order and the plan for Global Negotiations is collectivist, redistributionist, anticapitalist, anti-West. It stands in roughly the same relationship to economic development as the proposed New World Information Order stands to the exchange of news. Both embody assumptions and recommendations that would eliminate the freedom needed to achieve the desired goals. Both, we are persuaded, are recipes for failure; the one, because it ignores the experience of every society that has ever achieved rapid, self-sustaining economic growth, the other, because it violates the rules that every society with a free press knows are necessary to sustain a free press.

What can the United States do about this situation at the United Nations? One thing we could do is, of course, simply get out, following that old prescription of the DAR and others who said: "U.S. out of UN, UN out of U.S." We could take our billion dollars a year and stay home, so to speak. Another thing we could do is hang in and emphasize the values and goals we share with most of the nations in the world—certainly most of the nations of the NAM—and continue to try to achieve them.

As I speak, President Reagan is meeting at a Mexican resort with the representatives of twenty-one other nations to discuss world poverty. The meeting, many expect, will be a step forward toward the implementation of the New International Economic Order. Now this Cancún summit is the latest in a series of North-South encounters through which the less-developed nations seek to bring about a new economic order. The developed nations can either play the role ascribed to them in the dominant development ideology (in which they are simply guilty parties from whom large amounts of resources should be transferred) or they can do what President Reagan and Secretary Haig are doing right now, at Cancún—trying hard to persuade other nations that there are better ways of achieving the goals they seek.

Why better? Better, because we know that economic development cannot be achieved by a redistribution of wealth, no matter how massive. As social scientists and many others have argued for years, economic development is a complex social process of transformation from within that involves whole populations in new ways of thinking, living, and working. There have been a great many empirical studies of development, examining the experience both of nations that have achieved high levels of development and eliminated poverty and of those that have not. Their conclusion is, of course, that economies thrive where there is freedom to innovate and experiment and that economies founder where there is no freedom to innovate and experiment, where there is no social mobility and no hope of profit from hard work. The studies of economic development by social scientists have again and again demonstrated that nations achieve economic development when they involve large portions of their own populations in those processes of social and economic change.

I believe that we should work harder at the politics of the United Nations, and I hope that if we work harder at politics, we may at least win back a few regular allies. We should not accept responsibility for crimes we did not commit, nor acquiesce in prescriptions for remedies we do not believe will work.

We are happy to talk about economic development in a global arena, but we will not buy into the 1974 formulation of the problem. We are happy to talk about the New World Information Order in UNESCO, but we will not buy into a New World Information Order that constructs obstacles to the free flow of information and would muzzle journalists in the name of national self-determination. By voting our values, stating our case, dealing with other nations as equals, and treating other perspectives with respect, we can, I think, at least remind our colleagues in the United Nations that there are alternative approaches to development, alternative views of freedom, alternative approaches to decolonization, to Palestinian refugees, to independence for Namibia, and that there are more effective ways of achieving the results that all of us presumably desire. By stating those alternatives more clearly and more consistently, I think we can perhaps best do our job, which I take it, is to represent the legitimate aspirations of the American people for a better and more peaceful world.

The Problem of
the United Nations

I propose to speak today about the United Nations and to begin, as professors are wont to do, by telling you that I shall make four points: first, that the United Nations is an important body, worthy of our attention; second, that the United Nations is not at all the institution its American founders hoped for; third, that it does not reflect or represent the world in the way representative bodies usually do; fourth, that the great question for the United States and other countries committed to national independence, self-determination, self-government, representative democracy, is whether the United Nations can be made a more effective problem-solving tool, which will help resolve differences, rather than exacerbate them.

I begin from the proposition that the United Nations is an important institution. It is not, as some like to pretend, a world unto itself, insulated, without consequences for events beyond its own institutional boundaries. For better or worse, the United Nations is not only influenced by its environment, it influences the environment. The patterns of interaction inside the United Nations—the alliances and the rhetoric that develop there—have consequences cumulatively important beyond Turtle Bay. The relationship between the United Nations and the outside world receives less attention, I believe, than it deserves.

My second point is even less controversial than the first— it is *that the United Nations is not what we Americans were*

Address before the Foreign Policy Association, New York City, January 26, 1982.

seeking when we played our role in its construction. By the end of World War II, U.S. leaders no longer believed it was possible for this country to remain aloof from foreign affairs, but we Americans were still looking for a way to avoid the entangling alliances and Old World patterns of power politics against which George Washington had so eloquently warned us.

From before the founding of this nation, Americans had been dreaming of a world assembly; and, from one point of view, the United Nations is simply the last in a long series of heroic efforts, spanning the centuries, to devise an equitable, peaceable, stable international order. In 1693 William Penn published a remarkable work entitled "Essay toward the Present and Future Peace of Europe." In it, Penn called for the establishment of a "parliament of princes" to adjudicate territorial controversies and uphold the rule of law. "If any of the sovereignties that constitute the imperial states shall refuse to submit their claims or pretensions" to this international parliament, Penn declared, "and seek their remedy by arms . . . all the other sovereignties, united as one strength, shall compel the submission and performance of the sentence, with damages to the suffering party, and charges to the sovereignties that obliged their submission." Thus, Penn reasoned, the peace of Europe would be preserved, friendship among princes would be cemented, princes might marry for love instead of for reasons of state, and, most important, "the reputation of Christianity will in some degree be recovered in the sight of infidels."

More than two centuries later, the first great experiment in international planning for international order—the League of Nations—came into being. We know how that ended. Two and a half troubled decades and one world war later, there met in San Francisco 282 delegates, 1,444 assistants, 1,589 members of the International Secretariat, 2,636 journalists, 2,252 army and navy aides, 800 Boy Scouts, 400 Red Cross workers, and 188 telephone and telegraph operators, who toiled mightily "to save succeeding generations from the scourge of war."

The deliberations there, Sir Harold Nicolson asserted, reflected the essential elements of traditional American idealism and added up to one grand fallacy—which began with the idea that one could and should apply to external affairs the institutions and practices of legislative procedure in liberal democracy. "Among peace loving peoples—and all others should be and had been suppressed—violence could or would be superseded by reason." What was reasonable and right would be determined by majority vote; and just as the equality of man led to one man, one vote, so the doctrine of the "sovereign equality of states" led to one state, one vote.

As Dean Acheson (who *was* "Present at the Creation") noted, the United Nations was oversold to the American people from the moment of its birth: " its [the charter's] presentation to the American people as almost Holy Writ and with the evangelical enthusiasm of a major advertising campaign seemed to me to raise popular hopes which could only lead to bitter disappointment."

To many, Acheson said, the General Assembly appeared as the town meeting of the world. In fact, even its authors never expected it would solve all problems. The United Nations Charter, as it emerged from San Francisco, had as its primary purposes the peaceful settlement of disputes and the mobilization of the international community against acts of aggression. As the distinguished United Nations undersecretary general for special political affairs, Brian Urquhart, has recently written, the charter describes a system for maintaining international peace and security which "assumes that all governments will play the roles assigned to them. Those involved in disputes will avail themselves of the means available in the Charter to settle those disputes peacefully. If they fail to do this, the membership of the United Nations, under the guidance of the Security Council, will take a series of steps designed to persuade them to do so. The governments concerned will heed and obey the injunctions of the Council. And if in the end the threat to peace persists, the Council, led by its permanent members, will apply enforcement measures, ranging from economic sanctions to military action, to restore peace and security."

The Charter of the United Nations made assumptions about the behavior of nations that were quickly belied by their actual conduct. Very quickly after 1945, it became clear that the vision of a basically united world of basically peace-loving nations could not be sustained. The Red Army declined to withdraw from the countries of Eastern Europe; Joseph Stalin declined to honor the promises of free elections made at Yalta; and Soviet efforts to expand into Greece and Turkey demonstrated to a world still weary from the last war that not all great powers could be counted on to respect either the independence of their neighbors *or* the UN Charter.

By 1947 General Marshall could remind Ernest Bevin, his British counterpart, that "the transfer of the vexatious problems to the United Nations unfortunately does not render them any less complicated or difficult."

The perspective, I believe, of America—let me emphasize that I am talking here about Americans—on the Charter of the United Nations reflected our national optimism and our predilection for faith in good works. It was idealistic to the point of utopianism. This distinctly American perspective was impatient with the constraints of international diplomacy, with the methods of the past. And it was doomed from the start.

In saying this, I do not state or desire to imply that the United Nations has had no successes as an effective instrument for keeping or restoring the peace. It played a positive role in disputes in the Congo in 1960 and the India-Pakistan War in 1965. It has more recently played a positive role in Cyprus and Lebanon, and it has from time to time been instrumental in bringing an end to the various Arab-Israeli wars. Few, however, could be found today who would seek to justify the United Nations solely or even mainly on grounds of a successful record of *conflict resolution*.

I am not at all surprised, and less bothered than some observers might be, by the failure of the United Nations to ensure peace in a world of fractious people. I am more bothered by far by the tendency of the United Nations to make conflict resolution *more difficult* than it would otherwise be, at least in a good many cases.

Last week, the Golan Heights resolution was considered and acted upon by the members of the Security Council. Before Christmas the Security Council unanimously passed a resolution declaring Israel's extension of legal jurisdiction to the Golan Heights null, void, and without legal standing. On January 5 the Security Council reconvened to consider what action to take since Israel had not complied. After three weeks of what is called debate, the council voted nine yes, five abstain, one veto. In the interim, tides of invective swept through the Security Council with hurricane force—accusing Israel of virtually every crime of which a nation-state is capable and indicting the United States as, at best, an accomplice. Nothing that happened during those weeks contributed to the solution of the Golan problem or to peace in the Middle East. Furthermore I suspect that virtually all participants in the process were aware of that.

The goal of peace in the Middle East and the resolution to the Golan problem rather quickly gave way to putting together the nine votes which would draw a veto—which was a prerequisite for a special emergency session of the General Assembly.

Eventually, after a good deal of politicking on several continents, the requisite nine votes were assembled, the veto was cast, and we will this week move on to a special emergency session of the General Assembly, in which dozens more speeches will be made attacking Israel for every crime of which a nation-state is capable and the United States as accomplice. The extraordinary discrepancy between the political divisions in the world inside and outside the United Nations was evident in the process on the Golan Heights. What interests me most is the fact that *the discrepancy between those political divisions inside the United Nations and outside the United Nations has grown so familiar that it is no longer even noticed.*

I desire, however, to notice it.

First, we might note that, in the Security Council, Jordan literally and very enthusiastically "represented" Syria, and the representatives of those two countries worked together tirelessly in the endless efforts to draft and pass a resolution. From their perfect harmony in this task, one could never have imagined that only two days later concern with Syria's hostile intentions would lead Jordan's King Hussein urgently to return to Jordan. An observer accustomed only to the politics of the "real world" outside the United Nations might also have been surprised to see the representatives of Western-oriented African states or a representative of a Western European democracy align themselves with the cause of the Soviets and Syria. The most interesting fact about the alignments in the Security Council and the General Assembly is that they often *do not* reflect the policies or political orientations of many member nations in the world outside the United Nations.

Politics—conflict, struggle—have by no means been purged from the United Nations. But they are regularly transformed in and by that arena in important ways:

1. In the process of being transformed from actual problems outside the United Nations to United Nations issues, the number

of parties to a conflict is dramatically *extended*. A great many countries who would never be involved at all in the issue of the Golan Heights, for example, become involved in that issue as the conflict is extended inside the United Nations to become a matter of concern to all the world. The United Nations is an arena in which many countries are brought into conflicts they might otherwise not become involved in.

2. The UN process breeds polarization which, as Yeselson and Gaglione observed in their stimulating study of the United Nations (which, like Moynihan's book, also was titled *A Dangerous Place*), "by constantly forcing states to choose up sides, progressively destroys neutral havens." Obviously extending and polarizing conflict is the very opposite of resolving it. For as conflict is extended, polarized, and publicized, flexibility is diminished, and the possibilities of conflict resolution decrease as heat and light increase.

This process of conflict extension, exacerbation, polarization, has progressed so far that Yeselson and Gaglione pointed out: "Use of the United Nations is a barometer of the hostility existing between nations. Nations interested in reaching agreement almost always ignore or avoid the U.N. . . . Bringing an issue to the U.N. is likely to be regarded as a hostile act." Naturally the United Nations' reputation for partisanship and conflict exacerbation severely limits its utility for conflict resolution. Politicizing and polarizing the whole UN make impartiality an issue of some importance when the occasion arises that the UN might serve as a neutral arena for conflict resolution or a referee in an ongoing conflict. Today, for example, in the search for independence for Namibia, UN impartiality has become an issue of real substance.

What, if anything, can be done to render the United Nations a more useful instrument of conflict resolution and a less hospitable arena for conflict exacerbation and extension?

The answer, I believe, is that we and others who share the goals of conflict resolution should work toward a significant alteration of both the political culture and the political dynamics inside the United Nations. Neither may be possible to achieve, but both are worthy goals.

Today the political dynamics of United Nations interactions are shaped by *blocs*, which have little or no reality outside the UN bodies. Elsewhere I have considered positive functions of the blocs. Here, however, I desire to emphasize only that they are above all the mechanisms for conflict extension and exacerbation. The Arab-African bloc draws virtually every state in Africa and in the Arab world into a bitter conflict with Israel and the United States and in turn strengthens the Soviet Union and the radical polarizers in the Arab world.

Moreover, the patterns of bloc conflict encourage "solidarity" with entities that have reality only in the United Nations.

Most serious, they breed a process in which the concrete national interests of real nations may be subordinated to the interest of a group that has no relevance to the welfare of its member states. Support by conservative Arab states for the PLO is a good example.

At the end of a year at the United Nations I have concluded that it is urgently important to strengthen the linkage between politics *inside* the United Nations and political realities *outside* it. The conflicts of the real world are ultimately less destructive of democratic institutions than the alignments and conflicts that have been bred and structured inside the United Nations.

In addition, cooling the rhetoric inside that institution would help a lot. Frequently it is too harsh, violent, and bitter to breed anything but hatred. Last week one delegate spoke with enthusiasm about another nation having "broken the back" of the United States. Invective has become so common that old hands refer to "routine denunciation" and "ritualistic verbiage."

Ironically, then, the first step toward bringing the United Nations into closer conformity with the ideal is restoring its contact with the real. The real interests of a vast majority of nations at Turtle Bay and of our own nation are self-determination, self-government, peace, democracy, development—precisely the ideals and the goals which inspired the founding of the United Nations. Anything which distracts from their pursuit is time wasted. Only greater realism can lead us closer to the ideals that inspired this very human institution.

The U.S. Role in the United Nations

I understand that the previous speaker has just called for U.S. withdrawal from the United Nations. I disagree. I know, indeed no one knows better, that the United Nations poses a problem for the United States. It's expensive, it's often ineffective, it seems particularly inclined to push policies that we do not desire to adopt, decisions from which we dissent, agreements with which we disagree. My analysis of the causes and the possible cures of these problems at the United Nations has undergone significant evolution during my nearly eighteen months now at Turtle Bay. . . . That is, incidentally, the average tenure of U.S. permanent representatives to the United Nations.

In that eighteen months I haven't become an expert on that institution. Eighteen months is not long enough to become expert about any complex institution, and God knows the United Nations is a complex institution. Eighteen months, however, is long enough to have observed a full cycle of United Nations activity. Eighteen months is long enough to have observed at first hand the relative powerlessness of the United States at the United Nations, to have felt in virtually all the arenas of that body our lack of influence, long enough to have watched others—the Soviets, the ASEAN states, Syria, PLO, and most recently, the British—exercise influence that we cannot even hope to approximate. We have observed in that eighteen months the operation of bloc politics, and, equally interesting,

Address before the Heritage Foundation Conference on the U.S. Role in the United Nations, New York City, June 7, 1982.

we have observed from time to time, the virtual paralysis of the blocs. We have observed the power of the Soviets and their principal clients, and from time to time their inability to shape outcomes in ways that they desire. We have watched the political ineffectiveness of the Latin Americans and reflected on how it compares with the effectiveness of the ASEANs. In that eighteen months, I have been deeply impressed with American incapacities at the United Nations, our inability in this organization to find reliable allies, to make persuasive arguments, to put together winning combinations.

To avoid possible misunderstanding I desire to emphasize that the lack of influence of the United States in the United Nations does not represent some sort of worldwide revulsion against the Reagan administration. The fact is that the United States has been virtually powerless in the United Nations for more than a decade. Our friend, the Senator from New York, Daniel Patrick Moynihan, wrote in his book, *A Dangerous Place*, that in 1974 the United States was frequently reduced to voting in a bloc of three, alongside Chile and the Dominican Republic. Since then we have lost Chile and the Dominican Republic as reliable voting allies. The analysis of voting patterns at the United Nations reveals that the decline in U.S. influence which began around 1966 or 1967 continued precipitously for about five to seven years, at which point it reached a low level around which it has stuck ever since through both Republican and Democratic administrations. This low level of influence persisted through the terms of Andrew Young and Donald McHenry as well as those of Daniel Patrick Moynihan and Jeane Kirkpatrick. That is another way of saying it has persisted through changes in U.S. permanent representatives, ideologies, and styles. Throughout we have continued to be the largest financial contributor, paying first 30 percent then 25 percent of the operating expenses of the organization.

There was a time when I believed that our impotence was a kind of inevitable consequence of the changed character of the membership of the United Nations. Certainly that composition changed. When the United Nations was established there were approximately fifty members and though they were not all democracies, most of the members were stable, older nation-states, experienced in international affairs, democracies who had some sort of commitment to international law, and to liberal principles.

A degree of falsification was introduced into the United Nations from the very beginning because of the presence of the Soviet Union, certain of its client states, and selected autocracies in an organization committed to the principles of freedom and democracy and self-determination. But that degree of falsification was relatively small and the facts of the United Nations were not too far from the principles enunciated in the charter.

Today there are some 157 members of the United Nations. There have been three members admitted during my eighteen months there. Most of the nations that have been admitted since the United Nations' establishment are new nations, former colonies. The big influx of the former colonies into the United Nations occurred alongside the beginning of the decline of U.S. influence. Someone noted that 1964 was a watershed year. During that year, seventeen new nations were admitted to membership, some fifteen of whom were African nations. Many of these new nations have unstable boundaries, their whole national history has been lived out in the postwar period during which the United Nations has been an important arena of international action. They have never known a world without the United Nations. Most of these nations are, to paraphrase my friend Dick Scammon, unrich, unpowerful, and unhappy. Most are miserably poor; most of them are not democracies. Many have tried democracy but have had a great deal of trouble establishing and maintaining democratic institutions.

These nations have had two overriding preoccupations which have dominated the United Nations agenda since then: decolonization, since they have been involved in establishing their own national independence; and economic development. Now, in principle, the United States should be the last country in the world to have problems with an organization whose agenda is dominated by decolonization and economic development.

As a former colony, we've been involved with decolonization literally all our national life. We have regularly, in the periods before and after World War II, supported national independence and aspirations to independence of the colonies of our best friends. We have not been a colonial nation. We have no apologies to make to the world for our colonial past. We do not share the colonial guilt of many European allies. Similarly, with economic development. Many of us think we practically invented economic growth as a process of internal transformation which is continually at work in our own society —destroying traditional barriers of class and caste, achieving a good life for all. We almost invented economic development assistance with President Truman's Point Four Program in the postwar period. (A little noticed fact, by the way, about the Point Four Program was that it was enunciated in President Truman's Inaugural Address of which point one was that the United Nations would serve as the foundation of American foreign policy henceforth.) Decolonization, economic development, and development assistance are utterly consistent with our national experience, our values, and our practices.

Why would we have problems with an organization most of whose members are concerned with them? It is an interesting question on which I have been reflecting for months now, and I have concluded that it was not the influx of new nations that accounts for the U.S. position at the United Nations. It is not the changed composition of the United Nations that accounts for our fall from influence to impotence.

I have also examined the hypothesis that the bloc system accounts for the absence of American influence in the United Nations. Certainly it makes its contribution. The United Nations functions a lot like a legislature with a multiparty system and the parties in that system are the overlapping blocs, some of which are cohesive such as the Soviet bloc, the ASEAN states, and the EC-10. Some of the blocs are loose and not cohesive, such as the Non-Aligned Movement which embraces some 96 nations, or the G-77 (once a group of 77) which is today a group of 126. Some of the blocs are based on geography like the Organization of African States, some on culture like the Islamic Conference. We are a country without a party in the United Nations and that fact, that absence of a party, certainly is relevant to our impotence in that body. But I do not think it explains the whole problem.

Yet another hypothesis with which I have attempted to explain U.S. impotence is the structure of the United Nations itself: the rules, especially the practice of applying in the General Assembly the principle of one man, one vote to an international assembly of terribly unequal nations. Under that practice, one nation, one vote, we have one vote, Vanuatu has one vote. Obviously, that kind of principle creates a disjunction between power and responsibility because some of the nations who have the power to influence decisions, financial decisions for instance, or the nations who have the resources to implement decisions, are not identical with those who have the power to vote to make them. An extreme example of that was the Golan Heights resolution, passed at one of the many recent special sessions of the General Assembly. It was a particularly obnoxious resolution which laid the framework for a challenge to Israel's credentials. Some eighty-six nations voted in favor of that resolution. Though I have not verified it, I am informed by a reliable source that the financial contributions of all eighty-six of the nations who voted for the resolution do not equal that of the United States. It is argued that only third world countries get a good deal from the United Nations. Nonetheless, I do not believe this or any other basic structural flaw accounts for our impotence.

There is, I fear, another explanation, which was implicit in the drama I saw acted out on the issue of the Falklands. Watching the British permanent representative, an enormously skillful diplomat, operating in relationship to the Falklands crisis was tremendously impressive. In his conduct I observed what a Western democratic nation could do inside the United Nations. The British have done it. They have made the organization function in ways that are responsive to their interests and their policy goals, and the fact that they were able to do it means it can be done. Why, then, haven't we been able to achieve our goals inside this organization?

My tentative conclusion is that it is due to our longstanding lack of skill in practicing international politics in multilateral arenas. It is also part and parcel of the decline of U.S. influence in the world. It is, I believe, a direct reflection of what has been a persisting U.S. ineptitude in international relations that has dogged us all our national life; an ineptitude that has persisted through centuries, through administrations headed by different parties, through different presidents, and is especially manifest in our multilateral politics. It has persisted through administrations that brought to the United National different styles of operation.

We have not been effective in defining or projecting in international arenas a conception of our national purpose. Through decades, we have not been good at politics at the United Nations.

It is a political arena and we have not understood it accurately or adequately as a political arena. We have not, therefore, been able to take an effective part in the politics of the United Nations. We have treated it as though it were something other than a political arena. It is strange that we Americans, who are very gifted at clubhouse politics, statehouse politics, the politics of voluntary associations, at legislative politics and presidential politics, should be so inept at international politics in multilateral arenas like the United Nations. The more one reflects upon it, the stranger it becomes. The explanation, I believe, is that we have not understood that the same principles of politics that apply in our national life apply in multilateral international institutions as well.

We have also suffered from too rapid turnover in our representatives. (I hasten to say that I am not making an application for long tenure.) The job is terribly difficult and frustrating. Nonetheless, in principle, we ought to have representatives who stay there long enough to come to know the scene. When a freshman senator goes to Washington we do not expect that he is going to be effective quickly in the U.S. Senate, we don't expect that he will become a power in the Senate until he has learned the rules and the players, and how to make the rules work for him and how to make the players responsive. But permanent representatives and assistant secretaries of international organizations turn over before they develop expertise. This means the two principal policy-making offices of our international organizations operation are involved in musical chairs—not staying long enough to really get to know the job well.

Another consequence of ignoring the political character of the United Nations is that we operate as though there were no difference between our relations with supporters and opponents, with no penalties for opposing our views and values, and no rewards for cooperating.

We have also operated as though we had no persistent, coherent national purposes which link issue to issue. We act too often as if we changed our minds and basic national interests as issues change, and certainly as administrations change. We have not cultivated reliable voting alliances in the way, for example, the British carefully have nurtured Commonwealth relations, or the French nurture relations with their former colonies. By not really learning the rules, the players, the game, we have often behaved like a bunch of amateurs in the United Nations. Unless or until we approach the United Nations as professionals—professionals at *its* politics—with a clear-cut conception of our purposes and of the political arena in which we operate, knowledge of the colleagues with whom we are interacting, and of their goals and interests, then we won't ever know whether the United Nations could be made a hospitable place for the American national interest. Until then it would be unreasonable even to think about withdrawing from the United Nations.

PART
FOUR

Israel: In and Out of the United Nations

Israel as Scapegoat

It is a great pleasure for me to be here tonight with the Anti-Defamation League of B'nai B'rith. I have long admired the ADL for its leadership in the field of civil rights, its effective and persistent opposition to all forms of prejudice and discrimination, and its commitment to an open society and the democratic way of life. It has been said that the price of liberty is eternal vigilance. The ADL pays this price day after day, year in and year out. It exemplifies the kind of involvement and commitment by private organizations that has made American society strong and free, diverse but at the same time unified, a model of ethnic and institutional pluralism that knows no equal anywhere in the world.

I have a special reason for feeling close to the ADL. We are, after all, neighbors; and in our part of town over at Turtle Bay, we don't take a friendly neighbor for granted. Indeed, we at the United States Mission derive a certain comfort in knowing that the ADL building stands just a block away. With its name boldly emblazoned above First Avenue, the Anti-Defamation League of B'nai B'rith serves as a constant reminder to the self-contained world of the United Nations that there is, in fact, another world out there.

But it is about the self-contained world of the United Nations that I would like to speak tonight. I have been at the United Nations for more than a year now, which is already

Address before the Anti-Defamation League, Palm Beach, Florida, February 11, 1982.

longer than a good many of my predecessors served. I have been able to observe the organization at close range and from a rather special vantage point. And I have concluded that some aspects of the United Nations work very well in ways that would make us all proud. For example, the refugee program, which won last year the Nobel Prize. Some of the other technical and humanitarian agencies of the United Nations, the so-called specialized agencies, do marvelous work in the world eradicating disease and sustaining unfortunate peoples. Obviously, we want to offer generous support to those activities. But these activities do not diminish our conviction that the United Nations is an organization that is in a profound and deepening crisis.

Nothing reveals the nature and the scope of this crisis more clearly than the manner in which the United Nations has dealt with the Arab-Israeli conflict. The Arab-Israeli conflict (or more specifically the campaign against Israel) is the focus of controversy at meetings that are—or should be—totally unrelated to this question. Thus a women's conference is suddenly transformed into a forum for the denunciation of Zionism—and it will be solemnly announced by the assembled delegates of what is euphemistically called the "international community" that, having carefully studied the problem, the conclusion has been reached that the biggest, most important obstacle to the realization of women's full enjoyment of equal rights in the world is Zionism. The opening of an African refugee conference is delayed as a result of efforts to bar Israel from participating. An international conference on Kampuchea becomes engulfed in controversy when the Israeli ambassador is suddenly disinvited from a dinner for all participants. A meeting of the International Atomic Energy Agency becomes so absorbed in negotiations and debate over a resolution to suspend Israel from membership that it almost forgets to worry about nuclear nonproliferation.

The General Assembly itself deals with the issue over and over and over again. When the assembly debates the issue of Afghanistan, which is one of the most important questions facing the world today, it adopts a single, straightforward resolution and then moves on to other matters. When the assembly adopts a resolution on Kampuchea, it does so, once it gets over the question of Israel's participation at dinner, and then moves on to other matters. This is not so with respect to Israel and the conflict in the Middle East. Six anti-Israel resolutions may be adopted under the report of the Special Committee to Investigate Israeli Practices in the Occupied Territories only to be followed by what is called "The Question of Palestine," when six more resolutions are adopted. And it is only at that point that we get to the item on the agenda entitled "The Situation in the Middle East" and the adoption of still more, always predictable, resolutions. They are called, around Turtle Bay, ritual denunciations.

If all this furious activity actually contributed in some way to bringing about peace in the Middle East, one could say that it served some useful purpose. But quite the contrary is true. In fact, it has now become standard practice for the General Assembly to denounce the one agreement that actually *has* contributed tangibly to peace between Israel and her Arab neighbors. That agreement, of course, is the Camp David Accords, which ended the long conflict between Israel and Egypt.

It is instructive, in fact, to contrast the way the Arab-Israeli conflict was approached at Camp David and the way it is dealt with in the interminable debates at the United Nations.

Three factors were responsible for the success of the Camp David approach. First, it was oriented toward the achievement of practical results. In this respect the negotiations were marked by a pragmatic, nonideological, incrementalist approach to solving the problem. Second, participation in the negotiations was limited to those parties seriously committed to reaching a settlement with each other, namely, Israel and Egypt. And finally, the parties were assisted in working out their differences by a mediator who had credibility to both sides. The mediator, of course, was the United States.

At the United Nations, none of these factors are present. First, the debates are intensely ideological, as are the resolutions that are ultimately adopted. The objective is never to find some common ground of agreement with Israel. The objective is instead to isolate and denigrate Israel and ultimately to undermine its political legitimacy. A related objective is to isolate those countries friendly to Israel, above all the United States. The only compromises made during negotiations on resolutions concerning the Middle East are not with Israel and certainly not for the purpose of promoting a peace settlement. Instead, compromises are negotiated within the majority for the sole purpose of enlarging the anti-Israel vote. In these respects the approach taken toward the Arab-Israeli conflict at the United Nations has nothing to do with peace, but is quite simply a continuation of the war against Israel by other means.

Second, participation in the debate is globalized, and the initiative is generally seized by those with the strongest ideological antagonism toward Israel. A decisive role is played by the Palestine Liberation Organization, which, far from being prepared to reach a settlement with Israel, is committed in its National Covenant to the view that the establishment of Israel is "fundamentally null and void" (Article 19) and that the goal of "liberation" can only be achieved through armed struggle (Article 21). The process of polarization is aided and abetted by the Soviets since it offers them a good anti-Western, anti–United States propaganda weapon and allows them both to divert attention from issues like Afghanistan and to pose as an ally of the third world. Many African countries have joined the anti-Israel majority in order to obtain Arab support for their own campaign against South Africa and because they are frequently subjected to considerable economic and political pressures. That obnoxious phrase "Zionism Is Racism" symbolizes the alliance between the Arab and the African countries in the United Nations. Thus, the waters at the United Nations are not only muddied but churned up by the participation of parties that have no direct interest in settling the Arab-Israeli conflict and, in many instances, are committed precisely to its perpetuation and intensification.

Given its failure to take a balanced approach to the Arab-Israeli conflict and its loss of credibility with Israel, the United Nations has been effectively eliminated as an effective world mediator. The time whan a Ralph Bunche could work on behalf of the United Nations for peace between Israel and the Arabs is long past. As a result, a valuable mediator has been lost, and the cause of peace has suffered a significant setback.

It is sometimes believed that despite what happens in the General Assembly and in some of the specialized agencies, the Security Council of the United Nations remains a citadel of reason and balance. Unfortunately, the Security Council itself has not been unaffected by the overall politicization of the United Nations. The recent prolonged debate over the question of Israel's extension of its civil law over the Golan Heights is a depressing illustration of this point.

Throughout this debate—which began in the middle of December and didn't conclude until last Friday—it was assumed that Israel's action, the extension of her jurisdiction over the Golan Heights, alone constituted a threat to international peace. Our government made clear at the outset that we opposed Israel's legislation because it purported or appeared to alter unilaterally the international status of the Golan Heights. We therefore joined in the initial Security Council resolution, in December, which both called upon Israel to rescind the legislation and declared that it was without international legal effect.

Yet this, as we pointed out in our statements, was hardly all there was to say about the problem. The state of relations that existed between Israel and Syria before the passage of Israel's Golan legislation was far from peaceful. A cease-fire had been in effect since 1973 based upon Security Council Resolution 338. This resolution called upon the parties to "start immediately" to negotiate the implementation of Security Council Resolution 242, which was passed after the 1967 war. It was Resolution 242 which established the only valid and enduring framework for negotiating peace between Israel and its Arab neighbors, namely, the withdrawal of Israel "from territories" it had occupied, in exchange for the recognition of Israel's existence within "secure and recognized" borders.

The central threat to peace which the Security Council should have addressed in December was the lack of progress in implementing Resolution 338's mandatory call for immediate negotiations in the framework of 242. But the Security Council would not reaffirm or even recall or even note Resolution 338 or Resolution 242. The facts are that Syria has refused to negotiate with Israel and her refusal has been and remains the chief obstacle to peace. Yet the Security Council took no note of these facts. Instead it ignored its own resolutions, ignored the facts, and directed its attack solely against Israel's Golan Heights legislation.

This pattern did not change even after December 29, when, with a little prodding from the United States, Israel submitted a letter to the secretary general reaffirming its readiness to enter into unconditional negotiations with the Syrians over the international legal status of the Golan. At that point the only constructive role for the Security Council to play was to facilitate such negotiations in accordance with Resolutions 242 and 338.

Instead it entered into more than two weeks of what is euphemistically called debate, during which a floodtide of invective flowed through the council, sweeping away whatever prospects might conceivably have existed for reason and compromise.

The Syrian delegate had already set the tone by declaring during the first Golan debate that it was necessary to turn the tide of "Israeli aggression which began long before 1948, with the arrival of the first colonists." This is the same Syrian delegate who frequently refers to Israel as a crusader remnant and suggests ominously that just as the crusades were defeated and the crusaders were driven out of the Middle East, the last crusade will be as well. The Syrian delegate opened the new round of debate by saying that peace, in his government's view, did not mean anything "identical to or remotely resembling the structural or institutional injustices inherent in the Camp David Accord." Cuba, entering the debate, described Israel's letter of December 29 as "an insolent rebuff of the council and the international community" and called on the council to "halt Zionist arrogance, which is one of the greatest threats to world peace." The PLO, which had been invited to participate in the council proceedings as if it were a member state (in clear violation of the council's own rules of procedure), praised the Soviet Union as "a great nation with a profound knowledge of what it takes to crush fascism," that is, Israel. This knowledge was relevant to the present discussion, according to the PLO, because Israel had "the same militaristic, expanisionist, and racist motives and aims as the fascists the Soviets fought in World War II." Nicaragua joined the chorus by attacking the United States for what it called our policy of support "for repressive regimes hostile to Israel's neighboring states." It accused us of trying to impose "the law of the jungle" in the Middle East as well as in Central America. Not to be outdone, the representative of Jordan reminded the council that Arnold Toynbee had once described Israel as "a fossil of Assyriac civilization."

The Syrian delegate was given another turn before the vote, which he used to praise Vietnam as a "heroic country" because it "broke the back of the United States and Israel." Just to make sure we got the point, he went on to praise Cuba, which, he said, "has defied the entire system that was imposed upon it by the United States of America." "Israel," he said, "was imposed by the United States of America on our region to destroy our life, to control us and a strategic route to the region, and also to control our oil and our wealth."

I found these remarks so illuminating about the thinking of the Syrian delegate that when he finished I-took the floor for the first and only time in the debate to thank him "for his very useful clarification of the issues," at which the Syrian delegate demanded to know what I meant. I was violating his right to understand, he asserted, citing a "right" new even in the United Nations' exhaustive list. Was my statement "constructive ambiguity or merely an example of imperialist obfuscation?" he demanded. I told him later that I thought it was an example of imperialist obfuscation but I wasn't sure.

The resolution before the council was consistent with the debate that had preceded it. It did not seek to promote negotiations for a peaceful settlement but rather to impose sanctions to punish Israel. In explaining our vote, I pointed out that the resolution constituted "an aberration, even a perversion of the very purpose which the Security Council is called upon by Chapter VII of the United Nations Charter to perform." That responsibility is to prevent "an aggravation of the situation," when the situation may be dangerous to peace. Far from doing that, the resolution before the Security Council would have itself become a source of aggravation of a dangerous situation. In spite of our best efforts, nine positive votes were accumulated for the obnoxious resolution. Therefore, exercising our constitutional right as a permanent member of the Security Council, the United States vetoed this harmful resolution, which opened the way for what is called a Uniting for Peace resolution. It might better be called a Uniting for Mischief resolution given the way it is used these days.

Under a Uniting for Peace resolution, an emergency special session of the General Assembly may be called when one member has vetoed a majority vote in the Security Council. Yehuda Blum, the Israeli ambassador to the United Nations, later, noting the repetition of the special session, commented, "Some emergency!" as people made the same speech for the fourth time. The session provided an occasion for the adoption of a fourth resolution on Israel's Golan Heights action that was much more extreme than the one presented to the Security Council. The most recent one, passed only last Friday, is the most objectionable and dangerous of all. The resolution called for comprehensive sanctions against Israel and for Israel's total isolation in all fields. It also harshly criticized us, by the way, for supplying military, economic, and technical support to Israel and for exercising our veto in the Security Council. Basically that resolution denies the legitimacy of the veto in the United Nations and the legitimacy of Israel's membership in the United Nations because it raises a serious question about whether Israel is "a peace-loving member state," which is charter language describing the requirements of membership. You have to be a peace-loving member state like Syria in order to be eligible for membership in the United Nations. The Golan Heights resolution suggests that Israel is in violation of the charter and of the resolution under the terms of which it was admitted. This unique action against a member state laid the groundwork for an attack on Israel's membership in the United Nations. It did not itself seek to expel Israel, but it lays the legal groundwork for an expulsion or suspension.

What did we do? We did what we always do in those situations, but a bit more effectively this time. We worked very hard to stimulate opposition to this resolution, which we pointed out to everyone was unprecedented in the seriousness of its attack. We lobbied in New York, in Washington, and in capitals, and we were actually only defeated by 4 to 1, which by United Nations standards is something of a victory. In December the vote was 127 to 2, and last week it was only 86 to 21. Last week also our European allies and the other democratic nations voted with us against that resolution against Israel. All the Latin American nations except those tied to the Soviets abstained, and that is good by United Nations standards. Fiji was the only full-fledged member of what is known as the third world to vote against that resolution. There should be a special fund for Fiji.

What happened? What happened there was one more example of what goes wrong at the United Nations. This organization, which was developed out of a vision of how to build a better world, how to replace violence with reason, how to contain conflict, how to resolve differences peaceably, has been transformed. Instead of being an effective instrument for conflict resolution, it serves all too often as an arena in which conflict is polarized, extended, and exacerbated, in which differences are made deeper and more difficult to resolve than they would otherwise be.

What can we do about that? We ought to do something, I think that's quite clear. We ought to do something because we know that the "ritual denunciations" that took place over the last six weeks do in fact take their toll. They take their toll because words matter. Words can destroy. What we call each other ultimately becomes what we think of each other, and it matters.

What can we do about this organization to which the United States contributes more than $1 billion annually? We can, first of all, take it seriously. We can face the fact and let everybody else understand that we believe that what happens there matters, that we know and we care. That's our slogan at USUN: "We take the United Nations very seriously."

Second, we can make certain that when we speak we are serious and credible. It is important to let countries around the United Nations understand that when we say that destructive exercises and attacks like those of the last six weeks matter to us, we mean it. It is important that the other nations understand that when we say that attacks on the membership of Israel or her right to participate matter, we mean it. We try very hard at the U.S. Mission to establish that kind of seriousness, and I believe we have. David Broder, *Washington Post* columnist, said that the president reminded him of Horton the Elephant. Horton, you may recall, was the Dr. Seuss elephant who faithfully sat on the egg till it hatched. Horton's slogan was: "I meant what I said and I said what I meant, an elephant's faithful 100 percent." We try at the United Nations to be faithful 100 percent and to be sure that everybody understands that we said what we meant. We try also to answer attacks against our own country and against our friends when those attacks are unfair and unjust. We try to be fair, balanced, and reasonable but also vigorous in our response to attacks against us and our friends and our principles.

Finally, I think what we can do and should do is pursue a consistent policy over time, letting our actions demonstrate that we are, indeed, serious people who notice and who care and who distinguish between actions and between countries who behave like friends and supporters of democratic institutions and freedom—and those who do not. If we do not act consistently, we cannot protect ourselves, our friends, and our principles.

I should like to emphasize that the policies we carry out at the United Nations are the policies of a president who is a very good friend of Israel and of Secretary of State Haig, who is another very good friend of Israel. Right now, in Geneva, Michael Novak and Richard Schifter, two other good friends of Israel, are very busy defending our principles and our friends and ourselves at the United Nations Human Rights Commission. There are a good many of us throughout the administration, beginning at the top. It is important for all of us to know that when we stand for ourselves, our friends, and our principles, there are organizations devoted to freedom and democracy and fidelity who, like Horton the Elephant, are standing with us.

A Miserable Resolution

Mr. President, the resolution before this emergency special session of the General Assembly is profoundly objectionable to the United States. We oppose it because it does not contribute to peace in the Middle East: it will make peace harder to achieve.

We oppose the end it seeks—which is revenge and retribution, not conciliation and compromise.

We oppose the means it recommends—which are unreasonably punitive and ill-suited to accomplishing any constructive purpose.

We oppose the use of the United Nations involved here because this body was and is meant to be devoted to building peace and security, and this resolution seeks neither. Instead, it uses this body as an instrument to deepen divisions and exacerbate conflicts.

We oppose this resolution because, like any other cynical use of power, it will leave this body weaker than it already is, less fit to achieve its noble purposes.

By damaging the prospects for peace, this resolution undermines the integrity—indeed, the very raison d'être—of the United Nations.

Last month in the Security Council the United States voted against a resolution on Israel's Golan Heights legislation because as we stated at the time, the resolution constituted "a perversion of the very purpose which the Security Council is called upon by

Statement in the Emergency Special Session of the General Assembly in explanation of vote on the situation in the Golan Heights, February 5, 1982.

Chapter VII of the United Nations Charter to perform." That purpose is to prevent "an aggravation of the situation." The resolution before us today, like the previous resolution, does not prevent an aggravation of the situation: it is itself a source of aggravation. It is also procedurally flawed in that it seeks to assign to the General Assembly responsibilities that Chapter VII of the charter properly and solely invests in the Security Council.

The United Nations has discussed the Golan Heights legislation now for nearly two months. As my delegation made clear at the outset, we opposed this legislation because it purported or appeared to alter unilaterally the international status of the Golan Heights. Therefore, on December 17 the United States joined other members of the Security Council in passing Resolution 497, thereby making clear our disapproval of the Israeli government's action in extending its civil law over the Golan Heights. We communicated the same message in our bilateral relations.

As we have stated often, the future of the Golan Heights, like that of all the occupied territories, can be resolved only through negotiations pursuant to Security Council Resolutions 242 and 338. Accordingly, we have called upon Israel to rescind its legislation and—most importantly—to reaffirm its commitment to a negotiated solution. In its letter of December 29 to the secretary-general, Israel did, in fact, reaffirm its readiness to enter into unconditional negotiations with the Syrians over the international legal status of the Golan.

At that point, the only constructive role for the United Nations was to facilitate such negotiations, in accordance with Resolutions 242 and 338. But the resolution before the Security Council did not even mention these resolutions and, needless to say, the current draft resolution doesn't either.

Mr. President, we must go back to basics. Israel is accused of threatening peace. Yet peace is not the situation that prevailed between Israel and Syria before Israel's Golan Heights legislation was adopted. Security Council Resolution 338, which was the basis for the 1973 cease-fire, called upon the parties to "start immediately" to negotiate the implementation of Resolution 242 so that Israeli withdrawal could be effected in exchange for recognition of Israel's existence within "secure and recognized" borders. But no such negotiations took place.

There is no one in this chamber who does not know which party has refused to negotiate peace or even to accept Resolution 242. Yet the resolution before us today and the speeches we have heard take no account of this reality.

Mr. President, the United States greatly desires to have cordial, cooperative, good relations with all the states in the region. My country has devoted enormous effort, in this administration and under previous administrations, to finding a basis for peace and reconciliation. We also want very much a strong United Nations acting in fidelity to the principles of its charter. For these very reasons we are appalled by this resolution which distorts reality, denies history, and inflames passions.

The draft resolution before us calls the Israeli legislation an act of aggression. But no shots were fired, no soldiers were brought into place. And the future of the Golan Heights is no less negotiable than before.

It describes the Israeli legislation as an annexation. It is not. The United States has not recognized it as such. The Security Council in Resolution 497 did not recognize it as such. To now call it annexation only creates an artificial obstacle to negotiations.

This resolution calls for comprehensive sanctions against Israel and for Israel's total isolation from the rest of the world. But can anyone truly believe that such proposals, advanced in a spirit of vindictiveness, will make a constructive contribution to peace?

Mr. President, the United States objects to this resolution because it makes the search for peace more difficult, and because it weakens this body. We also object to it for less disinterested reasons—we object to the barely veiled attack on the United States present here in the paragraph that "strongly deplores the negative vote by a permanent member."

The right to cast a veto is vested by the charter in the five permanent members of the Security Council. The sole purpose of this provision is to permit one of the permanent members to block a proposed action of the council if for any reason this action is deemed seriously flawed. The United States used the veto for the purpose for which it was intended—to block action which we deemed ill-conceived and imprudent and, moreover, one incompatible with the pursuit of international peace and security to which this body is dedicated. It is not at all appropriate that an action taken in conformity with the spirit and the letter of the charter should be deplored.

Furthermore, as everyone present understands, this resolution raises basic questions which go to the heart of the relationship of a member state to the United Nations. This is a profoundly serious matter, filled with ominous portent. Questions of membership in this body and its associated agencies should not—indeed cannot—be settled by majority passions. The United Nations or any similar organization can only exist if the principle of majority rule is balanced by respect for minority rights. This resolution strikes twice at the principle that minorities also have rights: first, when it deplores our use of the veto, and second, when it attempts to submit questions of membership to the General Assembly. Respect for the United Nations means respect for its charter.

We hope that the authors and supporters of the resolution will think deeply about this aspect of their approach, for the health, even the survival, of the United Nations depends on respect for both majority rule and minority rights. Nothing is more clear than this.

Mr. President, suppose this resolution passes, as regrettably I suppose it will, what will this exercise have achieved?

- An Israeli withdrawal from the Golan? Of course not.
- An embargo of economic, technological, or military goods destined for Israel? Of course not.
- A restoration of the occupied territories? Of course not.
- A resolution of the problems of Palestinians? Of course not.
- Peace in the Middle East? Of course not.
- Will it intimidate the United States, causing it to abandon its Middle East policy, its friendship with Israel, its search for peace in the region? Of course not.

What then, will this resolution accomplish?

What has already been achieved by these weeks of harsh, seemingly endless attacks on Israel, on the United States, on the spirit of reason, moderation, on peace itself? To raise the question is to answer it.

There is, in my country, a child's rhyme, "sticks and stones may break our bones but words will never hurt us." The rhyme is profoundly mistaken. Words have consequences.

Words express the ideas, the values, and the truths we live by. They are the principal means available for reason to explain purposes and dispel misunderstandings. The United Nations was conceived as a place of reason, a place where reason would replace violence as the tool for settling disputes.

This miserable resolution before us today demonstrates the sad truth that any instrument can be made to serve purposes remote from its raison d'être: words can be used as weapons; ploughshares can be turned into swords, and the United Nations itself can be used to polarize nations, spread hostility, and exacerbate conflict.

The use made of the United Nations in this resolution and in the weeks preceding it is indeed worth "strongly deploring" and my government strongly deplores it.

Naturally we shall vote no.

Golan Again

Mr. President, my country opposes the resolution sponsored by Jordan for reasons which are of importance not only as regards the proper disposition of the current matter before us —that of Israel's Golan Heights legislation—but also out of concern for the future of the United Nations and the ability of the Security Council to perform a positive role in the maintenance of world peace and security.

The resolution with which we are confronted today constitutes, we believe, an aberration, even a perversion, of the very purpose which the Security Council is called upon by Chapter VII of the United Nations Charter to perform. Article 39 vests in the Security Council the responsibility to deal with activities that threaten world peace and security. The role the Security Council is called upon to perform is, by definition then, a constructive role: to prevent "an aggravation of the situation." This resolution, we believe, would do the opposite. Far from preventing aggravation, it would become a source of aggravation.

Indeed, it has already succeeded in exacerbating the terribly difficult problems of the Middle East, in dividing people whose cooperation is needed to solve problems, in sowing suspicions, and feeding hostilities. A flood tide of invective has flowed through this hall threatening day after day to overwhelm the spirit of reason and compromise with hatred and cynicism.

The United States has tried hard to demonstrate its determination to be fair and reasonable in confronting the situation in

Statement in the Security Council in explanation of vote on the situation in the Golan Heights, January 20, 1982.

the Golan Heights. We have refused to be drawn into vicious exchanges, or distracted from the search for real solutions that will render more safe and secure the real lives of actual people in the region.

We will not be deterred from our course. We will continue to search for constructive means to achieve peace for Israel and her neighbors.

We believe that a good place to begin is indeed with the implementation of the resolutions of the Security Council of the United Nations. We believe that Security Council Resolutions 242, 338, and 497 can serve as the basis of that constructive search. We urge the implementation of all three.

Mr. President, on this occasion, and in this place where there has been so much talk of aggression, repression, and the desire of peoples to live in peace, I cannot forbear to mention the problems of another people in the world who are just now being denied peace and self-government. What an extraordinary institution this is that, in the more than a month since the massive, brutal repression of the people of Poland got under way, there has been no mention here of the violations of their human rights, of the violations of the United Nations Charter, the Helsinki Final Act, or the Universal Declaration of Human Rights that have occurred there. We should like on this occasion to express our solidarity with the people of Poland as well as with those of the Golan and to affirm the commitment of my government to work for the rights of all peoples currently denied freedom, self-determination, and self-government.

Mr. President, we do not approve Israel's annexation of the Golan Heights. Indeed, we do not even believe such annexation has occurred. We believe we should get on with negotiations which will demonstrate that fact.

Delegitimizing Israel

In a letter to President Kittani, which has been circulated at my request as a document of the General Assembly, I stated the reservations of my government with regard to the "resumption" of the Seventh Emergency Special Session on "The Question of Palestine." I desire to repeat these reservations here.

The Seventh Emergency Special Session adjourned "temporarily" on July 19, 1980, having adopted a resolution which authorized "the President of the latest regular session of the General Assembly to resume its meetings upon request from member states." It seems plain that the purpose of this "temporary" adjournment was to allow for a resumption in the same time frame should events warrant. Almost two years have passed. During those intervening twenty-one months, two regular sessions of the General Assembly, two different emergency sessions, and one special session have been held. Yet now, at the request of a group of members and notwithstanding the passage of a substantial period of time, the Seventh Emergency Special Session has been reconvened without regard to the views of other members, or the developments that have taken place in the interim. Clearly, this dubious procedure of a "resumption" has the effect of undermining the provisions of the rules of procedure for convening an Emergency Special Session.

This procedural irregularity provides a fitting framework for the work of this session, which is already on its way to

Statement in the General Assembly at the Seventh Emergency Special Session, April 23, 1982.

creating new, further obstacles to peace between Israel and her Arab neighbors.

Let me be clear. My government shares the concern of those who are alarmed at the escalation of violence in the Middle East. We are profoundly distressed at the increase of tensions and conflict, the spreading of fear and suspicion, the deepening sense of hopelessness with respect to resolving "The Question of Palestine" and achieving peace and stability in this region rent by violence and hate.

But who among us sincerely believes that the exercise in which we are now engaged—this "resumed" Emergency Special Session—will take us closer toward that goal?

Who among us believes that the cause of peace is served by still another round of bitter denunciation of Israel?

Who among us, I wonder, believes that peace is even the *goal* of this assembly?

This assembly can repeat its familiar and unbalanced charges, it can issue flamboyant ultimata, and adopt ever harsher resolutions, all with the usual predictable effect. That effect will be to increase—not to reduce—tensions; to inflame— not to calm—passions; to widen—not to narrow—divisions; and to make war more—not less—likely to take place.

The fact that this institution, conceived to resolve conflicts, is thus used to exacerbate and embitter divisions among nations is the cruelest of ironies.

But that is not the end of the irony. It is even worse that the United Nations, by its own actions, is being driven further and further away from the very framework of peace which *it* established fifteen years ago. I refer, of course, to Security Council Resolution 242. That resolution remains the only realistic framework for a just and lasting peace in the Middle East. But it is not reaffirmed, it is not even recalled in the current United Nations resolutions, which—to the contrary— violate the spirit of Resolution 242 and undermine its balanced approach to peace.

Security Council Resolution 242, along with Resolution 338 which was adopted in 1973 and which calls for immediate negotiations to implement 242, is built around four main principles:

First, it links Israeli withdrawal from territories occupied in 1967 to the establishment of peace with the Arab parties to the conflict.

127

Second, it stipulates that Israel should then withdraw to secure and recognized boundaries established in the agreements of peace.

Third, it affirms that agreements of peace should also provide for security arrangements, including demilitarized zones, and guarantees of maritime rights through all the international waterways of the area.

Fourth, it affirms that the goal is true peace, as distinct from "declarations of non-belligerency" or their equivalent.

It was precisely according to this resolution of the United Nations Security Council, and the principles set forth therein, that peace has been achieved between Israel and Egypt, leading to the return of the entire Sinai to Egyptian sovereignty—a process that is due to be completed this very Sunday. That process, which is based on mutual respect and reasoned argument, stands in stark contrast to a different approach which insists on Israeli withdrawal in the absence of peace. The second approach cannot possibly achieve its putative goal, which is a negotiated peace; but, by ensuring confrontations, it can produce spurious "evidence" that peaceful settlement of disputes with Israel is impossible.

My government believes that peace can only be achieved through respect, reason, and compromise. We recognize that while the Camp David process looks toward a comprehensive peace, it has not yet achieved that goal. It constitutes the greatest concrete step toward peace, however, in the history of the Arab-Israeli conflict. And yet it is but a step. There remains a great distance still to be traveled. But we believe peace is possible—real peace, peace in accordance with Security Council Resolutions 242 and 338.

We certainly do not underestimate the obstacles to a peace settlement in the West Bank and Gaza. Yet we believe that Camp David offers the only viable basis for a settlement that will determine the final status of these territories. Camp David actually goes beyond Resolutions 242 and 338, which call for an agreement among states, by affording the indigenous populations of the West Bank and Gaza the opportunity to participate in the negotiations toward a settlement. Such a settlement can only be achieved through negotiations between the parties concerned—in this instance Egypt and Israel, as well as Jordan and the representative of the Palestinian people. These negotiations still await the establishment of a self-governing authority in the West Bank and Gaza and the agreement of Jordan to enter the talks.

This painstaking and protracted process will require hard bargaining, compromise, and arrangements that establish trust and new patterns of interstate and human relationships. But that is the only way that a just and lasting peace can be achieved. Only such an approach can hope to satisfy to the greatest degree possible the rights of all the parties concerned. Only such an approach can work.

We are now reaching a point when new efforts will be devoted to the completion of the Camp David process. It would be a great tragedy if this process must go forward in the face of opposition from the United Nations. The peace process might suffer, and more certainly the United Nations itself would suffer.

Mr. President, there are, as everyone knows, members of this body who desire to deny membership and/or participation to another member state. There will be, we understand, an effort to pass, in this special session, a resolution that prepares the way for questioning Israel's credentials and the right to participate in the various bodies of the United Nations. To this end, one draft resolution circulating in the corridors now asserts that Israel is not a peace-loving member state, and has repeatedly violated the provisions of the charter.

But Mr. President, neither this special session nor the draft resolution now circulating in the corridors is consistent with the purposes of the United Nations Charter. Neither seeks (in accordance with Chapter II) to maintain "international peace and security," nor "to develop friendly relations among nations," nor "to achieve international cooperation in solving international problems"; least of all do they make this institution "a center for harmonizing the actions of nations in the attainment of . . . common ends." This special session is one more event in an ongoing process whose goals are to delegitimize a member state—Israel—to deny it the right to self-defense, to secure borders, to survival.

This special session and its accompanying draft resolutions are one more clear example of a strategy whose goals and tactics are clear: use a United Nations body to make "official" demands incompatible with Israel's security and survival, so as then to be able to complain that noncompliance with these impossible demands "proves" Israel an international lawbreaker—unworthy of membership in the international community of peace-loving states.

Mr. President, if this organization, established to seek, maintain, and strengthen peace, is used to make war by other means; if its arenas, established to provide a rational basis for discussion and settlement of international disputes, are used as battlefields in a holy war; if its procedures, designed to ensure fairness, are twisted to ensure desired political outcomes—then the purposes and structures of this organization are transformed. And the United Nations itself is transformed. It becomes, quite literally, a different organization, inspired by different purposes, dedicated to different goals, characterized by different modes of behavior; for an institution is, finally, nothing more or less than the regular interactions of its members. When the goals and behavior of the members change, the institution has changed as well.

Mr. President, how much falsification can an institution stand without destroying itself entirely? This world body cannot endure as a moral and political force if its energies are devoted to increasing conflict and conducting vendettas against targeted countries. If the United Nations prefers to make political war rather than peace, it must suffer the consequences in terms of its credibility and reputation. And if, in violation of its own rules, it should decide to exclude the democratic state of Israel from participation, it will inevitably reap the whirlwind.

It is not too late, Mr. President, for a majority of member states to reverse the trend toward irresponsibility and destruction. The time to begin is now, before this trend gathers an irreversible momentum.

Condemning Israel:
The Iraqi Reactor

The issue before the Security Council in the past week—Israel's attack upon the Iraqi nuclear reactor—raises profound and troubling questions that will be with us long after the conclusion of these meetings. The Middle East, as one prominent American observed last week, "provides combustible matter for international conflagration akin to the Balkans prior to World War I," a circumstance made all the more dangerous today by the possibility that nuclear weapons could be employed in a future conflict.

The area that stretches from Southwest Asia across the Fertile Crescent and Persian Gulf to the Atlantic Ocean, is, as we all know, torn not only by tension and division, but also by deeply rooted, tenacious hostilities that erupt repeatedly into violence. In the past two years alone, one country in the area, Afghanistan, has been brutally invaded and occupied, but not pacified. Afghan freedom fighters continue their determined struggle for their country's independence. Iraq and Iran are locked in a bitter war. And with shocking violence, Libya, whose principal exports are oil and terror, invaded and now occupies Chad. Lebanon has its territory and its sovereignty violated almost routinely by neighboring nations. Other governments in the area have, during the same brief period, been the object of violent attacks and terrorism. Now comes Israel's destruction of the Iraqi nuclear facility. The danger of war and

Statement in the Security Council on the complaint by Iraq, June 19, 1981.

anarchy in this vital strategic region threatens global peace and presents this council with a grave challenge.

My government's commitment to a just and enduring peace in the Middle East is well known. We have given our full support to the efforts by the secretary general to resolve the war between Iran and Iraq. Our abhorrence of the Soviet Union's invasion and continued occupation of Afghanistan—against the will of the entire Afghan people—requires no elaboration on this occasion. For weeks, our special representative Philip C. Habib has been in the area conducting talks which we still hope may help to end the hostilities in Lebanon and head off a conflict between Israel and Syria. Not least, we have been engaged in intensive efforts to assist in the implementation of the Egyptian-Israeli treaty, efforts that have already strengthened the forces for peace in the Middle East and will, we believe, lead ultimately to a comprehensive peace settlement of the Arab-Israeli conflict in accordance with Resolutions 242 and 338 of the Security Council.

As in the past, United States policies in the Middle East aim above all at making the independence and freedom of people in the area more secure and their daily lives less dangerous. We seek the security of all the nations and peoples of the region: the security of all nations to know that a neighbor is not seeking technology for purposes of destruction; the security of all people to know they can live their lives in the absence of fear of attack and do not daily see their existence threatened; and the security of all people displaced by war and violence.

The instability that has become the hallmark and history of the Middle East may serve the interests of some on this council—it does not serve our interests and it does not serve the interests of our friends, be they Israeli or Arab.

We believe, to the contrary, that the peace and security of all nations in the region are bound up with the peace and security of the area.

It is precisely because of my government's deep involvement in efforts to promote peace in the Middle East that we were shocked by the Israeli air strike on the Iraqi nuclear facility and promptly condemned this action, which we believe reflected and exacerbated deeper antagonisms in the region.

However, although my government has condemned Israel's act, we know it is necessary to take into account the context of this action as well as its consequences. The truth demands nothing less. As my president, Ronald Reagan, asserted in his press conference:

> I do think that one has to recognize that Israel had reason for concern in view of the past history of Iraq, which has never signed a cease-fire or recognized Israel as a nation, has never joined in any peace effort for that. . . . it does not even recognize the existence of Israel as a country.

With respect to Israel's attack on the Iraqi nuclear reactor, President Reagan said: "Israel might have sincerely believed it was a defensive move."

The strength of U.S. ties and commitment to Israel are well known to the members of this council. Israel is an important and valued ally. The warmth of the human relationship between our peoples is understood. Nothing has happened that in any way alters the strength of our commitment. We in the Reagan administration are proud to call Israel a friend and ally.

Nonetheless, we believe the means Israel chose to quiet its fears about the purposes of Iraq's nuclear program have hurt, not helped, the peace and security of the area. In my government's view, diplomatic means available to Israel had not been exhausted, and the Israeli action has damaged the regional confidence that is essential for the peace process to go forward. All of us with an interest in peace, freedom, and national independence have a high stake in that process. Israel's stake is highest of all.

My government is committed to working with the Security Council to remove obstacles to peace. We made clear from the outset that the United States will support reasonable actions by this body which might be likely to contribute to the pacification of the region. We also made clear that my government would approve no decision that harmed Israel's basic interests, was unfairly punitive, or created new obstacles to a just and lasting peace.

The United States has long been deeply concerned about the dangers of nuclear proliferation. We believe all nations should adhere to the Non-Proliferation Treaty. It is well known that we support the International Atomic Energy Agency and will cooperate in any reasonable effort to strengthen it.

We desire to emphasize, however, that security from nuclear attack and annihilation will depend less on treaties signed than on the construction of stable regional order. Yes, Israel should be condemned; yes, the IAEA should be strengthened and respected by all nations. And yes, too, Israel's neighbors should recognize her right to exist and enter into negotiations with her to resolve their differences.

The challenge before this council was to exercise at least the same degree of restraint and wisdom that we demand of the parties directly involved in the Middle East tensions. Inflammatory charges, such as the Soviet statement that the United States somehow encouraged the raid, or that we knew of the raid beforehand, are false and malicious. One can speculate about whose interests are served by such innuendo. Certainly the spirit of truth, restraint, or peace are not served by such innuendo. Certainly the process of peace is not forwarded.

Throughout the negotiations of the last days, my government has sought only to move us closer to the day when genuine peace between Israel and its Arab neighbors will become a reality. We have searched for a reasonable outcome of the negotiations in the Security Council, one which would protect vital interests of all parties, and damage the vital interests of none, and which would ameliorate rather than exacerbate the dangerous passions and division of the area. In that search we were aided by the cooperative spirit, restrained positions, and good faith of the Iraqi Foreign Minister Sa'dun Hammadi. We sincerely believe the results will move that turbulent area a bit closer to the time when all the states in the region have the opportunity to turn their energies and resources from war to peace, from armaments to development, from anxiety and fear to confidence and well-being.

Exacerbating Problems

The United States profoundly regrets and strongly condemns the senseless act of violence that occurred on April 11, 1982, at one of Islam's most sacred mosques—the Dome of the Rock. We extend our condolences to all those who have suffered physically and spiritually from this act.

Last Friday, April 16, President Reagan met with six ambassadors delegated by the Islamic countries represented in Washington. I should like to read the official report of that meeting. President Reagan, it said,

> expressed his deep personal sorrow and that of all Americans over last Sunday's violence at the hands of a deranged individual in an area sacred to three of the world's great religions.
>
> The President expressed his sympathy with the concern of the Islamic world over the disruption of the tranquility of one of its most holy shrines. This concern is shared by the members of all faiths. He reiterated his conviction that the peace of the holy places of Jerusalem must be maintained and confirmed the dedication of the United States to encouraging the conditions necessary for the wellbeing of all those who draw their spiritual inspiration from that city.
>
> The President called upon all the governments and peoples of the Middle East to work to decrease tensions in the area and prevent further acts of violence and loss of life.

Statement in the Security Council on the Dome of the Rock Incident, April 20, 1982.

We understand that this goal—to decrease tensions in the area and prevent further acts of violence and loss of life—is also the chief objective of the Security Council.

We have considered the matter carefully in our government; regrettably, we do not believe that the resolution before us helps to achieve our shared objective. For these reasons we think it serves no constructive purposes but will further embitter the peoples of the region and deepen the divisions that could lead to conflict. Thus, as much as we condemn the act of violence that occasioned this debate of the Security Council, we must oppose this resolution which, in our view, would make new acts of violence more—not less—likely to take place in the future.

We voted against the resolution because it contains language in the preambular and the operative paragraphs which implies that the responsibility for this terrible event lies not with the individual who was responsible for the incident but with the Israeli authorities who have unequivocally denounced the act. The text also implies that Israel has hindered the efforts of the Higher Islamic Council to perform its responsibilities for the administration of the holy places whereas the evidence is that Israel has, in the main, carefully respected the council's role. To eliminate any misunderstanding, Mr. President, I may add that our vote does not affect our longstanding position on the status of Jerusalem. As President Reagan explained to the Moslem ambassadors last Friday, the U.S. position remains as previously stated, that is, that we support an undivided city whose final status can only be determined through negotiations among all concerned parties.

Beyond Sadat

The death of Anwar Sadat was, of course, an event with the potential of significantly altering the shape of the world. Anwar Sadat was a world leader, a man whose life has profoundly affected events and alignments in his part of the world—a part of the world with unique centrality for all those other parts dependent on its strategic resources. Sadat's death introduces one more element of potential instability into this troubled area of oil, Islam, Israel, and instability, an area that bears a disturbing resemblance to the Balkans in the period just prior to World War I.

Let me be clear. Egypt's political system has shown a reassuring capacity to cope in an orderly, constitutional fashion with the succession crisis, and Sadat's chosen successor, Vice President Mubarak, has stated clearly his commitment to continuing Sadat's policies—specifically including the peace process rooted in the Camp David accords. U.S. Secretary of State Alexander Haig has spoken out forcefully to warn other nations against attempting to take advantage of Sadat's assassination to provoke or profit from increased instability. Nonetheless, during the period in which Egypt's new president establishes his leadership and consolidates power, that nation will feel the trauma of Sadat's brutal murder and sudden removal. It is a special kind of trauma which has been felt by Americans, Bangladeshis, Italians, and other peoples whose

---

Address before the American Gas Association, at the Waldorf Astoria, New York City, October 12, 1981.

leaders have been brutally cut down by assassins' bullets. Regardless of the type of regime, the sudden loss of an esteemed ruler is shocking. Because leaders embody collective identity and aspirations, a violent destruction of a powerful leader resonates and is felt as a threat throughout a polity.

Inevitably, therefore, there is and will be discussion of possible policy consequences of this tragic event. Such discussion began even before Sadat's burial. "For American policy in the Middle East, can there be life after Sadat?" an American journalist wrote, and answered, "Yes, of course, but that policy can succeed only if we finally learn not to tie policy wholly to the survival of strong men." Repeatedly in the past days it has been said that the death of Sadat resembles the fall of the shah, because once again a powerful leader, important to the United States, whose government rested upon personal power, has been abruptly removed from the scene. And, in fact, the death of Sadat, like the fall of the shah, illuminates and underscores the vulnerability of policies that depend—or seem to depend— on a single individual. Some commentators, like the one quoted above, rush to the conclusion that the United States should not rely on policies that depend on men, overlooking the fact that in the Middle East, as in various other parts of the world, the realities of politics force us to heavy reliance on relations with individual rulers.

Such regimes are characteristic of the area. The fundamentalist theocracy headed by Khomeini is no less dependent on personal leadership than the preceding monarchy was dependent on the shah. Presidents Qaddafi and Nimeiry, Kings Hussein and Khalid differ with regard to their goals, their policies, their methods, and their styles, but they all head regimes which depend heavily on their personal leadership. The tradition of paternalistic authority is strong in the Arab world. It rests on strong authoritarian, patriarchal family structures in Arab societies, and there is coherence between society and polity. The truth is that we cannot control the governments of the area or choose the rulers. We cannot structure their institutions, transform their beliefs, or, by moving a magic wand, make the Arab states that stretch across North Africa into South Asia into replicas of modern, secular, democratic nations living harmoniously with one another. We must deal with them as we find them. Instead of being modern, secular, and democratic, they are quite the contrary—authoritarian, traditional, profoundly religious, subject to the kinds of instabilities characteristic of personal autocracies. These include periodic rebellion, chronic succession crises, and complicated, persistent rivalries that have culminated repeatedly in war. To the traditional sources of instability and conflict have been added modern weapons, modern education, communication and transportation, modern ideologies, oil, Israel, and Soviet ambitions. These new elements have exacerbated rivalries and conflicts, extending both their scope and intensity. These conflicts and rivalries—historic and modern—constitute a second important element of the context which shapes conditions and limits for our relationships with the region and the nations that comprise it.

It is easy to infer from the reality of Arab identity—based in what my Georgetown University colleague Michael Hudson terms "ethnicity and religion"—an assumption that there is unity among Arabs. Nothing could be more mistaken. Arab nations remain profoundly divided among themselves and frequently within their own borders.

Today, *Iraq* is enmeshed in a seemingly endless war with Iran. *Libya's* Qaddafi has stepped up his violent campaign to spread Islamic radicalism through North Africa and the Middle East, has invaded Chad outright, and is involved in a critical struggle with the Sudan. *Syria,* whose 25,000 troops more often disturb the peace in Lebanon than enforce it, is threatened internally by pressures from fundamentalist Sunni Moslems and also by intense hostility from Iraq. *Lebanon,* meanwhile, has almost succumbed to the complicated and violent struggle among Maronites and Moslems, Syria and Israel, the PLO and Haddad forces. The government of *Morocco* is challenged by the violent demands of the Polisario. In 1979 the Saudi regime was the object of an attempted coup, an unholy alliance by religious extremists and political radicals. Even more than Saudi Arabia, the government of Jordan has felt the destabilizing effects of radical politics introduced into the area under the cover of Palestinian nationalism. Although Jordan expelled Palestinian guerrillas after the conflict of 1970–1971, the effects of Palestinian radicalism on Jordan's politics remain strong. Nearby, *Iran* teeters on the brink of anarchy; the fanatical theocrat who replaced the shah has managed to hold onto power in the midst of an almost incredible carnage. Executions, bombings, and war have decimated Iran's polity and economy. But still the Ayatollah Khomeini hangs on, snuffing out lives like the mad queen of Alice in Wonderland.

And, of course, over the whole region hangs the threat of Soviet expansion. Soviet armies on the borders of Iran, Soviet weapons and advice in Syria, Cubans in "democratic" Yemen, threaten the independence of all nations in the region.

War, assassinations, coups, ethnic separatism, religious fundamentalism and secular revolutionaries, and the Soviet appetite disturb the peace of the Arab world. And we have not even come to Israel.

Today, another unifying factor has been added to language and religion around which peoples of the region can coalesce: it is, of course, radical Palestinian nationalism, which is closely related but not quite identical with hostility to the state of Israel.

"It is difficult to emphasize sufficiently the importance of the Palestine issue for the politics of legitimacy in the Arab world," Michael Hudson wrote. Most Arab scholars would agree. In the decades since the establishment of Israel, the Palestine issue has undergone a subtle change. On the foundation of the objective problem of Palestinian refugees has been built a myth: the myth that the Palestinian problem is, in Hudson's words, *the* "barrier to the integration of the Arab homeland." Alongside this myth has developed the extraordinary belief that *only* the presence of Israel stands in the way of achieving Arab unity and integration, and peace and stability in the Middle East. According to this mythology, Israel, then, is *the* barrier to Arab self-realization. Although patently false, it is not too surprising that Israel should have become a special object of hostility in this region filled with hostilities.

Israel is modern in the midst of traditional societies; democratic in the midst of authoritarian societies; egalitarian in the midst of class-based societies; Jewish in the midst of Moslem cultures. Its ties to the United States and the West stand, moreover, as both a problem and a provocation to Soviet appetites in the region.

In this Arab world where faith and politics are linked, traditionalists and radicals, Saudis and Libyans can unite in hostility to the state of Israel—whose right to exist they deny, whose very existence they refuse even to acknowledge, whose name they refuse to utter, calling Israel instead the "Zionist entity" or the "deformed Zionist entity." Not only, then, has Palestinian nationalism become centrally identified with pan-Arab nationalism, but the PLO, using fair means and foul, has won wide acceptance as *the* spokesman for Palestinian rights and interests preaching a brand of Palestinian nationalism and radical politics that links the struggle for the destruction of Israel to the triumph of violent, radical, Soviet-sponsored revolutionaries in Nicaragua, El Salvador, Africa, the Middle East, indeed everywhere. The PLO has then linked the destruction of Israel to the Soviets' global agenda.

The PLO wins acceptance from modern Arab nations because their leaders have been persuaded that the link between faith and politics calls for the destruction of Israel, and the PLO is the group most militantly dedicated to that cause. For let us be clear, the PLO is not only an instrument of Palestinian nationalism, it not only declines to recognize Israel, it is dedicated, as it reaffirmed in 1980, "to liquidate the Zionist entity, politically, economically, militarily, culturally, ideologically." The ideological appeal of *jihad*—which provides a partial sense of Arab unity—is reinforced by terror, selectively, effectively, ruthlessly employed. The ideology that links faith, politics, the destruction of Israel, and Palestinian nationalism is continually reinforced by violence and fear. Note, however, that the same linkage covertly commits traditional Arab rulers to strengthening the radical forces—carriers of radical politics hostile to their own survival. The PLO thus enlists traditional Arab rulers in their own destruction. Never did the dialectical "cunning of history" operate more clearly to enlist the powerful in the struggle for their own replacement.

This brief overview of the dynamics of the politics of the Middle East makes clear, I hope, not only that there are multiple political and military problems in the region which are unrelated to the PLO or the Israel/Arab problems, but also that there exist at least three separate major problems for U.S. policy:

First, an appetite control problem: preventing Soviet appetites for expansion from leading—on the model of Afghanistan—to the straightforward invasion or occupation or incorporation by other means of other Moslem lands into the Soviet empire;

Second, preventing the transformation of independent regimes fundamentally friendly to the United States, or at least

141

compatible with our national interest, such as Saudi Arabia and Jordan, into hostile regimes. This problem is *not* identical with the first one. The Ayatollah Khomeini is neither friendly nor a client of the U.S.S.R.

Third, protecting Israel against her sworn enemies. The United States is tied to Israel by security interests—she is the only state in the region that *welcomes* U.S. bases; by common values—she is the only functioning democracy in the area; by honor, because we have repeatedly sworn to protect her right to survive; by the fact of membership in a common Judeo-Christian civilization. Protecting our civilization, its values and institutions, commits us to protecting Israel. Failure to do so would compromise the moral basis of our foreign and national security policy.

The political importance of Anwar Sadat was that he pointed the way to positive answers to all these problems. A devout Moslem, a revolutionary leader, and a friend of the United States *and* of Israel, Sadat embodied a solution to all these major policy problems confronting the United States. The fact that he was also a man of extraordinary personal courage, honor, and vision made his message the more powerful. Anwar Sadat demonstrated, with dignity and grace, an alternative way of being a serious Moslem dedicated to the Arab cause and committed also to a solution to the Palestinian problem.

Sadat's loss must not be underestimated; but his contribution of an alternative Arab response to existing problems should also not be underestimated. The model remains even though the man is gone from our midst.

That model demonstrated that it is not necessary to compromise basic commitments to live in the modern world. It reminded us that the cause of the Palestinians is not identical with the cause of the PLO. Sadat honored the one, rejected the other. Sadat understood that dealing with the PLO was not the only route to a solution of the Palestinian problem, and was not compatible with a stable regional order. Finally, Sadat established for our times that to be a good Moslem it is not necessary to be hostile to Israel. He illustrated to a whole disbelieving world that it is possible to be a good friend of the United States, live at peace with Israel, and remain a modernizing, revolutionary, nationalist Moslem leader.

This alternative model of nationalist Arab leadership may

have cost Sadat his life and so contributed tacitly but significantly to the role of terror in the Middle Eastern decision
process. Certainly the peace process created by Sadat, Menachem
Begin, and the United States constitutes a threat to the war
process from which our common adversaries profit. However,
it is well known that while bullets can kill men they cannot
kill visions.

Sadat's vision—and ours—is of regional order based on
respect for the independence and security of all nations. It is
a vision capacious enough to accommodate all those peoples
willing to live in peace and mutual respect with their neighbors.

Sadat's enemies loved to pretend that he had betrayed
"the" Arab cause when he made a separate peace; and, reinforced by confusion, fanaticism, anti-Semitism, and terror, this
charge was potent enough to produce a diplomatic boycott that
stretched from Morocco to the Soviet border. In fact, Sadat
never ever abandoned the Palestinian cause. Now that his death
has removed his clear head from policy processes, it is crucially
important, if the Camp David peace process is to move forward,
if peace compatible with Israel's security—indeed her survival—
is to be had, to be clear about what Sadat did and intended.

First, he struck an extraordinary deal which involved
Israel's returning all occupied Egyptian land including Sharm
el-Sheikh and its naval base, the three strategically important
airfields in eastern Sinai, the oil fields developed by Israel—all
in return for what? For the acceptance of Israel's right to exist
and survive, plus normal diplomatic relations. Nothing more,
nothing less. For this Sadat was ostracized. For this, Arab
nations broke diplomatic relations with Egypt, boycotted Sadat's
funeral, and—in the case of some—rejoiced at his death.

As we set about advancing peace in the post-Sadat period,
it is vitally important that we bear in mind that *the* issue has
been and is the existence of Israel. *This* was the issue that
separated Sadat from many of his "rejectionist" Arab brothers;
above all it was the issue that separated Sadat from the PLO.
This is, of course, the issue Israel cannot compromise, the issue
no friend can ask her to compromise. To his dying day Anwar
Sadat insisted that his separate peace did not imply indifference
to Palestinian aspirations and well-being; that the PLO was not
the custodian of Palestinian aspirations; further, that Israel's
existence was not incompatible with Arab self-fulfillment, and

that frank friendship with the United States was the route to regional order, national independence, and economic development in the Middle East.

It is shocking that so soon after his death, influential Americans should be proposing solutions down the pathways Sadat scorned—negotiating with his deadly enemies.

Powerful forces hostile to U.S. interests and Israel's survival are at work today diminishing his legacy. It is the job of all who honor Sadat's achievements to remember well and think clearly about his example.

The Peace Process Continued

Distinguished friends and members of the American Committee of the Weizmann Institute of Science:

It is an honor and a pleasure for me to be here this evening. Yours is a most outstanding organization. Its efforts in support of the Weizmann Institute in Rehovoth have been instrumental in keeping alive and helping to achieve Dr. Weizmann's hopes for bringing together in constructive ways spirituality and science, as well as his goal of enhancing human dignity by technological achievement. Like the American Founding Fathers, he believed that science and democracy in cooperation could open unprecedented, unparalleled opportunities for human fulfillment.

On May 15, 1948, the day of Israel's birth, Weizmann wrote a message addressed to David Ben Gurion, Golda Meir, and other Labor party leaders of the Provisional Government conceiving the new state.

"It will be our destiny to create institutions and values of a free community in the spirit of the great traditions which have contributed so much to the thought and spirit of mankind."

The Weizmann Institute is such an institution.

The vision of science and democracy collaborating in the creation of a better world is one important aspect of Chaim Weizmann's legacy. The state of Israel itself is another aspect

---

Address before the American Committee of the Weizmann Institute of Science, Chicago, Illinois, September 12, 1982.

of his legacy, as it is of all those who worked for its establishment.

Dr. Weizmann was a pragmatist interested in results. His invaluable scientific assistance to Britain during World War I and his active role in negotiations contributed to the issuance, in 1917, of the Balfour Declaration favoring a Jewish national home in Palestine. His wise counsel and diplomatic skill as president of the World Zionist Organization between the two World Wars were key factors in the establishment of the state of Israel. As Israel's first president, he deserved much of the credit for the successes of its early trying years. He believed deeply in the Jewish nation. Yet the state, like science, always remained for Dr. Weizmann means to other ends—to the life of the spirit.

In his autobiography, *Trial and Error*, Dr. Weizmann, after discussing the challenges faced by the Jewish Yishuv as it prepared in late 1947 for the transition to statehood, observed:

"But all of these matters, whether in the realm of finance or constitutional arrangements, really deal with externals of the situation. As the state is merely a means to an end, it is necessary to envisage the end; or, to change the figure, the state is merely a vessel into which the contents still have to be poured, and it is necessary to know what the contents are likely to be."

It was in this context that Dr. Weizmann spoke of the pressing need to offset what he called "the frightful spiritual and intellectual losses we have suffered in the last war" through the creation of scientific institutions in Israel to, in his words, "ensure the intellectual survival of the Jewish people." And it was in this context that he spoke of the challenge of peace, along with justice, and civil and intellectual freedom, as a pressing need.

Another aspect of Dr. Weizmann's remarkable life and legacy for us all was his vision of Arabs and Israelis living and working together harmoniously to create a Middle East in which all would share the benefits of scientific achievement. The first official agreement between Zionist and Arab leaders was that signed in 1919 by Weizmann and an equally gifted Arab leader, Emir Feisal, the sherif of Mecca, who in 1921 became the king of Iraq. In a letter written by Feisal to Felix Frankfurter, then a leader in the American Zionist movement, Feisal described Weizmann as a "great helper to our cause" of working together

146

"for a reformed and revived Near East." "Our movements," he wrote, "complete one another; the Jewish movement is national and not imperialist; and there is room for us both." To this Frankfurter replied that he cherished the relationship he had established with Dr. Weizmann and "knew that the aspirations of the Arab and the Jewish peoples were parallel, that each aspired to reestablish its nationality in its own homeland, each making its own distinctive contribution to civilization, each seeking its own peaceful mode of life."

Dr. Weizmann believed strongly that the United Nations Partition Plan of 1947 would be implemented and that a Jewish state would arise peacefully. He had faith in the United Nations, and he had faith in peaceful accommodation.

"We extend our hand in peace and neighborliness to all the neighboring states and their peoples and invite them to cooperate with the independent Jewish nation for the common good of all. The State of Israel is prepared to make its contribution to the progress of the Middle East as a whole," declared the Proclamation of Independence of the state of Israel.

Nonetheless, Israel's birth was not as peaceful as Weizmann hoped, nor has her history fulfilled the dreams of peace of Israel's Founding Fathers—one of whom heads her government today. Israel's security has been chronically endangered by the refusal of neighboring states to accept her right to exist, to negotiate differences, to establish normal diplomatic relations.

Weizmann's vision has thus far remained largely a mirage. In the past thirty-five years Israel has made astounding progress in scientific achievement. Israel's neighbors, however, have derived little benefit from Israeli science. Instead, they, like Israel, have devoted vast amounts of their resources and the resources of others to the continuing conflict, to a succession of wars, and to seemingly never-ending preparation for more of the same.

Moreover, the fact of war was accompanied by the development of a myth that denied the very possibility of peace. In an area rent by historic rivalries and bitter intra-Arab strife, a myth developed that only Israel disturbed the harmony of "the" Arab nation, that only Israel prevents the unity and fulfillment of the Arab world.

According to this myth, Israel's destruction is the precondition of peace. Peace therefore could never exist for Israel.

The result was an escalating cycle of bitterness and war

which deprived Israel and her neighbors of the security and peace that is a prerequisite to regional development.

That cycle was abruptly halted by President Anwar Sadat and Prime Minister Menachem Begin—each of whom displayed extraordinary imagination, daring, courage, and statesmanship in his determined effort to create peace where there had been only war and plans for war, peace where there had been only fear, resentment, distrust, hate. It is easy today and tempting to forget and understate the risks run and price paid by Egypt and by Israel for the process we call Camp David. For embracing a settlement consisting of a peace treaty, mutual diplomatic recognition, a commitment to secure boundaries and Israeli withdrawal from the Sinai, Egypt suffered ostracism within the Arab world, including a diplomatic boycott that stretched from Morocco to the Soviet border. President Sadat, a devout Moslem, suffered calumny and finally death at the hands of fanatic coreligionists who mistook making peace for betraying the Arab world.

If the sacrifice of Sadat is too easily understated, too easily forgotten, so too is the sacrifice of Israel. When, on April 25th, Israel returned the Sinai to Egypt, thus fulfilling her commitment under the Peace Treaty, she made the largest sacrifice and took the largest risk for peace of any nation in this century. For Israel, the Sinai was less a spoil of war than a guaranteed buffer to protect the Israeli state against her most powerful Arab neighbor, Egypt. Returning the Sinai also meant sacrificing a colossal human and economic investment—billions of development dollars had been poured into the Sinai.

The voluntary withdrawal from and relinquishment of the Sinai are powerful testimony to the will to peace of Israel's government and people. And also of her prime minister. There should be no obfuscation of this fact.

This great leap forward to peace was, of course, accomplished in the framework of the Camp David Accords, which is surely one of the most dramatic cases of successful conflict resolution in our times.

The Camp David accords constitute a model of successful conflict resolution in an era and a region where disagreements are almost routinely settled by force rather than by reason and compromise. What accounted for their success? Were there elements beyond the personal genius and generosity of Anwar Sadat, Menachem Begin, and Jimmy Carter? I think so.

I believe it is possible to identify three factors that contributed to the success of the Camp David approach. First, the negotiations were oriented toward practical results. They were pragmatic, nonideological, and incrementalist. Second, the negotiations were limited to those parties who had an important stake in the outcome and were seriously committed to reaching a settlement with each other, namely Israel and Egypt. Finally, the parties were assisted in working out their differences by a friend—credible to both—who also had a stake in achieving a peaceful settlement. I speak, of course, of the United States.

It was crucial, I believe, to the success of the Camp David effort that negotiations were limited in their participation, goals, and means. Limitation of the participants to parties who had a great deal to gain by peace meant that no one was present who stood to gain by the continuation of conflict. Limitation of goals kept the negotiations focused on practical problem solving rather than on grand proclamations or sterile recriminations. Limitation of the means—reliance on negotiation—meant that no settlement was possible except one understood as fair and beneficial to both parties. There was no question of one party imposing its will on the other. Agreement was required. The good will, intelligence, imagination, and restraint of Menachem Begin, Anwar Sadat, and Jimmy Carter were, of course, also crucial. So was their willingness to pay the price and assume the risks of a bold break with entrenched, even institutionalized, hostilities. Their achievement dramatically altered the realities and possibilities for the region. Still, as Ambassador Sol Linowitz observed, "the wisdom of Camp David was its recognition that the best hope of enduring peace lay in a phased process—one in which agreements attainable at one stage became building blocks for future progress on more important issues."

One of the most difficult of the remaining issues, surely, is the Palestinian problem. "It is difficult to emphasize sufficiently the importance of the Palestine issue for the politics of legitimacy in the Arab world" wrote Michael Hudson, specialist on Arab politics and my sometime Georgetown colleague. No one who has been at the United Nations would be inclined to underestimate it. On the foundations of the objective problem of

Palestinian refugees there was constructed an elaborate ideology and a political organization with menacing military power: the Palestine Liberation Organization. The solution to the Palestinian problem has been severely complicated by the armed power of the PLO and the threat it constituted to the security of Israel. Now, thanks to the sacrifices of Israel, the determined efforts of the Lebanese government, and the diplomacy of a brilliant, skillful, and tenacious American diplomat, Ambassador Philip Habib, the military threat to Israel from PLO rockets based in Lebanon has been eliminated and the evacuation of the armed PLO from Beirut and southern Lebanon has been achieved.

These important events open new opportunities for Lebanese, Israelis, Palestinians, and the region. They constitute, we believe, a hopeful occasion for new progress in the process of restoring control of Lebanon to the Lebanese people and government, in building the peace for which Israelis have longed, and in providing for the legitimate rights of the Palestinian people as foreseen in the Camp David Accords.

Recently President Reagan offered some proposals designed to stimulate the process. These proposals, which have been discussed by the president and Secretary Shultz in the last days, are well known to all of you. I desire only to make three points in relation to them.

First, that the president's proposals are built on and wholly consistent with the Camp David Accords. Concerning these proposals former President Jimmy Carter commented, "There is absolutely nothing in the President's speech . . . nor in the information he sent to the Israelis which is contrary to either the letter or the spirit of Camp David." All the arrangements proposed by President Reagan would be based, as the Camp David Accords provide, on United Nations Security Council Resolutions 242 and 338.

Second, the proposals made by President Reagan are fully consistent with the security of Israel, to which the commitment of President Reagan and the U.S. government is clear, and has recently been underscored.

Third, President Reagan's proposals are designed to stimulate and encourage negotiations and agreement. As Secretary Shultz asserted Friday, "the President has now articulated a reasonable basis for a negotiated compromise among the parties."

The president enunciated these views because the United

States is a partner in the Camp David process. President Carter's role was central and important in that process, as the U.S. relationship with Israel has been central and important throughout her history.

Chaim Weizmann wrote to President Harry Truman on May 13, 1948, "the leadership which the American government took under your inspiration made possible the establishment of a Jewish state. . . ."

In his autobiography, Weizmann tells us, moreover, "my first official act as President of the State of Israel and my last on American soil, was to accept the invitation of the President of the United States to be his guest in Washington. . . ."

Of that visit, Weizmann wrote, "we passed from ceremonial to practical matters and discussed the critical months that lay ahead. The President showed special interest in the question of a loan for development projects, and in using the influence of the United States to insure the defense of Israel. . . ."

Nearly thirty-five years have passed since Israel's first president made that official visit to Washington. During those years, the Israelis have demonstrated a vocation for self-government, a talent for nation building, and an impressive capacity for economic development. During those years Israeli energies have been continuously diverted from these constructive endeavors by a brutal need to defend herself. During these years the United States has remained concerned and committed to Israel's security.

Repeatedly the U.S. government has joined in the search for peace in the region that would end the chronic insecurity which has been a basic fact of life throughout the region. Today, as in the past, we are partners in the search.

The American and Israeli governments have not always agreed about all matters as, indeed, they do not wholly agree at this moment. But disagreements have occurred in a context of shared values and interests—as they do now. There is no crisis in American-Israeli relations today. There is discussion among friends.

On the occasion of his election Dr. Chaim Weizmann ended his cable of acceptance to Ben Gurion saying, "I pray that the struggle forced upon us will speedily end and will be succeeded by (an) era of peace and prosperity for the people of Israel. . . ."

That is our prayer as well. We pray that the long struggle

will speedily end and will be succeeded by an era of peace and prosperity for the people of Israel, Lebanon, Jordan, Egypt, the West Bank, the Gaza Strip—indeed, all the people of the area. The government of the United States is ready and willing to work with others to translate that prayer into a reality for the region.

Thank you. Good night.

PART
FIVE

Some Troublesome Problems
of Foreign Policy

Southern Africa

Namibia, the United Nations, and the United States

Because a free press is indeed the absolutely essential ingredient of a free society, absolutely essential to democratic institutions, it is a very special pleasure to be associated with the celebration of the responsible coverage by a free press of the multifarious events in the world.

Since my very recent university experience has been mentioned, I may note that the transition from the classroom to the cabinet, from the critic to the criticized, from a strictly private person to a not so private person, is traumatic as well as dramatic. I often feel, to paraphrase both the president and the late W. C. Fields, that altogether I think I'd rather be at Georgetown. However, I'm not. Instead, I am at the United Nations, which is a very odd place. I'm trying to learn a new language there.

As everybody in this room also knows, I'm sure, all professions have their own language or, if you prefer, their own jargon. They develop distinctive words and phrases and acronyms to describe their distinctive activities and problems. As a newcomer to the United Nations and to the diplomatic world, one moreover who cares as much as you do about words, I'm aware of the importance of learning the rudiments of that new language of the new profession and world in which I am involved—new modes of communication as well. Indians prefer smoke signals, Victorians wrote letters, teen-agers rely on telephones; with

Address to the Overseas Press Club, Waldorf Astoria, New York City, April 29, 1981.

diplomats, I've learned, nothing is regarded as having really happened unless it's been sent and received by cable; and I've also learned that those cables are collectively called "the traffic" and that reading "the traffic" is a very important activity of diplomats and related persons. I now start reading "the traffic" at about 7:30 every morning. "The traffic" communicates in a language of its own that features very odd abbreviations. I read, for example, within the first day or two that I was at the United Nations, a cable which said "See GOL ASAP." I thought to myself, "Who in the world is GOL ASAP, and how will I know where to find him?" It took me a little while to figure out that GOL ASAP meant "government of Lebanon as soon as possible." It's an example of the problem. There isn't even a glossary or a vocabulary list that goes on the back of the cables. You just learn as you go.

I also have learned that, among other things, the United Nations, and diplomatic missions and diplomats in general, do not become "involved" in issues or active in relation to them, they are "seized" of them. Now, in the beginning I found this very odd. It's an interesting expression, as anybody interested in words knows, because being "seized" by something suggests that it's not something one wills, not something that happens by a deliberate act, but something that one is struck by, if you will, like a fit, possessed by some sort of outside force, which operates independently of anyone's desires. More and more, I may say, that seems to me to describe accurately the condition of that world body in which I now reside vis-à-vis certain issues which claim the attention of all of us there and develop a life of their own.

Right now, as we say at the United Nations, we are seized of the Namibia question, which has riveted the attention of that world body for at least a week, most intensively the last week. It has become the occasion on which some twenty-five or so —depending on the day you count them—foreign ministers descended from Algiers, where they had (among other things) received and discussed *The Council on Namibia Report*, which (among other things) called for severe, comprehensive, mandatory sanctions against South Africa for having blocked the Geneva Conference of last January, which it was hoped would bring independence to Namibia under the United Nations plan embodied in Resolution 435. Another interesting thing about reading United Nations documents is that they almost always include references to at least seven other resolutions, which, if you take documentation seriously, involves you in a process of infinite regression. Tonight I am not going to tell you about all the other resolutions to which you get referred if you look up Resolution 435. If you are really interested, you can check them for yourselves.

There are various interesting aspects of the current discussion, but two are especially so. One is that, like the other discussions I have witnessed more than participated in, in my brief time there, this one seems, first, to have moved beyond the control of virtually all the key participants; and second, it seems to have at best an ambiguous relationship with the putative goal of the exercise, which is to achieve independence for Namibia. It's a fascinating process—watching a United Nations initiative take on a life of its own. It reminds me a bit of watching someone throw a basketball in a fast-moving game. Once the ball is in the air, it develops a momentum of its own and frequently has an unpredictable outcome decided by the skills of the players and by unpredictable interactions among them.

The United States and I, seized of the issue of Namibia, are confronted by two quite different questions. The first is, What can we do or should we do to help bring independence to Namibia? And the second question is, What can we do and should we do *in the United Nations* in relation to the Namibia debate? The distinction between the two questions is important.

The United Nations, like most political arenas, structures whatever passes through it. I don't have to tell a group of journalists that the medium often shapes the message. The United Nations, which was established as a problem-solving institution, of course, sometimes becomes part of the problem. In the past few days I have become almost convinced that it would be easier to create an independent, stable, democratic Namibia than to participate constructively in this United Nations debate, which presumably has that as its goal. I will come back to this matter, but first I'd like to touch on a prior question which occurs to me as I take part in this extraordinary process.

The question is, Why, of all the issues the nations in the world might confront and deal with, why is the United Nations seized with Namibia? Why is the United Nations not dealing, for example, with the Libyan invasion of Chad, which deeply disturbs and threatens neighboring countries, or with the Soviet threat to Poland? Why is the United Nations not dealing with the more than a million destitute and desperate African refugees? Why is it not dealing with the destruction of Lebanon? Why does it focus so much attention, so intensively, on a territory with fewer inhabitants than there are refugees in Africa today?

It is an interesting question. The reason apparently is that the United Nations is an institution that specializes in certain kinds of issues, among which "decolonialization" is central. In fact, it specializes in certain kinds of decolonialization. Another qualification for becoming a major issue, one that remains in the forefront of United Nations attention, seems to be that the issue not be seriously linked to a major concern of a major power. It is probably relatively safer for the United Nations to focus on the "continuing illegal occupation" of Namibia (as they say there) than on the continuing illegal occupation of Afghanistan. So be it. We must, at least for now, play it as it lays; so we are seized with Namibia.

What is Namibia anyway? As I am sure everybody here knows, it is a large, ethnically heterogeneous territory, rich in minerals, poor in political experience. Namibia has been an intermittent matter of concern to the United Nations since 1947. It has a white population that comprises about 12 percent of the total and one dominant tribe, the Ovambo, who comprise about 47 percent of the total population. It has a tiny black and colored middle class. It is a society in which most of what is worth having is securely held in the hands of the Afrikaaner, the German, the English, that is, the white, population.

As everyone knows, Namibia is still ruled by South Africa, a medium-sized power which, though important in Africa, does not constitute a major threat in the international arena to anyone except its immediate neighbors, whom it worries a great deal, and some of its own population, whom it worries in a different way. But it is not a major power, and that, surely, is one reason it is safer for the United Nations to focus on it than on Afghanistan.

Vis-à-vis Namibia, the Reagan administration confronted on arriving in office a failed conference, a ruptured negotiation. We were not in a position to start from scratch on this issue, but neither could we merely continue. In approaching this issue we formulated goals. Our principal goal, as we have stated repeatedly, is independence for Namibia. The United States is not a colonial power. We are committed to national independence and self-determination for all people. We desire independence for all African states, indeed for all the states in the world, among which we would like to see an authentically independent Namibia. That is not our only goal. Namibia has the largest known uranium deposits in the world, and a second goal we have is to prevent this mineral-rich territory from being permitted to slide into the Soviet sphere of influence, which has expanded markedly in Africa. A related strategic goal is to keep the vital waterways around Namibia out of hostile hands. A third goal we think about in connection with Namibia is that dealing with the problem of Namibia should not inhibit our good relations with surrounding African nations or our good relations with our allies with whom we associate on this problem, in the Western Contact Group.

Our goals are complicated by the presence of more than 30,000 Cuban troops in neighboring Angola. Although many argue that the independence of Namibia will more or less automatically produce Soviet-Cuban withdrawal from Angola—why would the Cubans stay, it is asked, if the MPLA no longer needed to worry about South Africa?—we doubt it. We tend rather to believe that the Cuban troops remain in Angola because of UNITA's resistance to the MPLA as much as because of fear of South Africa's coming over its border. We think they stay in the area, also, because the Soviets desire a forward position there. In sum, then, the United States has multiple goals vis-à-vis the region; achieving those goals is complicated by the very high feelings of the various parties to the conflict.

Being a political scientist whose profession is the analysis of political problems, I am led next to identify the actors who are involved in this problem. One of these actors is SWAPO. Now SWAPO, as everyone knows, is a coalition whose ethnic base is the Ovambo, who constitute about one-half of the Namibian population. SWAPO is the oldest, best-established party devoted to independence in Namibia. Like a great many "national liberation movements," SWAPO is a mixed bag, which contains some merely nationalist elements, some persons who are simply dissatisfied with the present government, some per-

sons of undefined ideology, and some who are enthusiastic supporters of Marxism-Leninism and closely tied, by training and
connections, to the Soviet Union, which is the principal source
of arms to the movement.

There are other political parties in Namibia, including the
DTA or Turnhalle Alliance, a predominantly white and multiracial
party historically tied to South Africa. Neither it nor any of
the other parties seems to be as strong as SWAPO, though one
cannot accurately estimate the popular strength of a group in
the absence of either free elections or careful opinion polls.
Since neither is available here, we have no reliable information
about the popular support for these groups. We do know, however, that there is a powerful tendency in the politics of Africa
for party preference to follow tribal identification.

South Africa, of course, is also a major party to this
conflict. It too is an ethnically heterogeneous, mineral-rich nation
—the most powerful in the area—which is a democracy on top
and an authoritarian system on the bottom. It is a democracy
for the whites and an authoritarian system for everyone else.
South Africa's white population identifies strongly with Europe
and cares about being accepted as a civilized Western nation by
other Western powers. That concern, indeed, constitutes an
important factor in the equation. South Africa is rich, strong,
tough, and—in the purest sense of the word—racist, because it
makes access to values depend on race. Still, it features a rule
of law which is, of course, a protection to the population, a
restraint on government, and a lever for peaceable change.

The United Nations is another party to the negotiations.
It is a would-be referee with somewhat tarnished credentials.
Since 1973, when the United Nations General Assembly passed
a resolution designating SWAPO the sole authentic representative of the Namibian people, the United Nations has tried to
serve both as a partisan for one side and as an impartial mediator. SWAPO has enjoyed permanent observer status in the
United Nations, and the United Nations has dispensed millions
of dollars in financial support for SWAPO under one or another
of its programs. Its Council on Namibia travels all over the
world "raising consciousness" on the issue. In the past the
United Nations has claimed that only the General Assembly was
committed to SWAPO. Recently, however, the United Nations
Security Council acted to deny the DTA the opportunity even

to be heard in the Security Council—while hearing SWAPO. The United Nations contains people who are presumably capable of behaving in a fair and evenhanded fashion if they set their minds to it, but the body itself has clear-cut public commitments to one of the parties.

Other parties to these interactions are the other nations of the Contact Group—France, the United Kingdom, Canada, the Federal Republic of Germany—all of whom have very large investments in Africa, which give them a special stake in staying on good terms with as many leaders of as many African nations as possible, and a proclivity, now quite strong, for believing that "colonial" questions become more dangerous the longer they are permitted to fester.

A very important counter in this whole drama with which the United Nations is seized is Resolution 435, which has acquired the status of a sacred text. United Nations resolutions seem to take on a life of their own even though they may be viewed as quite unsatisfactory by all parties concerned with them. The fact that they have finally become a matter of consensus, if even a consensus of the moment, gives them a special status in this body, one of whose principal activities is seeking consensus. Resolution 435 provides for independence for Namibia and for free elections to be conducted under United Nations supervision. In fact, this resolution is filled with gaps. It leaves unanswered questions concerning what kind of regime will emerge and even who will govern Namibia during the period before a government is elected.

We, the United States, are another actor in this drama. What kind of government would we like? What kind of settlement would we like? One thing we would like is a framework that provides more stability than 435 alone. We would like some constitutional guarantees.

What will we, the United States, accept? We will accept anything that will achieve our goals, which, as I have said, are nothing less than an independent, stable, democratic Namibia which cannot readily be incorporated into the expanding Soviet sphere of influence. Does that mean we will accept Resolution 435? Of course it does, provided that it is completed or, augmented, so that a way is found also to provide the basic minimums of civilized government. Those basic minimums include protection for minorities and a framework that would protect

161

Namibia's independence once it is won. Those do seem to us to be among the minimum requisites of civilized government, and we are reluctant to be parties to the construction of any government anywhere that does not provide them.

What is going to happen in that glass house where everyone throws stones? We, the United States, are going to go right on working with the problem, with our allies, with the front-line states, with South Africa, with the United Nations, and with the other interested parties. We are, I think it is fair to say, flexible, determined, and optimistic about the means of achieving those goals. I, who am by temperament not given to optimism, am quite optimistic about the possibilities today of achieving an independent, stable, democratic Namibia provided that the dynamics of interaction inside the Security Council do not destroy what diplomacy achieves. But God alone knows what we will be able to achieve in the Security Council. Immanuel Kant described the categories through which we perceive reality and their effect on what we perceive. I think that the glasses through which we perceive reality at the United Nations frequently distort the objects being examined. Perhaps the time has come to seek a new oculist.

Southern Africa

Fair Play for Namibia

In considering this vote, I should like to emphasize that the United States believes it a very important matter of principle that all individuals with relevant information to impart to the Security Council be permitted to speak under Rule 39 of the Security Council's provisional rules of procedure. We believe there are two important issues here. One is whether the United Nations, through the Security Council, is and should be willing to listen to a party to any important question before it, assuming that the application has been made according to the rules of the body. And second is whether it matters whether the United Nations and the Security Council through which it acts are willing to listen to any such group.

No one here asks that the Security Council agree to agree with the analysis or the position of the DTA. We ask merely that the Security Council hear the representatives of this group of Namibians.

We do not purport to know how many Namibians support this party or any other party. We will not know the answer to that question unless or until free elections are held in that country, if indeed they can ever be arranged. We only know that some Namibians support this party, and the question therefore seems to us whether the members of the Security Council should stifle in this arena the expression of the DTA's opinion merely because the majority of this council expects to

Statement in the Security Council on the situation in Namibia, April 21, 1981.

disagree with that opinion. Is a majority of the Security Council ever justified in refusing even to listen to an argument of a group which some of its members desire to have heard? We think not.

We think further that the stakes here are very high. By its actions on such a fundamental matter of principle—fairness, a democratic spirit, evenhandedness—the United Nations, and the Security Council, defines itself. The Security Council damages its capacity to act as a forum, as a peacemaker, as an impartial mediator who can be trusted to treat all parties fairly. If the Security Council were to deny the DTA the right even to be heard, then the Security Council damages precisely those principles on which the United Nations itself is based—the principles of reason, discussion, representation. It is as easy to damage these principles of reason, discussion, representation as it is easy to silence dissent.

I hope the members of the Security Council will consider very carefully before they vote which course—listening to the DTA or not listening to the DTA—will be most consistent with the principles of the United Nations and the peace and independence of Namibia.

Southern Africa

Solving the Problem of Namibia

It seems to me that it is time that we focus again on the goal of this meeting and this special session of the Security Council. Presumably that goal is to produce an independent, stable, self-governing Namibia. As I understand it, there is no disagreement on that goal.

A number of charges have been made in the past few days, and I have followed with interest those charges. There have been charges that the Western countries, the Contact Group, have failed to achieve the goal of an independent, stable, self-governing Namibia. There have been charges that the Western countries, the Contact Group, have failed to bring South Africa to her knees. There have been charges that the Western countries are responsible somehow for the continuation of racism and colonialism in Namibia, in South Africa, indeed in Africa. It has been suggested that because the Western Contact Group, like the African countries, like the Eastern bloc, have substantial economic relations with South Africa, they are somehow responsible for the continuation of racial discrimination in South Africa.

I have asked myself repeatedly in the course of these negotiations and discussions how the charges which are being made here relate to the accomplishment of the goal on which we are presumably all agreed—the goal of an independent, stable, democratic Namibia. Repeatedly it has been suggested that be-

Statement in the Security Council on the situation in Namibia, April 23, 1981.

cause we have not already succeeded, we should not try again, that we should try some other course than the continuing search for an internationally acceptable peace arrived at through peaceable negotiation, an internationally acceptable independent Namibia arrived at through international negotiation. It has been suggested, for example, that we should commit ourselves to comprehensive compulsory sanctions. But, Mr. President, I think that if we are realistic—and if we are not realistic we waste our time and that of everyone else present—if we are realistic then we will understand that resolutions do not solve problems, sanctions do not solve problems, declarations do not make peace, declarations do not secure independence.

Is it not past time that we consider here realistically the practical, actual alternatives to a continuing search for an internationally acceptable solution in Namibia?

Mr. President, my government has no other objective than to achieve authentic independence and self-government for Namibia, and indeed I believe that all the Western Contact Group has no other objective than this. We have no territorial objectives in Africa. We have no aspiration to station thousands of our troops in African countries. We have no desire to send armed surrogates to subvert the independence of the new states of Africa. We have no desire to divide this body or to divert its attention from the problem of self-government for Namibia to the creation of divisive diversions here.

Mr. President, solving problems is much more difficult than adopting resolutions, but the problem of an independent, stable, self-governing, democratic Namibia will be solved because it must be solved, and it will be solved eventually by the force of arms or by the exercise of reason. No one has spoken much here about the true alternatives to the continued search for a negotiated, internationally acceptable solution to the Namibia problem, but I think it is past time that we face those alternatives squarely. And I should like on behalf of my government to pledge ourselves to the continued effort, to the maximum of our abilities and ingenuity, independently and with our colleagues in the Contact Group and our associates here in the United Nations, to the unflagging search for an internationally acceptable, truly, authentically independent, stable, democratic Namibia.

Southern Africa

Fair Play for South Africa

The United States believes that South Africa's credentials should not be rejected and opposes the denial of South Africa's right to participate in the General Assembly.

Mr. President, the questions of procedure involved here have substantive implications of great import to the United Nations. In 1974 the United States made plain its strong opposition to the ruling of the General Assembly that, by rejecting the credentials of the delegation of South Africa, the General Assembly had, in effect, decided to refuse to allow the South African delegation to participate in its work. This afternoon the United States delegation reiterates its position. Involved here are the most fundamental questions of membership and the rights of membership. The fact that South Africa's intention to resume its seat today was not known is irrelevant to the exercise of these rights. Neither is it relevant that South Africa is in arrears in the payment of its financial assessments. Only the Charter of the United Nations is relevant. The provisions and requirements of that charter should be our only guide. Under the law of Article V and VI of that charter, a member state may be suspended or expelled from the United Nations only upon the recommendation of the Security Council as confirmed by the General Assembly. Yet depriving a member state of the right to participate in the work of the only universal, parliamentary organ of the United Nations is a principal consequence

Statement in the United Nations General Assembly in explanation of vote on South African credentials, March 2, 1981.

of suspension and expulsion. And that is also the consequence of denying a state the right to participate in the General Assembly. Consequently, the right of participation can only be denied in accordance with Articles V and VI of the charter.

The Security Council has never recommended that the Assembly should suspend or expel South Africa. For this reason, the General Assembly's action in 1974 was without legal foundation. On so fundamental a question as rights of membership, the passing of time has not given the Assembly a better legal basis for doing in 1981 what it did improperly in 1974. No one has shown that South Africa's credentials fail to meet the requirements of the Rules of Procedure. To refuse to consider those credentials as required by the rules is to use the guise of credentials to try to accomplish a suspension that lies beyond the powers of the General Assembly.

Redefining Asian-American Ties

Those two great indicators of one nation's involvement with another, war and trade, provide all the proof that is needed that American ties to Asia have become so multifarious in this century, so complex, so intertwined, that they are today already part of the national fabric.

Three times in the last half century, more than in any other part of the world, the United States has fought a bloody war in Asia. Asia's role in our trade is no less important. In 1980, for the first time in our history, U.S. trade with the countries of Asia surpassed trade with any other region in the world, including Western Europe. Making policy toward Asia is, then, one of the primary tasks of any American administration. It is rendered more delicate by the memory, still vivid for many Americans, of the bitterly controversial questions that have surrounded aspects of our Asian policy three times since World War II: Who "lost" China and how? Who involved us in a "no-win war" in Korea? Who was responsible for our disasters in the Vietnam War?

Obviously, Asian policy can arouse intense passions and has; it can produce lethal political folly and has. How then should we think about the distant lands that are so important to our prosperity, our politics, and our peace?

I am not a specialist on Asia. I have no special responsibilities for Asian policy in this administration. The comments that follow, therefore, take Asia as an example of a more general

Address to the Asia Society, New York City, April 14, 1981.

orientation which I believe informs our approach to foreign policy. That general orientation begins and ends with the concrete. It eschews the abstractions that mystify relations among nations.

George Orwell noted that the whole tendency of modern prose is away from concreteness. We of the Reagan administration propose to try to reverse that tendency. We agree with the famous European philosopher of the past century who held that the concrete is the real and the real is the concrete. The more complicated the reality, we believe, the more intense the temptation toward, and the greater the cost of, oversimplification.

The language of contemporary politics is filled with abstractions that complicate the intellectual problems they purport to illuminate. None of the verbal prisms through which we view reality are the source of greater distortions than those simple, putatively geographic concepts, North and South, East and West. Many of the difficulties that engulf the contemporary world ensue when we attempt to understand the world and make policy by way of these metaphysical and meta-empirical terms. Nowhere is their power to distort reality and delude us more evident than in their application to Asia.

The first striking point about the notions of North and South, East and West is, of course, that although they purport to describe geographic categories, they do not do so. Not all the countries south of the equator fall into the category termed "the South." Australia and New Zealand are good examples of exceptions. Certainly, Asia itself does not fit neatly in the geographic category "South."

It may be argued that I am belaboring the obvious, that everyone knows that North applies not to geography but to a condition of development defined, above all, in economic terms and that, understood in this fashion, Asia is still *under*developed. But that too is not true.

Some Asian countries feature a subsistence level, land-based economy, low mobility—social and geographic—and the poverty and primitive technology associated with what are often termed "underdeveloped" societies. The Brandt Commission identified as the world's poorest countries some twenty-nine nations, several of which lie in southern Asia. The OECD defines southern Asia as including eight nations—India, Bangladesh,

Pakistan, Burma, Afghanistan, Sri Lanka, Nepal, and Bhutan—where the average income is about $150 per capita. Although some notable successes in economic development have been registered in these countries, too many people live in these parts of Asia for a good life to be possible with their existing technologies, and many live barely above the level of subsistence, utterly vulnerable to every natural disaster.

The concept of South might have been modeled on these nations, and they are an important part of Asia. Yet they are no more Asian than the countries of the region that have achieved an advanced stage of industrialization, large exports of manufactured products, and a wide enough distribution to have an important internal market. I speak, of course, especially of Japan, Singapore, Hong Kong, Taiwan, Korea. The meteoric rise of Japan to the status of an economic giant with a gross national product surpassing $1 trillion is well known to all—a fact, by the way, that proves that democratic capitalism is not irrelevant to all except Western countries. It has now become clear, moreover, that the Japanese achievement was not an anomaly with no relevance for the rest of the region.

South Korea's 10 percent annual income growth from 1962 to 1976 is unprecedented and unequaled. Korea's extraordinary increase in exports was accompanied by distribution policies that encouraged the dramatic expansion of internal markets. Singapore, whose per capita income now stands at approximately $2,700 a year, and Hong Kong, which is not far behind, are nations in which the dynamics of continuing progress have been securely established. In consequence, their futures appear as bright as their past. These nations are as different from the stereotype of "South" as nations could be. There is almost no policy imaginable that would be equally relevant to all the Asian nations we have so far mentioned, and we have not even yet referred to China. Although progress has been most dramatic in Japan, Singapore, Hong Kong, Taiwan, and South Korea, notable strides have also been made in Malaysia, Thailand, Indonesia, and the Philippines. It should be emphasized, moreover, that the social, cultural, political differences are, if anything, even more pronounced than the economic ones. But if Asia is neither North nor South, still less is it East or West.

Whether we focus on how they organize their economies or on their relations to the Soviet Union, we are forced to

recognize the diversity of the Asian nations and the undesir-
ability of thinking about policy toward them in terms of an
East-West dichotomy. Some of those nations—Afghanistan,
Vietnam, Laos, Kampuchea—are indeed linked to the Soviet
Union. Moreover, 80,000 Soviet troops in Afghanistan and
many thousands of Vietnamese in Kampuchea guarantee that
these nations will remain linked to the political empire that is
so often termed "East." But east of them lies China, which also
features a command economy and is not integrated into the
Soviet empire. To the contrary, China provides in itself a
particularly striking example of the inappropriateness of trying
to deal with Asia in terms of any simple East-West dichotomy.
Although a socialist country, it has in recent years allowed a
much greater scope to market forces within its economy and
increasingly has recognized the indispensability of productive
economic relations with the market areas of other nations and
has planned for rapid modernization. Over 55 percent of China's
trade is now going to the United States and Western Europe,
to Japan and the non-Communist countries of Southeast Asia.

The United States, of course, welcomes the steps that the
Chinese have taken toward liberalizing their economic and
political systems and welcomes their expanding ties with us and
the other nations of our region. Indeed, the Reagan administration has committed itself to a relationship with the People's
Republic of China based on the Shanghai communiqué and the
communiqué normalizing relations between the two countries.
Given the mutual good will of the American and the Chinese
people, the relationships which have begun so recently will continue to expand and develop, while we maintain our cordial
relationship with Taiwan on the basis of the Taiwan Relations
Act.

Suppose then that we agree that these simple concepts,
North and South, East and West, do not apply to the lands
ranging from Iran in western Asia to Japan in the Far East, lands
that are the home of 2.5 billion people comprising, incredibly
enough, 56 percent of the world's population. Suppose we
agree that the remarkable diversity of these nations makes it
difficult to set forth any valid generalizations about the Asian
continent, except that it is different from some other parts of
the world. Suppose we agree that sensible policy cannot rely on
these categories. What then should we do to rid ourselves of

this misleading intellectual framework? How are we to make language describe rather than distort reality?

The answer must be to ground our thinking and our policies in what Edmund Burke described as "due attention to the concrete circumstances which give to every political principle, its color and discriminating effect." To purge ourselves of disabling, distorting, and ultimately defeating intellectual habits we should recommit ourselves to knowing what we mean. The reward should be clearer thinking and better policy, for, as Orwell also said, thinking more clearly is the prerequisite to political regeneration. In this administration we are firmly committed to clearing away the trampled intellectual underbrush that blocks the path to political regeneration.

Problems of the Alliance

It is sometimes said, by cynics, that the United Nations is a microcosm of the world. On my most pessimistic days, I fear this may be the case. If it is, we are in even worse trouble than most of you here dream, as regards the alliance or almost anything else.

At the United Nations, the alliance is not very strong. At the United Nations, the United States frequently stands alone on controversial issues, some of which are very important to us, some of which are very important to others. At the United Nations, our European allies often prefer a posture of nonalignment between us and the Group of 77 on the so-called North-South issues, which consume much of the time of that organization. On some other issues, they vote with our adversaries. Just this past week, the United States cast a lone veto in the Security Council on an obnoxious Golan Heights resolution. We voted no. The Soviets, Arabs, and miscellaneous others voted yes. Some five of our closest associates abstained. That's a common pattern on Middle Eastern and some other questions. A more ominous pattern was manifest on the El Salvador resolution in the last General Assembly. The resolution on El Salvador reaffirmed the Franco-Mexican communiqué, which opposed elections and supported the "negotiated" settlement advocated by the guerrillas. The resolution was cosponsored by five of our NATO partners. Nine of the European Ten finally sup-

Address to the Committee for the Free World, January 23, 1982, in Washington, D.C.

ported it. Only the United Kingdom abstained. Abandoned by our allies on this issue of great importance to us, we voted with some twenty Latin nations, including most of the Latin democracies.

At the United Nations, the NATO countries vote together mainly on administrative and budgetary matters, on which we are also joined by the Soviet Union, and on some—but not all— of the most egregious of the Soviet propaganda resolutions. If we regarded voting at the United Nations as the litmus test of the alliance, we would have to conclude that the alliance was not in very good shape.

I shall argue here today that that is not a fair or even a relevant test; that the alliance is in better shape than this test would reveal; and that just as the lack of allied agreement should not lead us to despair, neither should it constrain the United States. The allies' failure to join us on issues not central to the defense of Europe should not threaten the alliance. Neither should our unilateral action on such issues. Like cooperation, independence must be mutual.

Much of the contemporary discussion about crisis in the alliance is an example of what Edward Banfield, in his *Unheavenly City,* called "crisis mongering," to which, he argued, Americans are particularly prone. Freud wrote about World War I that he was less disappointed than many of his contemporaries with what the war revealed about human nature because he had never expected so much of it. Having never expected so much from the Western alliance, I am less dismayed by its performance.

To deal adequately with the question of whether there is a crisis in the Atlantic alliance and, if so, what are its characteristics and what we might do about it, it is necessary to go back to basics: What was the alliance supposed to be, anyway? In judging a tool, one should ask, What is the tool for? Is it able to accomplish the task for which it was intended? It is that question—what NATO is for—that I want to address in my remarks today.

I propose to begin where the Atlantic alliance began—at the end of World War II—and desire to remind us all that NATO represented a dramatic abandonment of the traditional American posture, stated by George Washington, who advised us to steer clear of "permanent alliances with any portion of the foreign world." In particular, he advised us not to entangle ourselves and our "peace and prosperity in the toils of European ambition, rivalship, interest, humor, or caprice." The conviction that the United States should avoid permanent alliances dominated the U.S. role in foreign affairs until World War II. As one historian noted, until the end of World War II and the emergence of the cold war, "the general public, the Congress and most public leaders believed that alliances caused wars instead of preventing them, and they opposed any such arrangements for the United States."

It follows, then, that for the United States NATO was not a preferred pattern of relating to the postwar world. It was not an arrangement that American leaders regarded as an ideal instrument for bringing peace to the world. On the contrary, the Atlantic alliance was founded on the shattered hopes for a very different structure of peace. In 1945 American leaders did not envision, and certainly did not wish for, the division of Europe that compelled the establishment of the Atlantic alliance. They cherished a vision of "one world" governed by the democratic principles embodied in the Atlantic Charter. Speaking to a joint session of Congress on March 1, 1945, President Roosevelt said that the Yalta Conference had been a success because it spelled "the end of the system of unilateral action, exclusive alliances and spheres of influence, and balances of power and all the other expedients which have been tried for centuries and have always failed." "We propose," he said, "to substitute for all these, a universal organization in which all peace-loving nations will finally have a chance to join." This universal organization on which Roosevelt based his hopes for peace was, of course, none other than the United Nations. This perspective, we know today, was idealistic to the point of utopianism, impatient with the constraints of international diplomacy and with the methods of the past. It was distinctly American. And it was doomed from the start.

These optimistic universalist plans were based on the even more optimistic assumption that the world order would be made up of democratic governments. Today, in the shadow of the Soviet-ordered repression in Poland, it is easy to forget that Yalta reaffirmed the principles of the Atlantic Charter, recognizing "the right of all people to choose the form of government under which they will live," and, in the case of Poland specifically, pledged that "free and unfettered elections" would be held "as soon as possible on the basis of universal suffrage and secret ballot." Roosevelt and Churchill no doubt took these words very seriously. But Stalin, who once wrote that "good words are a mask for the concealment of bad deeds," clearly did not. A Soviet puppet regime was already in place in Warsaw. The Red Army had occupied all of Eastern Europe, with the exception of most of Czechoslovakia. Words and dreams could neither conceal nor change this reality.

Stalin used words to great effect at Yalta. He argued that Poland was a question of both honor and security: honor because of past Russian grievances against Poland and security because Poland was a neighbor and had been a corridor for attack against Russia. This was, of course, the kind of falsification of history to which we have since become accustomed. It was Poland that had grievances against Russia, not Russia which had grievances against Poland. Stalin's falsification of history, however, concealed the real reason for the failure of the U.S. vision of the United Nations and for the division of the postwar world. The real reason was Soviet imperialism. The consolidation of the Soviet hold over Eastern Europe—the lowering of the Iron Curtain—necessitated the creation of NATO as one of a system of defensive alliances, designed as protection against Soviet expansion in Europe.

The American alliance system, of which NATO is only the most highly developed example, is thus rooted in the cold war. It was a specific response to the Soviets' effort to gain control of the governments of Greece and Turkey and other governments in Eastern Europe over whom they had not been able to consolidate power immediately following the war. The Inter-American Treaty of Reciprocal Assistance, the so-called Rio Treaty, which was signed almost two years earlier than the NATO Treaty, in September 1947, established a mutual collective security agreement for the Western Hemisphere. NATO was explicitly concerned with mutual security arrangements in Western Europe.

NATO was established for the specific purpose of protecting Western Europe against being overrun or subverted by the Soviet Union. Neither Yalta nor the NATO Treaty was intended to ratify or recognize the division of Europe, much less to legitimize the consignment of the eastern half of Europe to the

Soviet sphere. On the contrary, the NATO Treaty opened with a reaffirmation of the United Nations Charter, which itself was based on the democratic principles of the Atlantic Charter. The Truman Doctrine also signified the refusal of the United States to acquiesce in the spread of Soviet totalitarianism in Europe and its determination to regard the evolution of Europe as a matter of concern for U.S. security.

Although the Atlantic alliance recognized that the nations of Western Europe shared with the United States an attachment to democracy and an aversion to nondemocratic institutions, the NATO alliance never was regarded by its members as having the responsibility for rolling back communism or even for acting in concert to encourage the independence of Eastern Europe. In Hungary in 1956 and Czechoslovakia in 1968, NATO was confronted with clear-cut, brutal Soviet invasions aimed at smashing indigenous national liberation movements in those two countries. But in neither case did the countries of the Atlantic alliance act, nor was their inaction generally regarded as a betrayal of the alliance, whose purposes were perceived as less broad even than the defense of freedom *in Europe.* But although the Atlantic alliance committed NATO neither to containing communism outside Western Europe nor to helping Eastern European peoples liberate themselves, it was not devoid of ideological content. Its ideological purposes derived from the democratic character of the governments it was pledged to protect. But no additional ideological content can be attributed to it, I believe, without either distortion or exaggeration or both.

I should also like to emphasize that since 1949 the members of NATO have pursued independent national policies, except on matters of common concern to the alliance, that is, matters involving the security of Western Europe. Little effort has been made to consult or to coordinate national policies oriented toward other goals. France and Britain, the Netherlands, Belgium, for example, had colonial empires of which they more or less peaceably, more or less traumatically, divested themselves after World War II. The process of decolonization went on without significant mutual consultation, no matter how violent or difficult it became. France's long war in Indochina did not trigger alliance support, even though the "national liberation" movement she fought had important and relatively clear ties to the Soviet Union. Neither did anyone propose that

France's long struggle in Algeria concerned NATO or that Belgium's problems in the Congo were the business of the Atlantic alliance. The pursuit of national foreign policy goals outside the Atlantic alliance was the norm. It was not regarded as disloyal or threatening to the alliance.

A greater strain was put on relations within the alliance when one of its partners actively opposed the policies of others. When the United States, for example, joined the Soviet Union in opposing the British-French-Israeli invasion of Egypt in the Suez adventure, that temporarily strained the alliance. When John Kennedy quietly supported national liberation movements in northern Africa against France's colonial rule, that was hardly welcomed by the French—but it was not regarded as a violation of the Atlantic alliance.

The United States' own understanding of the limits of commonality among members of the alliance has been manifest in various important initiatives. The Kennedy administration saw the prospect of Soviet missiles in Cuba as a serious threat to the security of the United States. However, it had recourse not to NATO but to the OAS and the Rio Treaty and took pains to brief the OAS ambassadors carefully and urgently before Kennedy's announcement of the U.S. response. Secretary of State Dean Rusk called a special meeting of the OAS, at which he invoked the Rio Treaty to justify U.S. actions.

This is one example—there are others—of the United States acting, and assuming it had the right to act, independently of the NATO alliance to protect its national interests. We did not consult in advance with European allies on that occasion. Instead, we informed them about the same time we were informing the world. NATO partners responded in various ways. President de Gaulle, a man who appreciated boldness and nationalism in foreign affairs, announced: "If there be a war, I will be with you, but there will be no war." Konrad Adenauer was also quick to express support. Britain and Italy had misgivings. Harold Macmillan pledged Britain's support at the United Nations but not in the Atlantic. And so forth.

The point is that collective action by NATO was neither expected, sought, nor forthcoming. It was generally understood that, like other members of the alliance, the United States had interests that lay outside the concerns and commitments of the Atlantic alliance, which she could pursue without prior consultation but with the hope of understanding and support from her European friends in such cases.

It is important to remember also, in considering the alliance, that it has proved very flexible; otherwise it wouldn't have survived for thirty-three years. One dramatic piece of evidence of that flexibility, of course, occurred when Charles de Gaulle announced on January 14, 1963, his new plan for France's national defense. De Gaulle, who had written that England is an island, France the edge of a continent, America another world, brusquely redefined and limited France's relationship to the alliance. Since then, as everyone knows, France has concentrated on the development of her own national defense, coordinating her relations and role within NATO with her national purposes. But this candid, forthright affirmation of French national identity and purpose has not ended France's role as a member of the Atlantic alliance. Neither then nor later was it argued that the pursuit of national policies independently of the alliance constitutes a betrayal of the alliance.

In assessing the present difficulties, the so-called crisis of the alliance, it is terribly important to understand that NATO has demonstrated unity only when it has confronted a possible threat to European security. During the Korean War, for example, Western Europeans were reluctant to join the police action in Korea, even though that war was carried out under the banner of the United Nations. The European contribution to the U.S. effort in Vietnam was even less. The NATO powers in both instances demonstrated that they did not see the Atlantic alliance as a party to a global effort to contain communism and that they did not accept American leadership beyond the very important, but quite specific, purpose of providing for the security of Western Europe.

Emphasizing this point in no way demeans or diminishes the importance of the NATO alliance to the United States or to its various members. It does, I hope, demystify a bit that relationship, which, from time to time, becomes overloaded with sentimental rhetoric and grandiose expectations.

As human institutions go, NATO has been a colossal success. I do not think there can be any question that since NATO was founded, nearly thirty-three years ago, the parties to the treaty have fulfilled their goal of safeguarding "the freedom, common heritage and civilization of their peoples, founded on the principles of democracy, individual liberty and the rule of law." Even neutral states in Europe have been able to maintain their freedom and independence by virtue of NATO's stabilizing influence. NATO has been a great success. It remains one. It was never intended to be an all-purpose instrument. It should, therefore, not be criticized for failing to be one.

Why then is there so much discussion in places like this of the crisis in the alliance? Partly, I believe, because as memory of the history and purposes of the Atlantic alliance grows dim, there is a tendency both to romanticize the alliance and to overload it with exaggerated expectations and demands concerning what it might be and do. Furthermore, the relative eclipse of other mutual security treaties, which were constructed to provide for hemispheric security and containment, encouraged some to treat NATO as though it were *the* instrument of our foreign policy.

The ultimate antidote for this delusion should be the fact that the most critical international involvements of the United States in the post–World War II period—the Korean and the Vietnam wars and the Cuban missile crisis—have not directly involved the Atlantic alliance. This fact testifies neither to the success nor to the failure of NATO but to its nonrelevance to some major aspects of U.S. foreign policy. More realistic expectations of the alliance will surely lead to a more positive assessment of its performance.

Another reason for contemporary concern about the condition of the alliance is, I believe, the certain knowledge that as the social and economic, political, and military environments of NATO change, these changes may affect the alliance itself. Most dramatic and important among the changes is the evolution of economic interdependence between East and West associated with détente. The Polish crisis has dramatized the potentially negative effects on the alliance of interdependence, by focusing attention on the different views of the NATO partners concerning economic policy. Concern about the long-range effects of these environmental changes on the alliance is, I believe, reasonable and realistic.

A third source of concern about the present and future of the alliance lies, I believe, in the conviction of people like us that ideas and culture matter, that they have consequences for politics and for foreign policy, and, indeed, that they ultimately shape the world. We are, therefore, naturally worried when,

181

for the first time, we hear significant numbers of people on both sides of the Atlantic questioning the value of the alliance. The fact that many Americans ask today whether an American alliance with Europe still serves *our* interests is itself indicative of the evolution of intra-alliance doubts in the United States, and it is every bit as important as the more widely publicized mass demonstrations in Europe for disarmament. The trends toward isolationism, globalism, and unilateralism in the United States, toward neutralism and pacifism in Europe, are equally reflections of unease about the alliance. Some Europeans are focusing on risks involved in alliance with the United States, risks that draw them, they fear, into conflicts that they might otherwise avoid; while Americans are saying that alliance with Europe imposes burdens and constraints on American foreign policy that can, perhaps, no longer be justified by the advantages of collective security in Europe.

European and American complaints against the alliance have not yet been translated into significantly different policies. We hope that they will not be. But as pressures and mutual recriminations mount, the time is fast approaching for a re-affirmation of the place of the alliance in a U.S. and Western strategy for defense and security. Obviously, Europe cannot insist on American support against the Soviet Union in Europe while at the same time supporting pro-Soviet forces outside Europe that may endanger U.S. security (as in Central America).

The growth of neutralism, isolationism, unilateralism—whatever one calls it—on both sides of the Atlantic constitutes an independent strain on the alliance and illuminates the fact that the alliance must be defended at the level of ideas. The defense of freedom is finally grounded in an appreciation of its value. No government, no foreign policy, is more important to the defense of freedom than are the writers, teachers, communication specialists, researchers—whose responsibility it is to document, illustrate, and explain the human consequences of freedom and unfreedom.

Central America

Nicaragua and Her Neighbors

In his letter requesting this meeting, the coordinator of the Nicaraguan government, Mr. Daniel Ortega Saavedra, made some extraordinary charges against the government of the United States. We naturally desire to respond to the grave charges that Mr. Ortega has leveled against our policies and our intentions.

The essence of Mr. Ortega's complaint is that the United States is about to launch a "large-scale military intervention" against his country. Thus he wrote, in the letter in which he requested the meeting, of "an ever increasing danger of a large scale military intervention by the armed forces of the United States [which] constitutes a grave threat to the independence and sovereignty of the Central American countries and to international peace and security." He spoke of the "interventionist strategy of the government of the United States" and of statements and "concrete actions that clearly evidence an intention to attack Nicaragua and intervene directly in El Salvador." To support his arguments, Mr. Ortega charges us with the "systematic repetition of . . . aggressive statements [which] seriously affects the normal conduct of international relations . . . with bellicose statements." The U.S. actions, Mr. Ortega asserts, violate the Charter of the United Nations, the "principles and goals" of the United Nations, and constitute a "grave threat to the independence and sovereignty of the Central American countries and to international peace and security."

Statement in the Security Council on the complaint by Nicaragua, March 25, 1982.

The attack made by Nicaragua is not haphazard; its charges are not random: The government of Nicaragua has accused the United States of the kinds of political behavior of which it is guilty—large-scale interventions in the internal affairs of neighbors, persistent efforts to subvert and overthrow by force and violence the governments of neighboring states, aggressive actions which disrupt the "normal conduct of international relations" in the region—acts and intentions inconsistent with the Charter of the United Nations. These charges—as extravagant as they are baseless—are an interesting example of projection, a psychological operation in which one's own feelings and intentions are simultaneously denied and attributed—that is, projected —to someone else.

Hostility is the dominant emotion and projection the key mechanism of the paranoid style of politics which, much to our regret, has characterized the political behavior of the Sandinista leadership. The principal object of Sandinista hostility, I further regret to say, is the government and people of the United States.

Nicaragua's new political elite has constructed a historical myth to justify its demand for full power. According to this myth, the United States is responsible for all problems and disasters—natural and social—that Nicaragua has ever suffered; the Sandinista anthem describes us as the enemy of mankind; and Sandinista ideology defines us as implacably opposed to national independence, economic development, and peace. Since the moment of their arrival in power the Sandinistas have predicted that the United States was about to overrun them. The Yankees are coming, they have reiterated. The counterrevolutionaries will get us if we don't silence criticism, mobilize the population, destroy freedom.

The familiar totalitarian assertion that they are surrounded by enemies internal and external has been heard again and again to justify the elimination of opponents and the concentration of power in a one-party elite. . . .

Given this pattern, it is no surprise that last week, as Commander Ortega leveled new charges against the United States, the Nicaraguan government suspended its constitution and promulgated a new Law of National Emergency that threatens to eliminate the limited liberty and pluralism that remains.

• All discussions in the Sandinista-controlled Council of State of the proposed media and political parties laws have been suspended.

• The Ministry of Interior has made an unspecified number of "preventive arrests" of people who are *suspected* of having ties with counterrevolutionaries.

• Radio Catolica has been closed down indefinitely, and all radio news programs, except official statements, are prohibited.

• *La Prensa* and all other media are required to submit news stories for prior censorship. Yesterday it was unable to publish since 50 percent of the paper was found objectionable.

• Opposition political leaders have been informed that they cannot leave the country; the passport of one politician was seized when he attempted to make a routine trip abroad.

• A new "patriotic tax" is to be imposed on businesses to help finance its latest mobilization campaign. . . .

It did not need to be thus. Nicaragua's new government could have satisfied the longing of its people for peace instead of making war on the people. They could have accepted the U.S. offer of friendship. The U.S. government did not oppose the Sandinista rise to power. It has not attempted to prevent its consolidation. The U.S. government gave the Sandinistas moral and political support in the crucial phases of the civil war, and negotiated the resignations of Somoza and Urcuyo, but this did not affect the Sandinista leadership's view of U.S. attitudes. With our help, the government of Nicaragua received more loans in two years from the International Development Bank than the Somoza government had received in any *decade*, but this did not affect the Sandinista leaders' attitudes toward us. A $75 million supplemental aid bill was rushed through Congress to assist in the job of reconstruction, and the United States provided more economic aid than any other government to the Sandinista regime during its first eighteen months in power.

Did this support from the United States alter the Sandinista leadership's hostility? Alas, it had no such effect.

By its words and deeds, the U.S. government—the Congress and the executive branch—demonstrated not only its respect for the sovereignty of the Nicaraguan political process, the right of Nicaraguans to determine their own government, but also our desire to give a boost to Nicaragua's new government, to help it overcome the devastation of civil war. But Sandinista ideology overcame the reality of U.S. assistance. The fact of U.S. support for economic reconstruction and national independence in Nicaragua proved less powerful than the stereotype—we remained the Yankee enemy of mankind.

Like others in this century who have seized power by force, the Sandinista leaders are haunted by the expectation that they will fall victim to the violent intrigues by which they won power and exercise it.

It is, of course, *they* who systematically seek to subvert and overthrow neighboring governments. El Salvador has the misfortune to be the principal target.

A clandestine support system established in 1978 at the time of the Nicaraguan civil war continued to operate after the fall of Somoza in July 1979 with a new final destination— El Salvador. The existence of this support system has been repeatedly and vigorously denied by Nicaraguan and Cuban spokesmen. Yet a considerable quantity of solid information shows that those denials are false.

Nicaragua offers a support system with three major components: external arms supplies, training, and command and control.

Within weeks after the fall of Somoza in July 1979, the Sandinistas began to cooperate in support of the Salvadoran insurgents by establishing training camps and the beginning of arms supply networks. This clandestine assistance initially involved local black markets and relatively limited resources. In 1980, after meetings in Havana had unified Salvadoran Marxists into a single military command structure, the Sandinista leadership agreed to serve as a conduit for an arms trafficking system of unprecedented proportions, originating outside the hemisphere. That structure remains in force today.

Arms and ammunition for the Salvadoran insurgents reach Nicaragua by ship and occasionally by direct flights from Havana to Nicaragua. Three Nicaraguan ships, the *Monimbo*, the *Aracely*, and the *Nicarao*, frequently transport arms and ammunition in their cargo to Nicaragua from Cuba. Salvadoran guerrilla headquarters near Managua arranges for their shipment into El Salvador. The timing of the resupply operations appears to be coordinated with the planned level of fighting, since before each surge in the fighting we have detected large deliveries.

When a clandestine shipment of arms is captured or a safehouse is found containing arms and terrorist supplies, it is often impossible to know with certainty whether the ultimate recipients are Guatemalan, Honduran, Costa Rican, or Salvadoran terrorists, since the arms supply networks established by Cuba and Nicaragua are funneling lethal military supplies to terrorists and guerrillas in all four countries.

A few examples, chosen from among dozens, will illustrate the pattern of arms flow.

• The Papalonal airfield provides a clear case of the direct airlift of weapons from Nicaragua to guerrillas in El Salvador. Papalonal is a commercially undeveloped area 23 nautical miles northwest of Managua, accessible only by dirt roads. In late July 1980, the airfield was an agricultural dirt airstrip approximately 800 meters long, but by early 1981 the strip was lengthened by 50 percent to approximately 1,200 meters. A turnaround was added to each end. A dispersal parking area with three hardstands—a feature typical of a military airfield—had been constructed at the west end of the runway. Three parking aprons were cleared, and six hangar/storage buildings were constructed on the aprons; the hangars were used to stockpile arms for the Salvadoran guerrillas. C-47 flights from the airbase corresponded with sightings in El Salvador, and several pilots were identified in Nicaragua who regularly flew the route into El Salvador. This particular route was closed in March 1981, but some air infiltration continues to this day, despite difficulties in pilot recruitment.

• Weapons delivery by overland routes from Nicaragua passes through Honduras. Several examples of this arms traffic can be identified. Honduran authorities have intercepted various shipments of arms en route from Nicaragua and in concealed caches in Honduras. In early January 1981, for example, Honduran police caught six individuals unloading weapons from a truck en route from Nicaragua. The six identified themselves as Salvadorans and as members of the International Support Commission of the Salvadoran Popular Liberation Forces (FPL). They had in their possession a large number of altered and forged Honduran, Costa Rican, and Salvadoran passports and other identity documents. This one truck contained over a hundred M-16/AR-15 automatic rifles, fifty 81mm mortar rounds, approximately a hundred thousand rounds of 5.56mm ammunition, machine gun belts, field packs, and first-aid kits.

• In April 1981, Honduran authorities intercepted a tractor-trailer truck which had entered Honduras at the Guasule crossing from Nicaragua. This truck was apparently heading for Guatemala. Ammunition and propaganda materials were hidden in the sidewalls of the trailer. The same arms traffickers operated a storehouse in Tegucigalpa, Honduras, with a false floor and a special basement for storing weapons.

• A special legislative commission established in June 1980 by the Costa Rican legislature confirmed in its May 1981 report that a clandestine arms supply link between Costa Rica and Nicaragua was established during the Nicaraguan civil war, and that the link continued to function between Costa Rica and El Salvador once the Sandinistas had come to power in Nicaragua.

• In April and July 1981, Guatemalan security forces captured large caches of guerrilla weapons at safehouses in Guatemala City. Several of the vehicles captured at the Guatemala City safehouses bore recent customs markings from Nicaragua, thus suggesting that the operation was part of the well-established pattern.

Within the past three months, shipments of arms into El Salvador reached unprecedented peaks, averaging out to the highest overall volume since the "final offensive" last year. The recent Nicaraguan-Cuban arms flow into El Salvador has emphasized both sea and—once again—overland routes through Honduras.

• Last month, a Salvadoran guerrilla group picked up a large shipment of arms on the Usulután coast after the shipment arrived by sea from Nicaragua.

• On March 15, 1982, the Costa Rican judicial police announced the discovery of a house in San José with a sizable cache of arms, explosives, uniforms, passports, documents, false immigration stamps from more than thirty countries, and vehicles with hidden compartments—all connected with an ongoing arms traffic through Costa Rican territory to Salvadoran guerrillas. Nine people were arrested: Salvadorans, Nicaraguans, an Argentine, a Chilean, and a Costa Rican. Costa Rican police so far have seized thirteen vehicles designed for arms smuggling. Police confiscated some 150 to 175 weapons, from Mausers to machine guns, TNT, fragmentation grenades, a grenade launcher, ammunition, and 500 combat uniforms. One of the captured terrorists told police that the arms and other goods were to have been delivered to the Salvadoran guerrillas before March 20, "for the elections."

Nicaragua's fraternal assistance to its neighbors is not limited to arms. Training is also provided. This coordinated Nicaraguan and Cuban political and military training creates the framework for the use of the arms by guerrillas operating within El Salvador and elsewhere in Central America. Since at least mid-1980, Salvadoran guerrillas have been trained in Nicaragua in military tactics, weapons, communications, and explosives at temporary training schools scattered around the country and on Sandinista military bases. At several military sites in Nicaragua, Salvadorans receive training under guidance from Cuban and other foreign advisers. For more specialized training, guerrillas transit Nicaragua for Cuba. They are provided with false identity documents to help them transit third countries. Guerrillas trained in Cuba are reinfiltrated through Nicaragua back into El Salvador. The attacks on Ilopango Airport in January 1982 and on the El Oro bridge in October 1981 were clearly performed by saboteurs who had employed the benefits of such sophisticated training.

Honduran police raided a safehouse for the Moranzanist Front for the Liberation of Honduras (FMLH) on November 27, 1981, in Tegucigalpa. And while the Honduran police were attempting to search the house, a firefight broke out. The police ultimately captured several members of this group. This cell of the FMLH included a Honduran, a Uruguayan, and several Nicaraguans. The captured terrorists told Honduran authorities that the Nicaraguan government had provided them with funds for travel expenses, as well as explosives. Captured documents and statements by detained guerrillas further indicated that:

- the group was formed in Nicaragua at the instigation of high-level Sandinista leaders
- the group's chief of operations resided in Managua
- members of the group received military training in Nicaragua and Cuba

Guerrillas at one safehouse were responsible for transporting arms and munitions into Honduras from Estelí, Nicaragua.

189

Command-and-control services are also provided by Nicaragua. Planning and operations are guided from this headquarters, where Nicaraguan officers are involved in command and control. The headquarters coordinates logistical support for the insurgents to include food, medicines, clothing, money—and most importantly—weapons and ammunition. The headquarters in Nicaragua decides on locations to be attacked and coordinates supply deliveries. The guidance flows to guerrilla units widely spread throughout El Salvador.

The pattern is clear. It continues to this day. We very much wish the government of Nicaragua would cease its efforts to repress its people and overthrow neighboring governments. We thought perhaps progress to this end was in sight. Frankly we are surprised by the Nicaraguan government's decision to expand and embitter regional conflict at this moment.

Mr. Ortega says it is because Nicaragua fears that the U.S. government is about to invade. But, of course, that is ridiculous. The U.S. government is not about to invade anyone. And we have so stated on many occasions.

It is true that once it became aware of Nicaragua's own intentions and actions, the U.S. government undertook over-flights to safeguard our own security and that of other states who are threatened by the Sandinista government. These over-flights, conducted by unarmed high-flying planes, and for the express and sole purpose of verifying reports of Nicaraguan intervention, are surely no threat to regional peace and stability. No, the threat to regional and world peace lies in the activities these photographs expose. One can understand the government of Nicaragua's preference that no such photographs exist.

The United States is frankly surprised and puzzled by Nicaragua's appeal to this council. As most members of the Security Council understand, Mr. Ortega's contentious charges come at a time when we and others are looking for a basis on which to settle peacefully the differences of the parties involved. The government of Nicaragua has attempted to broaden and deepen the conflict. Only last week the government of Nicaragua stated a desire to negotiate, but then, after two high government officials visited Cuba, called for this meeting to air baseless charges in this most public and important forum.

The United States seeks peace in Central America. We have repeatedly attempted to explore ways with the Nicaraguans in which our governments could cooperate in alleviating the tensions in the area. We have submitted proposals to the Nicaraguan government, and we have received no response. Instead, the Nicaraguan government replied—in October—as it has today—by sending Daniel Ortega to the United Nations to deliver an attack on the United States.

Assistant Secretary of State Thomas Enders went to Managua last August, to try to communicate with the leaders of the government of Nicaragua, to offer a way out of confrontation if they would restrain their military buildup and cease their support for insurgencies in neighboring countries. At that time we offered a specific agenda for discussions; we offered to consider their concerns if they would consider ours. We also agreed to restrain public rhetoric while this proposal was considered.

The response was not long in coming. On September 15, Humberto Ortega made a major speech in Managua during which he vilified the United States, and on October 5, Nicaraguan Junta Coordinator Daniel Ortega addressed the United Nations General Assembly, attacked the United States for past intervention in Central America, accused the United States of causing the world's economic problems, and attacked us harshly.

In recent weeks our secretary of state has met with the foreign minister of Mexico in yet another attempt to engage the Nicaraguans in a meaningful dialogue. And how has the Nicaraguan government again responded? By again sending Mr. Ortega to the United Nations, apparently in search of a propaganda victory—and an exacerbation of conflict.

The Nicaraguan government has said it wants peace; it has stated that it wishes better relations with the United States. But, unfortunately, its actions do not match its pretensions. If the Nicaraguan government was genuinely interested in alleviating tensions, would it continue to act as a conduit for war materiel aimed at subverting the government of El Salvador? Would it have undertaken a campaign of systematic violence against the Indian communities on the East Coast, displacing 25,000 Indians from their ancestral homes on the pretext of a security threat from a peaceful, democratic neighbor? Would it have doubled the number of Cuban military and security advisers in the past year? Would it have continued seeking to augment its military forces and arsenal? Would it have declared a state of siege effectively neutralizing the opposition? And, most im-

191

portantly, would it have continued incessantly to pour arms into El Salvador, even increasing the flow of arms, bullets, and now propaganda just when the people of El Salvador have been given an unprecedented opportunity to express their views?

Given this history, we are understandably skeptical when the government of Nicaragua declares it wants peace, or that it wishes better relations with the United States. How, we ask, is this professed interest in peace reconciled with Comandante Humberto Ortega when he states that the opposition will be "hanged from the lampposts"? Or with Comandante Bayardo Arce when he tells us that the Nicaraguan government will continue to pour arms into El Salvador, no matter what we do or say?

In spite of this harsh response on the part of the government of Nicaragua, our offer to engage in a dialogue was repeated by Secretary of State Haig at the OAS General Assembly meeting in December 1981. Secretary Haig said "the United States has made proposals to Nicaragua to normalize relations. If Nicaragua addresses our concerns about intervention and militarization, we are prepared to address their concerns. We do not close the door to the search for proper relations." Again, the Nicaraguan government has not responded to our offer.

On February 24, 1982, President Reagan said "we seek to exclude no one [from the benefits of our Caribbean Basin Initiative]. Some, however, have turned from their American neighbors and their heritage. Let them return to the traditions and common values of this hemisphere and we would welcome them. The choice is theirs."

Finally, just a few weeks ago, the president of Mexico offered his good offices in the effort to reduce tensions between Nicaragua and the United States. We welcomed that initiative. . . .

And now, even as representatives of the Mexican and U.S. governments are consulting on this initiative, the government of Nicaragua, fully aware of what is going on, has once again made a move that can only increase tensions, not reduce them.

Although we find its actions puzzling, we have not interposed any objections to the request of Nicaragua that an opportunity be granted for their head of state to present an exposition to the council, even though the government of Nicaragua, for whatever reasons, chose to ignore procedures well established in both the Charter of the United Nations and the Charter of the Organization of American States. As members of this council know, Article 52 of the United Nations Charter encourages efforts to achieve the peaceful settlement of disputes through regional arrangements and gives priority to them. Article 23 of the OAS Charter specifically singles out the role of the OAS in settling regional disputes before such disputes are referred to the Security Council.

The government of Nicaragua should be among the first to recall the existence under the OAS of the seventeenth meeting of foreign ministers which dealt in 1978 and 1979 with events in Central America threatening to the peace of the region. Indeed, in 1979, the Nicaraguan Government of National Reconstruction termed the resolution of the seventeenth meeting of foreign ministers as "historic in every respect." That meeting was never terminated. The question of Central America remains before the OAS. Just yesterday, in the Permanent Council of the OAS, the foreign minister of Honduras made serious proposals for efforts to bring peace to Central America.

The Organization of American States, thus, not only has jurisdiction of this matter in accordance with the provisions of the United Nations and OAS charters, but it is also formally seized of the matter. It is clear that the OAS is the appropriate and primary forum for consideration of the matters addressed by Nicaragua.

We appeal once again to the government of Nicaragua to join with us and other neighboring governments in resolving differences, ending interventions, and living in peace in this hemisphere.

Central America

Sandino Betrayed I

By way of reply, I should like to begin by thanking the various members of the United Nations who have spoken today in support of the principles of national self-determination, national independence, strict respect for territorial integrity, the principles of nonintervention in the affairs of other states. Those are principles which are very dear to my country and which the United States in its foreign affairs does its very best to honor in a serious and consistent fashion.

I should like also to express the sincere agreement of the United States with the principles of international law which were cited by the distinguished representative of Guyana and various other speakers today, particularly with reference to the use of force and threats of force in the affairs of nations. We are profoundly committed to the principles of nonuse of force in international affairs and committed also to following and abiding by the principles of the Charter of the United Nations concerning the use and nonuse of force.

I should also like to express the solidarity of the United States with all those people who hope for change, for democracy and development in Central America.

I cannot forbear noting that there have been some rather odd disjunctions between some aspects of political reality and political symbolism today. I find it interesting, as an observer of political affairs as well as a representative of my country, to hear the government of Vietnam speaking with such con-

Statement in the Security Council in right of reply, March 26, 1982.

viction about the principle of respect for national independence. I trust that members of the United Nations would all agree that respect for the principle of national independence should apply in Kampuchea as well as in the rest of our countries. Similarly I found it interesting yesterday to listen to the representative of Angola pay homage to the principle of respect for national independence since Angola is a nation, of course, whose national independence is in some sense subject to the will of 30,000 foreign troops who occupy that land with the consent of that government, which is here invoking the principle of national independence.

I find it, I suppose, particularly interesting to listen to the representative of the government of Cuba commenting on peaceful affairs in this hemisphere and respect for the principles of national independence and nonintervention. Cuba is a very strange nation which today, as members of this council know, maintains some 40,000 soldiers in Africa alone, where those troops dominate two countries, doing for the Soviet Union there what the Gurkha mercenaries did for nineteenth-century England. In Central America, Cuba is attempting to export aggression, subvert established governments, and intervene in a most persistent and massive fashion in the internal affairs of more than one nation in that region. In Nicaragua alone it maintains no less than 1,800 to 2,000 security and military personnel. In other words, as Assistant Secretary Thomas Enders noted yesterday in his testimony before the Congress of the United States, "Cuba is a would-be foreign policy giant superimposed on an economic pigmy whose peoples have had to sacrifice all hope for a rising standard of living in order to gain advantages in foreign affairs." Those advantages are largely purchased for it by some $3 billion annual economic aid from the Soviet Union and a great deal more military aid, of course. My country naturally welcomes any move of the government of Cuba toward greater concern for economic development and well-being of its people.

Finally, commenting on the use of language and the realities of politics, it occurred to me that members of the council might be interested in a recent article concerning Sandino and Sandinismo in Nicaragua, since we are discussing here the letter of the coordinator of the Nicaraguan junta. A distinguished writer, Pablo Joaquin Chomorro y Cardinale, was assassinated in the final days of the Somoza regime, as you perhaps know. His death was a precipitating factor in the successful revolt against the Somoza regime, leading eventually to the installation of the current junta in Nicaragua. Pablo Joaquin Chomorro was a very highly respected writer whose name is from time to time invoked by the leaders of the revolution but not as often as that of Sandino. And he was, of course, the editor and publisher of *La Prensa*, the last remaining independent newspaper in Nicaragua—which may or may not have been permitted to publish today. Chomorro wrote:

> Sandino should be exalted precisely as a contrast to the Communists who obey signals from Russia and China. Sandino fought against the United States Marines but he did not bring Russian Cossacks to Nicaragua as Fidel Castro did in Cuba. There is a great difference between the Communist Fidel Castro who in his false battle for the independence of his country has filled it with Russian rockets, soldiers, planes and even canned goods, and a Sandino who defended the sovereignty of his ground with homemade bombs but without accepting the patronage of another power. For this reason, Sandino was great because he was not handed over to Communist treason as Castro but fought within an Indo-Hispanic limit. Naturally the Communists who attacked and slandered Sandino when he was in the mountains now try to use him because they have no moral scruple to restrain them. Sandino was a pure product of our land, very different from the products exported by Russia or China and as such we must exalt and preserve his memory. The value of his exploits is a Nicaraguan value, not Soviet, and his nationalism is indigenous not Russian. Sandino is a monument to the dignity of our country and we must not permit the Communists with whom he never communed to besmirch his memory in order to use his prestige and to succeed, someday, on the pretext that they are fighting imperialism in delivering over our land to Russia as Castro did with Cuba.

I would finally like simply to mention that there has been a good deal of talk of change in Central America today and there has been a good deal of invocation of hope for change for the people of Central America. The government of the United

States hopes very much for change in Central America; we hope it will be as peaceable as possible and bought at as low a price to the people of Central America as possible. An example of peaceable change may be observed this very weekend in El Salvador, where free elections with a free press, free assembly, with competition among parties and candidates, will take place. The risks of free election are, as every officeholder knows, very great. When a government risks a free election, it risks being defeated. It takes a very brave government who is more committed to freedom and democracy than to retaining power to run such a risk. My government congratulates the government of El Salvador for being willing to risk its power for the sake of freedom.

Central America

Sandino Betrayed II

As this discussion of Commander Ortega's letter to the Security Council draws to a close, I should like to make several observations concerning his complaint against the United States and also concerning the debate that has taken place in this chamber in the past days.

First, I desire to reiterate that the great fear cited by Commander Ortega that the United States is about to invade Nicaragua is groundless. The United States has no intention of invading Nicaragua or anyone else. I have already emphasized the Sandinista leadership's past misunderstanding of the attitudes of the U.S. government. I desire to reiterate once again that the U.S. government did not attempt to prevent the Sandinistas' accession to power. It helped them. The United States did not attempt to prevent their consolidation of power; we helped them. The United States did not oppose their efforts to reconstruct Nicaragua's economy; we helped them. The record concerning U.S. economic assistance—direct and indirect—to the government of Nicaragua is clear. There is no need to labor it. I shall not do so.

Second, I have also reiterated the attachment of my government to the principles of nonintervention in the internal affairs of other states, our respect for territorial integrity and national independence, to the peaceful settlement of disputes, and to those principles of the United Nations Charter that govern

Statement in the Security Council on the complaint by Nicaragua, April 2, 1982.

the use and nonuse of force. Obviously, none of this means that the United States renounces the right to defend itself or that we will not assist others to defend themselves under circumstances consistent with our legal and political obligations and with the Charter of the United Nations.

Unfortunately, not all governments which have participated in this debate are equally attached to principles of nonuse of force, respect for territorial integrity, or national independence. There is an interesting correlation between the nations who have *supported* Nicaragua's complaint against the United States and those who *opposed* the resolution calling for withdrawal of Soviet troops from Afghanistan.

The principles of nonintervention and respect for national independence cited in this debate did not lead Angola, Cuba, the German Democratic Republic, Grenada, the Lao People's Democratic Republic, Libya, Madagascar, Mozambique, Seychelles, the Syrian Arab Republic, the Soviet Union, or Vietnam to join 116 other nations in calling for an end to the occupation of Afghanistan. All those nations opposed the Afghanistan resolution.

Zeal for national independence and noninterference did not move the governments of Algeria, Benin, the Congo, India, or Uganda to seek an end to the occupation of Afghanistan. All abstained.

It is not, moreover, only the national independence of Afghanistan which inspires so little response from among those who have expressed solidarity with these principles in the last few days: Neither Angola, nor the Congo, nor Cuba, nor the German Democratic Republic, nor Grenada, nor the Lao People's Democratic Republic, nor Libya, nor Mozambique, nor Seychelles, nor the Soviet Union, nor Vietnam, Algeria, Benin, India, Madagascar, Mexico, Panama, Uganda, Tanzania, nor Zimbabwe was moved by these principles to support the call for an end to the continuing military occupation of Kampuchea.

Will members of this council be surprised to be reminded that the government of Nicaragua was itself not prepared to extend to the people of Afghanistan and Kampuchea the rights to peace, national independence, and territorial integrity it seeks for itself now? Nicaragua supported *neither* the resolution calling for an end to the occupation of Afghanistan *nor* Kampuchea.

199

This sort of selective invocation and application of universal principles does not strengthen either the principles or the organizations dedicated to their realization and implementation. It breeds cynicism. It harms the United Nations. It mocks the search for peace.

Third, I desire to clarify the position of my government with regard to the jurisdiction and role of the United Nations and regional organizations. Despite efforts by the government of Nicaragua to indicate otherwise, it should be clear that the U.S. government believes that any member state has the right under the charter to bring before the Security Council an issue which seriously threatens international peace and security. As members of the council know, the United States did not oppose Commander Ortega's request to present an exposition to this council, even though we were objects of that complaint. But while the charter grants that right to all members, it is equally clear that the charter encourages the resolution of disputes through regional arrangements.

The Charter of the United Nations contains a chapter relating expressly to regional organizations. Paragraphs 2 and 3 of Article 52 of the charter contain the explicit provisions designed to encourage resolution of regional disputes in the relevant regional organization. These paragraphs read as follows:

> 2. The Members of the United Nations entering into such arrangements or constituting such agencies shall make every effort to achieve pacific settlement of local disputes through such regional arrangements or by such regional agencies before referring them to the Security Council.
> 3. The Security Council shall encourage the development of pacific settlement of local disputes through such regional agencies either on the initiative of the states concerned or by reference from the Security Council.

Those who attempt, as the government of Nicaragua has attempted, to describe the legal obligations of members of the regional organizations without reference to these provisions ignore *inter alia* fundamental provisions of the charter. It is an elementary rule of interpretation of treaties that effect must be given to all provisions of the charter—*ut res magis valeat quam pereat*. In this context it is worth recalling Article 2, paragraph

2, of the charter, which requires good-faith fulfillment of the obligation assumed by each and every member. Ignoring the existence of undeniably relevant provisions of the charter would appear to raise serious questions. Nicaragua's studied avoidance of those provisions in a long communication ostensibly devoted to an analysis of the subject demonstrates not only that its concern is less with law than with politics, but that it is prepared to seek political advantages even at the price of serious legal distortions.

Unfortunately, there have been other evidences, inside the chamber and outside it as well, that the government of Nicaragua is less concerned with rights than with advantages.

Its failure to support the national independence of the peoples of Afghanistan and Kampuchea; its continuing efforts to undermine and overthrow neighboring governments, especially El Salvador; its importation of heavy offensive arms; its militarization of Nicaraguan society—all establish that we are dealing here with a government that seeks for itself rights it is not willing to grant others.

Nicaragua invokes the principle of nonintervention, but claims the right to intervene in the internal affairs of neighboring states. Nicaragua demands that others respect its national independence, but does not respect the sovereignty or right to national self-determination of its neighbors. Nicaragua claims the right to seek advisers and arms wherever it chooses—as an exercise of its sovereignty—but would deny its neighbors the same right. Nicaragua claims the right to live in peace while fomenting internal war in neighboring countries.

The facts, as I stated last week, are that the government of Nicaragua is an active party to a massive intervention in the affairs of her neighbors. The government of Nicaragua is engaged in training guerrillas, directing command-and-control centers. It is involved in infiltrating arms and guerrillas, destroying electric power stations, blowing up bridges, terrorizing civilians. Her leaders come before the Security Council of the United Nations seeking international protection for these activities.

The government of Nicaragua espouses and practices a very particular conception of nonintervention, a very particular conception of nonalignment; the kind that, in the end, saps the meaning and power of both.

The letter of Mr. Daniel Ortega Saavedra, and the Security Council debate that it has prompted, remind me of a statement by the late French philosopher George Bernanos, who once said that "the worst, the most corrupting of lies are problems poorly stated." Mr. Ortega states "the problem" as having to do with the danger posed by the United States to the independence and sovereignty of the countries of Central America. This definition of the problem merely obfuscates the real issue that is at stake in Central America, which is a conflict between two concepts of organizing society, two ideologies—if you will—one democratic and the other totalitarian.

The elections held Sunday in El Salvador symbolize one of these approaches, the democratic one, while the Nicaraguan regime's systematic refusal to hold elections symbolizes the other, totalitarian approach.

That election, with its enormous turnout of voters, was a tribute to the Salvadoran people and to the vitality of the democratic idea.

What a stolid, courageous, unflinching people these Salvadorans are! Despite the possibility of massive violence at the polling places and threats of retaliation by guerrilla forces against voters, the Salvadorans still voted in huge, unprecedented numbers. Why did they do so?

In Monday's *Wall Street Journal*, there was an interview with one of these voters, Ana Maria de Martinez, who "was typical of some voters who thought they would beat the crowds by showing up early at the polling stations. This mother of two children got to the National Technical Institute, a polling place, around 5 A.M. But so did a lot of other people, and by 9 A.M. she was still two blocks from the gate entrance. 'I'll wait here all day if I have to,' she said, fanning her face with her wallet. 'The rest of the world seems to have made decisions about El Salvador. Now it's my turn.' "

Some people said that free and fair elections could not be held in El Salvador. They were wrong.

But there were others who have been against elections in principle, regarding them as a tool of the bourgeoisie and a misrepresentation of the popular will which could best be expressed through armed struggle. In El Salvador this view, preferring the bullet to the ballot, is held by the various guerrilla factions, whose coordinating front is appropriately named after Farabundo Marti, the Salvadoran Communist. One of these guerrillas, Comandante Ana Guadalupe Martinez, is quoted in this week's issue of the *Economist* of London as saying that "elections are there to ratify a popular government. . . . If laws exist which represent the people, elections are not very important."

The idea that the will of the people can be better expressed through a revolutionary elite than through free elections is, of course, a fundamental tenet of Leninism. It is, I need hardly point out in this forum, fundamentally at variance with Article 21 of the Universal Declaration of Human Rights, which states:

> The will of the people shall be the basis of the authority of government; this will shall be expressed in periodic and genuine elections which shall be by universal and equal suffrage and shall be held by secret vote or by equivalent free voting procedures.

The FMLN is not the only element in Central American politics that opposes free elections as defined in Article 21 of the Universal Declaration of Human Rights. The Sandinista leadership also opposes such elections. Indeed, they have called the Salvadoran election "an absolute denial of democracy and civilization." They did not always speak thus. One month before achieving power, in June 1979, when they were still seeking supporters, the Sandinistas promised the Organization of American States that they would hold free elections when they assumed power. Once in power, however, they quickly reneged on that promise.

In the spring of 1980, the Sandinistas consolidated their control over the Council of State, enlarging it and packing it with their own supporters to ensure a permanent majority. In July 1980 Sandinista Defense Minister Humberto Ortega announced that there would be no need for elections since the people had already "voted" during the revolution. Elections could not be held, it was said, until the people had been "re-educated."

The following month, in August 1980, Humberto Ortega announced that elections would be put off until 1985. Even then, it was stated, these would not be "bourgeois" elections—the kind of elections, that is to say, called for in the universal declaration, but rather "people's elections," in which, in the words of Interior Minister Tomas Borge, power "will not be raffled off." Meanwhile, no "proselytizing activities" on behalf of any candidate, no discussion of candidacies would be permitted before candidates were officially designated by an electoral agency, which itself would not be created until 1984. Violations would be punished by terms of three months to three years in jail.

Meanwhile, vigilante mobs have been encouraged to intimidate the opposition. The MDN and the Social Democrats, two of Nicaragua's principal opposition parties, have repeatedly been the victims of semiofficial mob violence. In a speech delivered last fall, Humberto Ortega stated that the Sandinista regime is "guided by scientific doctrine, by Marxism-Leninism" and threatened to hang dissenters against the regime's policies "along the streets and highways of the country." Shortly thereafter four Nicaraguan business leaders who signed a letter protesting against this speech were arrested and sentenced to seven months in prison.

The Sandinistas' description concerning elections is part of a larger policy of revolution by obfuscation. They have pretended to be democrats. For a long time they pretended not to be Marxist-Leninists, and today they pretend there is no contradiction between Sandinism and Marxism-Leninism.

As those familiar with the history of Augusto Cesar Sandino know, his nationalism provoked suspicion and criticism from those who supported submission to Moscow's so-called internationalism. His desire for "absolute sovereignty," for a "free country," and for leaving the solution of economic and social problems to democratic decision was naturally rejected by Communists as bourgeois and counterrevolutionary. The Communist attacks against Sandino, therefore, began when he was in Mexico. Because he refused to adjust his fight for "Country and Liberty" to the plans of the Mexican Communists, the secretary general of the Mexican Communist Party called him a traitor and denounced him upon his death.

It is particularly instructive, in light of the different attitudes toward free elections today in El Salvador and Nicaragua, to contrast Sandino's views with those of Jose Agustin Farabundo Marti, the leader of the Salvadoran Communist Party, who joined Sandino's struggle for a time but was eventually sent home because of his Communist ideology. "My break with

Sandino," he said, came about "because he did not wish to embrace the Communist program which I supported. His banner was only for independence, a banner of emancipation, and he did not pursue the ends of social rebellion." Years later this account was confirmed by Sandino himself, who said that "on various occasions attempts were made to distort this movement of national defense, converting it rather into a battle of a social character. I opposed this with all my strength."

In its effort to consolidate totalitarian power at home and mortgage the national independence of Nicaragua to Moscow and Havana, the Nicaraguan regime stands squarely in the tradition of Farabundo Marti, whose descendants, acting in that tradition, tried unsuccessfully to sabotage through violence the free elections in El Salvador and who, if they came to power, would adopt the same contemptuous attitude toward free elections that those who call themselves Sandinistas have adopted in Nicaragua.

It is hardly a coincidence that many of the countries who have supported Comandante Ortega's letter in the course of this debate share his regime's principled opposition to free elections. These countries include Cuba, Vietnam, Angola, the Soviet Union, Laos, Mozambique, Grenada, Iran, the German Democratic Republic, and Poland. In none of these regimes, which call themselves "people's democracies," are governments chosen by or accountable to the people. All of them oppose— because they fear—the free expression of the will of the people through free elections as called for in Article 21 of the Universal Declaration of Human Rights.

I have already expressed to the council my government's surprise at Nicaragua's decision to bring its complaint to the Security Council at precisely the moment when there seemed to be progress toward direct negotiations among the nations most directly involved. We have noted as well that this is not the first time that U.S. initiatives aimed at resolving disputes have been met by deliberate escalations.

Why did the Nicaraguans come, at this time, to this forum, with their harsh rhetoric and wild charges? To distract attention from El Salvador's elections? If that was their purpose, then they have failed.

To distract attention from the intensified repression going on in Nicaragua since the government declared an "emergency"?

If this was their purpose, they have largely succeeded. Not much note has been taken here of the new repressive measures aimed above all at the press. Yet strict prior censorship has prevented the appearance of *La Prensa*, which not only is prohibited from printing news on a great many subjects but also has been forbidden to print blank spaces. Even the pro-Sandinista *El Nuevo Diario* ran afoul of the censors' vague standards and strict enforcement. A twenty-four-hour suspension was imposed after it announced the government had declared a state of siege.

It has been suggested, too, that Nicaragua's complaint here merely reflects a (not unwholesome) desire to let off steam and express its frustrations at having a superpower for a neighbor. But this is a serious international forum, not a Turkish bath. It has also been suggested that being the object of such a complaint is a kind of occupational hazard of superpowers, that this complaint is analogous to that made against the Soviet Union on Afghanistan. An analogy would exist, we are quick to note, only if the United States had forcibly eliminated the government of Nicaragua, shot its chief of state, and moved in 100,000 combat troops to subdue and occupy the country. But, of course, my government has no intention of doing any such thing.

We desire to live at peace with all our neighbors. We shall continue our efforts to develop a constructive relationship with the government of Nicaragua. Secretary of State Alexander Haig has made clear that we are prepared to work on the basis of mutual respect to that end.

Various proposals have been offered for conciliation among the nations of the region and the hemisphere. The United States, interested in the constructive resolution of tension and conflict, remains ready to do its part to ensure peace in the region and to enhance the prospects for democracy and development for all our people.

PART
SIX
On Managing Freedom

Managing Freedom

The pleasure I feel in addressing you today is of a very special sort. It is the kind of pleasure one feels upon being reunited with members of one's own family after a prolonged and perhaps traumatic separation. It is the kind of pleasure that Samuel Johnson called "the wine of life" and that St. Augustine said "rejoices the soul." It is, in short, the pleasure of homecoming.

Receiving an honorary degree is naturally gratifying, but sharing a graduation with some of one's own students is a very special pleasure. So is the opportunity to see once again my many friends in this university's faculty, student body, and administration.

Although I am not in residence, I remain objectively and subjectively a member of this community. That is the reason why I could not possibly oblige the request that one member of this community made to me that I withdraw from this commencement because of some views that I presumably hold. I have earned my right to membership in this community. It is my sober calculation that, in the past fifteen years, I have graded at least 10,000 examinations, at least 3,500 term papers, read at least 100 dissertations—including one whose author is receiving a doctor's degree today—given at least 3,000 lectures and 738 makeup exams, attended 4,714 committee meetings, and eaten 892 hotdogs from Wisemiller's. In the

Commencement address, Georgetown University, Washington, D.C., May 24, 1981.

process, Georgetown University has become part of me. It is an identification I cherish.

I cherish it because this university is, in my firm opinion—an opinion based on detailed knowledge—a serious and distinguished university. Moreover, I like it. I like the way its history is intricately intertwined with that of our nation. Born the same year as the nation's Constitution, situated on the river that George Washington walked beside, Georgetown has for two centuries embodied and communicated the moral and intellectual commitment and discipline that characterize our civilization at its best.

Of course, not everyone has always shared this benign view of the university and of its founders and owners and managers, the Society of Jesus. One of the nation's Founding Fathers, I discovered, wrote to another of the nation's Founding Fathers not long after the establishment of Georgetown: "I do not like the reappearance of the Jesuits. If ever there was a body of men who merited damnation on earth and in hell it is the Society of Loyola's. Nevertheless we are compelled by our own system of religious toleration to offer them an asylum." Thus wrote John Adams to Thomas Jefferson. Oh well, it's never been possible to please all the people all the time.

There are three other things that I especially like and admire about Georgetown University. The first is the intelligence and good will of its students. The second is the dedication of its faculty. And the third is the moral seriousness of its Jesuit Community. Together these three qualities constitute all the necessary ingredients of a great university.

We come here today, however, neither to praise nor to blame Georgetown but to talk about you, the graduates, and to a lesser extent your parents. I know rather more than the average commencement speaker about both of you. I have read the statistical profiles of your class since before you entered as freshmen. Moreover, I know a good deal firsthand about the anxieties and the gratifications and the expenses of parents. I've been there—indeed, I am there. But what do I know about your futures?

I know that students, all of you, are now and will for some time continue to be faced with more freedom and more choices than any other comparable generation in human history, in part but not only because this is an extraordinarily free society, one that permits us to live where we like, to read and write what we choose, to worship according to our conscience, to practice any profession we are able. Those freedoms were also enjoyed by Greeks in Athens' Golden Age providing they happened to be free and not slave, providing they happened to be citizens and not foreigners. But we, you and I, enjoy freedoms of which the Athenians never dreamed because contemporary technology has given us unprecedented powers and their attendant choices. You graduates are blessed and cursed with the freedom and the necessity to define yourself, to choose from among the dazzling array of attitudes, values, roles, your own—what has come to be called—life style. You are free to choose the city in which you will live, the church to which you will go or not go, the profession for which you will prepare.

Once your role would have been settled at birth. The son of a swineherd, you would have been a swineherd. The son of a merchant, you would have been a merchant. And the daughter of either, you would have been the wife and mother of more swineherds and merchants.

Of course, all of you have already experienced the extraordinarily broad freedom available to students here. You came to Georgetown because you chose to. You studied whatever you liked—with just a few requirements here and there. You could go to class or not go to class as you chose, and sometimes you chose one way and sometimes you chose the other. You could learn your lessons well or fool around. You could get your papers in on time or apply for an extension. You could read, write, think what you liked. And, right now, you are confronted with decisions about where you will spend the summer and how you will spend it, and what you will be doing a month from now.

Erich Fromm is not the only modern writer to have understood that so much freedom is not necessarily easy to bear. But you have already learned that there are constraints that go with this freedom—existential constraints—and more of them than appear at first sight.

Already you've learned you're not free to stay up all night without getting tired or to waste time all semester and keep your QPI where you want it. Already you've learned you can't overeat all term without getting fat. Already you have learned that you probably cannot be as musical as Mozart, as tall as John Thompson.

Perhaps you also have already learned what the distinguished Spanish philosopher Ortega y Gasset wrote:

> It is our privilege to try to be whatever we wish, but it is vicious to try to pretend to be what we are not and to delude ourselves by growing habituated to a radically false idea of what we are. When habitual behavior of a man or an institution is false, the next step is complete demoralization and thence to degeneracy. For it is not possible for anyone to submit to the falsification of his nature without losing his self-respect.

All of us confront limits of body, talent, temperament. But that is not all. We are, all of us, also constrained by our time, our place, our civilization. We are bound by the culture we have in common, that culture which distinguishes us from other people in other times and places. Cultural constraints condition and limit our choices, shaping our characters with their imperatives.

The contemporary American version of the Judeo-Christian heritage, our heritage, still commands: worship God, value life, respect law, seek justice, honor truth. Eight hundred years before the birth of Christ, the prophet Micah summarized it: "And what doth the Lord require of thee, but to do justly, and to love mercy, and to walk humbly with thy God."

We, graduates, parents, all of us, we are the heirs of the Greeks, the Hebrews, the Romans, the early Christians who invented Western civilization. They are part of that "great cloud of witnesses" which St. Paul said surrounds us, encouraging us "to run with patience this race that is set before us." These constraints define us. This culture constrains and limits who you are and how you will run the race. I am sure that I speak for the entire Georgetown family when I express my hope and my prayer that what you carry from here will help you stay the course.

Personal Virtues, Public Vices

It is, of course, extremely pleasurable to hear pleasant comments made about oneself. (I have had a good deal of experience with the contrary kind of comments in the last year or so.) I do not for one minute believe that I deserve such compliments, but I thank Congressman Kemp, the Ethics and Public Policy Center, and, especially, the selection committee. I am a willing beneficiary of their excessively generous appraisal.

Like most human actions, their award has produced unintended and unanticipated consequences. It stimulated me to reflect a bit about integrity and courage in the light of what I have learned in the past two years about public life. This led to my setting down some reflections on the complicated relations between personal and public morality. I propose now to impose those reflections on you, my captive audience.

I shall, as professors are wont to do, make an argument in three parts: first, I shall emphasize that there are important differences between personal and public morality.

Second, I shall insist that in public life, extremism in pursuit of virtue surely *is* a vice.

Third, I will suggest that accommodation, tolerance, compromise, patience, moderation, are not only political virtues, but that, in normal times and places, they are the *only* means to the public good.

The case I shall make is not new, but it is the kind of argument that requires repeating from time to time to guard oneself against the temptations of impatience, intolerance, intransigence.

Address before the annual Ethics and Public Policy Dinner at which the writer received the Shelby Cullom Davis Award, Washington, D.C., September 29, 1982.

The difference between personal and public morality has been observed by many—most—students of politics. Aristotle noted that "the good citizen may not be a good man" if he serves a bad state. The same distinction is present in the idea of "reasons of state" that almost always purport to justify acts—undertaken in the name of a government—like lying, cheating, stealing, murdering, that sort of thing—that would be not at all acceptable if committed by private persons.

The distinction between private virtue and the public good, valid everywhere I believe, is basic to our own liberal democratic tradition. It is present in the fundamental assumptions of market economics, liberal democracy, cultural freedom—all of which assume that the public good is best served by the pursuit of personal interests.

Adam Smith believed an "invisible hand" assured that an economy based on the decisions of millions of self-interested individuals would produce more wealth for more people than a centralized economy based on the decisions of planners consciously seeking the public good. James Madison made a parallel argument: that the public interest was best served when each pursued his private interests through politics. John Stuart Mill wrote persuasively in his essay *On Liberty* that truth and such public goods as innovation, science, progress, were better served through the pursuit of individual interests. In the eighteenth century, wags were wont to sum up this principle by saying that public virtues flowed from private vices.

The distinction between private and public morality is by no means limited to the Aristotelian and utilitarian traditions: it underpinned Machiavelli's advice to *The Prince* and Reinhold Niebuhr's analyses and recommendations in *Moral Man and Immoral Society*.

When the distinction between private and public morality is denied or confused, strange errors result.

One standard confusion is to imagine that the personal habits of rulers determine the moral quality of a government. As in, "Joseph Stalin was a very sincere person"; or "Heinrich Himmler loved animals"; or "the Commandant at Auschwitz was a good family man"; or "the Khmer Rouge led simple, dedicated lives." Each may be true, as has been asserted. None is really relevant to the institutionalized mass murder for which the individuals were responsible. I am not suggesting that the character of leaders has no relevance to the moral quality of regimes, but that no simple, direct relationship exists.

The flip side of the tendency to infer qualities of regimes from life styles of leaders is the demand that government leaders (and their wives or husbands and children) reflect preferred public virtues in their private lives.

Americans tend to judge the moral quality of government by the personal morality and motives of its high officials, and to assume that when good men with good motives and good personal habits lead a government, good government results. But this is not necessarily the case.

Take, for example, the United Nations, that extraordinary organization to which I am posted, as the saying goes. Although I am known as a critic, I should like to state it here and now that the United Nations is filled with good people. The secretary general, Javier Pérez de Cuellar, is a man of great intelligence, high integrity; he is an unusually fair, reasonable, decent man. The Secretariat is staffed by agreeable, intelligent persons about as reasonable and efficient as other large bureaucracies with which I have been associated.

The same can be said for my colleagues, the representatives of other countries: most are talented, experienced, multilingual diplomats—thoroughly civilized people.

The moral problems posed by the United Nations' double standards are institutional—rooted in the subtle institutionalized interactions of power and persuasion, of menaces and promises, as one colleague put it—in the ongoing game of bloc politics.

There are important differences between moral governments and moral individuals. Private morality depends on such personal virtues as honesty, generosity, reliability, industry, fortitude. Public morality concerns the polity and depends on institutional relationships and policies which protect and enhance democracy, freedom, accountability, order, justice. A responsible person, for example, is one who can be counted on to honor his obligations, but a responsible government is one in which rulers are held accountable through periodic competitive elections for their use of public office. It is true that the moral quality of rulers sets the tone for the political class and seeps downward into the political culture, and it is also not unreasonable to suppose that the values and predispositions present in leaders' private lives affect their behavior in office as well as out.

It is also true that a relatively virtuous people is necessary to a virtuous republic. But a passion for the cultivation of personal virtue has never been the distinguishing characteristic of political men, and it is unreasonable to expect that political leaders will be paragons of personal virtue as well as persons of high political skill. Politicians are at least as prone as others to ordinary hypocrisy and venality, and their personal moral failings should be treated in about the same way as the comparable failings of others in the society. There is no good reason, for example, to judge a congressman who is unfaithful to his wife more (or less) harshly than a private citizen guilty of the same offense—*providing* that the congressman has not used the powers of office to expedite his pursuit of pleasure.

Personal virtue is a good in itself, but it is not a sufficient means to the end of good government and one might as well be clear about it.

A second, more perilous distortion of the relationship between private and public virtue results from extremism in the use of public power to promote private virtue. If virtuous persons can be produced by governments, then there is no excuse for a government failing to abolish evil—no excuse except that the very effort increases the evil it seeks to eliminate.

History is pockmarked not only with moral revolutionaries' failing to achieve their goals through government, but with the terrible consequences of their efforts. Heretics tortured and killed in Spain's Inquisition, Calvin's Geneva, Robespierre's France, Moscow's purge trials, Pol Pot's murderous Utopia, testify to the consequences of the unfettered pursuit of virtue through politics.

Governments can encourage the cultivation of private virtue. They can provide a framework in which we may pursue virtue (or happiness), but they cannot make us virtuous (or happy), and the effort to use the coercive power of government for that purpose not only fails to produce private morality, it undermines public morality as well.

The public good differs from private good, above all, because it concerns the whole society. It is necessarily inclusive and takes account of all sectors of a society. Our political system is structured not merely to represent all interests, but to take account of the well-being of all parts—and to force on governments minimal concern for and responsiveness to all

216

sectors of a complex society—all geographic sectors, all economic, all social groups.

No autocratic government, no purely majoritarian government provides as much continuing institutional protection for all social groups as does the American political system. Our institutions, as our morality, do not permit, much less encourage, governments to sacrifice a generation, a class, or economic well-being for a decade; government does not permit our decision makers to be too generous with someone else's interests, or too indifferent to them.

All this is directly relevant to many criticisms with which the Reagan administration is faced today. There is abroad the perennial, predictable disappointment of some, perhaps many, of the strongest, earliest supporters of Ronald Reagan with his presidency, his administration, its policies. It has been nearly two years, and some portion of what was desired has not been achieved. We are reproached for having been taken in by the bureaucracy and done in by creeping moderation. We are reproached for having failed to adequately increase defense spending, decrease taxes, trim the budget and the bureaucracy, prohibit abortion, permit prayers in school.

These charges are, in a certain sense, true.

And it is surely true that some of the president's earliest, strongest, sincerest supporters have been disappointed.

The administration of Ronald Reagan has not, in the last twenty months, either dismantled the Soviet Empire or the welfare state, disavowed accumulated entitlements, or definitively disestablished the liberal establishment. We *have* accomplished a good deal in all these domains: inflation is down and military strength is up; ordinary Americans keep a larger share of their earnings, but taxes are still too high. Economic growth—including the number of employed—is up, but so is unemployment. The expansion of Soviet power has been halted—no new country has been added to the Soviet sphere since Ronald Reagan became president—but they have not yet been persuaded to forgo aggressive expansionist policies in Central America, Africa, Southeast Asia. Certainly we have not restored U.S. influence in the United Nations to levels comparable to that of the Soviets.

We have achieved no miracles because we are not miracle makers, conducted no revolutions because we are not revolutionaries. To the contrary, most of the people in the administration can be accurately described as conservatives of various breeds—lib-cons, neo-cons, trad-cons, and con-cons. There are also authentic moderates in our midst. These personal political convictions matter, and matter quite a lot, but they do not alter the fact that we operate in a system that systematically moderates initiatives for change.

Respect for all groups in a society, and institutionalized deference to their views and values, is built into the American political system. The interlocking system of elections, jurisdictions, and decisions not only reminds our elected officials of this close dependence on the people, as John Adams intended, it also effectively blocks a pattern of decisions that ignore any significant portion of the electorate. The fact that our congressmen are constrained as much by their constituencies as their parties means that, to pass its bills, this administration, like any other, must put together shifting coalitions. That makes it—the executive department—sensitive to almost everyone.

The dynamics of the American political system precludes the successful practice of purist politics and guarantees chronic frustration to all persons whose public policy preferences deviate significantly from the status quo. That includes most of us some of the time and some of us most of the time. The Reagan administration is no more able than any other to escape the powerful moderating, aggregating, consensus-building pressures that the American system puts on our governors. And that, as always, is a good thing for the United States.

* * * *

Now, I've learned a bit in the past two years about the hazards of media exposure. And I can imagine that some reporter somewhere, hearing of my remarks, will write a lead or a headline which says: "Kirkpatrick Says Administration Has Failed to Achieve Its Goals."

And, at the next presidential press conference, someone who read that story will ask the president: "Do you agree with Ambassador Kirkpatrick's judgment that the administration has failed in all spheres?"

And, after the president says, "I certainly don't agree with that statement, but I feel sure she didn't say that," someone, somewhere, will write a lead that says: "The president today disagreed sharply with his representative to the United Nations," and so forth.

It is not so; I don't think the Reagan administration has failed. I think President Ronald Reagan has made substantial progress toward accomplishing almost all the administration's objectives. I think he is not only a principled man with a clear sense of the public good, but a leader skilled at compromise and consensus building. In the long run these skills, operating in this system, will produce the results his strongest supporters—including me—desire, providing, of course, that we do not grow too discouraged, too impatient, too soon. Remember, no important goals have been abandoned nor principles compromised.

I have at the United Nations a colleague with a new technique for dealing with the problem of being misunderstood or having his words and phrases taken out of context. His statements consist entirely of words and phrases which sound good no matter how they are excerpted, no matter whether they are understood or misunderstood. He makes whole speeches of words like:

> Human aspirations . . . economic development . . . solar
> energy . . . an end to hunger . . . rededicating ourselves
> and redoubling our efforts . . . world community . . .
> global negotiations . . . ideals and dreams. . . .

That sort of thing. It doesn't even matter in what order they occur. I swear, if anyone interprets my speech as an attack on the administration—or anyone—my next speech will consist entirely of "world community . . . constructive solutions . . . solar energy . . . human aspirations . . . hopes and dreams . . . global negotiations. . . ."

Good night.

Index

Acheson, Dean, 94
Adams, John, 210, 218
Adenauer, Konrad, 179
Afghanistan, 12–13, 31, 33, 35, 70–75, 86, 110, 112, 131–32, 141, 158, 171–72, 199, 201, 206
  Afghan Communist party, 73
  Afghans, 69
  freedom fighters, 74, 131
Africa, 13, 18, 21, 24–25, 27, 29, 32, 35, 86, 96, 98, 101, 141, 158–61, 165, 179, 195, 217
  front-line states, 162
  northern, 138–39
  southern, 16, 22, 165
  See also South Africa
Agence-France Presse, 58
Algeria, 179, 199
Algiers, 156
Allen, William Sheridan, 64
Amin, Idi, 49
Amnesty International, 51–52
Anarchy, 47, 139
Angola, 13, 35, 159, 195, 199, 205
Anti-Defamation League of B'nai B'rith, 109
Anti-Semitism, 143
Apartheid. See South Africa
Arab countries, 111, 138, 140, 149, 174
Arab-African bloc, 98

Arab-Israeli conflict, 95, 110–12, 127–28, 132
Arce, Bayardo, 192
Arenas, Reinaldo, 50
Aristotle, 214
  Aristotelianism, 214
ASEAN (Association of South East Asian Nations), 83–84, 99–100, 102
Asia, 13, 18, 21, 29, 32, 169–71
  East, 23
  South, 70, 138
  Southeast, 217
  Southwest, 23, 131
Atlantic Alliance. See NATO
Atlantic Charter, 176, 178
Augustine, Saint, 209
Auschwitz, 214
Australia, 84, 170
Autocracy, 22, 101, 217

Bahais, 69
Balance of power, 176
Balfour Declaration, 146
Balkans, 131, 137
Banfield, Edward, 175
Bangladesh, 137, 170
Barrios, Jaime Chomorro, 66
Bayh, Birch, 9
Begin, Menachem, 143, 148–49
  See also Israel

Beirut, Lebanon, 150
Belgium, 178–79
Ben Gurion, David, 145, 151
    See also Israel
Benin, 199
Bernanos, George, 202
Bevin, Ernest, 95
Bhutan, 171
Bill of Rights, U.S.
    See United States
Biological Weapons Convention of 1972, 72
Blum, Yehuda, 115
Bolivia, 50
Boniato prison, 51
Borge, Tomas, 65, 204
Brandt Commission, 170
Brazil, 24
Broder, David, 117
Bunche, Ralph, 112
Burke, Edmund, 40, 173
Burma, 171
Bush, George, 9

Calvin, John, 216
Camp David Accords, 111, 114, 128–29, 137, 143, 148–51
Campins, Luis Herrera, 52
Canada, 84, 161
Cancún, Mexico, 89–90
Capital (financial), 22
Caribbean, 16, 23, 32, 83
Caribbean Basin Initiative, 192
Carter administration, 9–10, 13, 17, 20, 30, 33, 39, 149–51
Casa award, 50
Casa de las Americas, 50
Castro, Fidel, 50, 52, 196
    See also Cuba
Central America, 16, 32, 35, 57, 59, 114, 182–83, 189–91, 193–97, 202–3, 217
    See also El Salvador; Nicaragua
Central Asia (U.S.S.R.), 73
Chad, 27, 86, 131, 139, 158
Chile, 50, 80, 100

China, People's Republic of, 74, 75, 86, 169, 171–72, 196
Chomorro, Pedro Joaquin, 63, 66
Chomorro y Cardinale, Pablo Joaquin, 195–96
Choto, Carlos, 58
Christendom, 3
Christianity, 93
Christian Democratic party, 58
Church, Frank, 9
Churchill, Winston, 177
Cold war, 28, 33
Colonialism, 18–19, 27, 165
Combinado des Este prison, 51
Commentary, 39
Commonwealth, British, 105
Communism, 29, 178
Communism and the Elephant, 85
Communists, 42, 73, 196, 205
Communist countries, 21
Communist movement, 4
Conflict
    exacerbation, 97
    resolution, 95, 97, 116, 206
Congo, 95, 179, 199
Congress, U.S.
    See United States
Consent of the governed, 5, 15, 46, 49
Constitution, 3, 6, 43–44
Constitution, U.S.
    See United States
COPPAL, 64
Correlation of forces, 14, 32
Correspondence of Poems, A (Cuadra), 51
Costa Rica, 187–88
Counterrevolutionaries, 65, 184, 204
Croce, Benedetto, 3
Cuadra, Angel, 50–51
Cuba, 13, 27, 35, 50–52, 84–86, 114, 140, 159, 179, 186–91, 195–96, 199, 205
    See also Castro, Fidel
Cuban missile crisis, 179–80
Culver, John, 9
Cyprus, 95
Czechoslovakia, 29, 177–78

Dangerous Place, A (Moynihan), 97, 100
Dangerous Place, A (Yeselson and Gaglione), 97
Daoud government, 71–72
Daughters of the American Revolution (DAR), 89
Decolonization, 80, 86, 91, 101–2, 158, 178
de Gaulle, Charles, 12, 179–80
Democracy
 people's, 6, 205
 representative, 92
 social, 6
Democratic capitalism, 171
Democratic civilization, 31
Democratic institutions, 28, 98, 117, 155
Democratic party (U.S.) 8–11, 17, 100
Democratic Turnhalle Alliance (DTA), 160, 163–64
Desnoes, Edmundo, 50
Détente, 13, 30, 33
Deterrence, 29
Development (economic), 21, 25, 33, 35, 48, 87, 89–91, 98, 101–2, 134, 144, 148, 170–71, 195, 206, 219
Dictatorship, 15, 22, 42, 54–55, 57, 59, 63, 67
Disarmament, 13, 85, 182
Dr. Seuss, 117
Dome of the Rock, 135
Dominican Republic, 80, 100
Duarte, José Napoleón, 55–56
Due process, 43, 62

East-West relations
 East-West conflict, 7, 13–16, 20–21, 25, 32, 34, 70, 83, 171
EC. *See* European Community
Economics, liberal, 13, 214
Economist, The, 203
Egypt, 111, 128, 137, 143, 148–49, 152, 179
Egyptian-Israeli treaty, 132
El Nuevo Diario, 206
El Salvador, 50, 54, 58–61, 141, 174, 183, 186–92, 197, 201–2, 204–5
 Chalatenango, 58
 Cinquera, 58
 land reform, 55, 57
 Popular Liberation Forces (FPL), 187
 San Jose de las Flores, 58
 San Pedro Perulapan, 58
Enders, Thomas, 191, 195
Ethics, 42
 of motives, 42–43
 of consequences, 42–43
Ethics and Public Policy Center, 213
Ethiopia, 13, 35, 86
Europe, 16, 21, 30, 35, 50, 88, 93, 102, 116, 160, 175–76, 178, 181–82
 Eastern, 28–29, 83, 94, 177–78
 Western, 29–30, 96, 169, 172, 177–78, 180
European Community (EC, "the 10"), 83–84, 102, 174

Falkland Islands, 103
Fanaticism, 22, 143
Farabundi Marti National Liberation and Democratic Revolutionary Fronts (FMLN/FDR), 54, 57–59, 203
Fascism, 114
Federalist, The, 44
Feisal, Emir, 146
Fertile Crescent, 131
Fields, W. C., 155
Fiji, 116
Ford, Gerald R., 9
Founding Fathers. *See* United States
France, 4, 12, 40–41, 44–45, 161, 178–80, 215
Franco-Mexican communiqué, 174
Frankfurter, Felix, 146–47
Free societies, 28, 31, 36
Freedom, 3, 7, 16, 20, 23–25, 27, 45, 63, 65, 73, 101, 146, 180, 182, 184, 197
 as political goal, 35–36, 47–49, 54–55, 91, 132–33, 214–15
 as a way of life, 210–11

Freedom House, 67
French PEN Club, 51–52
French Revolution, 40–41, 44
Freud, Sigmund, 175
From My Wheelchair (Valladares), 51
Fromm, Erich, 211

Gandhi, Mahatma, 18, 86
Gaza, 128–29, 152
    See also Israel
Geneva, 27, 41, 48, 50, 118, 156, 215
Geneva Protocol of 1925, 72
Genghis Khan, 71
Georgetown University, 139, 149, 155, 210–11
Germany, 60
    East 13, 27, 199, 205
    Thalburg, 64
    West, 161
Global Negotiations, 85, 89, 219
Golan Heights, 95–97, 103, 112–16, 119–22, 124–25, 174
    See also Israel
Gorky, U.S.S.R., 49
Great Britain, 5, 99, 146, 161, 175, 178–80
Great Depression, 8
Greece, 94, 177, 211–12
Grenada, 86, 199, 205
Group of 77 (G-77), 83–85, 102, 174
Guasule crossing, 188
Guatemala, 50, 187
    Guatemala City, 188
Gurkha mercenaries, 195
Guyana, 84, 194

Habib, Philip C., 132, 150
Haig, Alexander M., Jr., 15, 90, 118, 137, 192, 206
Hallucinations (Arenas), 50
Hammadi, Sa'dun, 134
Hassan, King, II, 27
Havana, 52, 186, 205
Heart with Which I Live, The (Valladares), 51
Hebrews, 212
Hegel, Georg W. F., 80

Heiden, Konrad, 63
Helsinki Final Act, 125
Higher Islamic Council, 136
Himmler, Heinrich, 214
Hispanics, 9–10
Historical method, 35
    historicism, 35
Hitler, Adolf, 60
Hmong tribe, 69
Hobbes, Thomas, 47
Hollywood Screen Actors' Guild, 10
Honduras, 67, 187–89, 193
Hong Kong, 24, 171
Hoover, Herbert, 11
Horton the Elephant, 117–18
How Israel Destroyed the Palestinian Elephants, 85
Hudson, Michael, 139–40, 149
Human rights, 39, 42–44, 48, 52–54, 64–65, 69
    as policy, 20, 39, 43
    as political weapon, 48
    violations of, abuses of, 20, 46–48, 50, 55, 62, 68, 125
    See also Rights; Right of; Right to; United Nations, Human Rights Commission
Hungary, 29, 178
Hussein, King, 96, 138

Impromptus (Cuadra), 50
Independence, 13, 18, 61, 65, 86, 91–92, 97, 101, 140, 143–44, 164, 166, 195, 202, 205
    as movements, 18
    as U.S. policy, 19, 25, 36, 72–75, 198–99
    as U.S. policy (Middle East), 131–33
    as U.S. policy (Europe), 175, 178
    in Central America, 183, 186
India, 86, 170, 199
India-Pakistan War (1965), 95
Indian Ocean, 16
Indians, Nicaraguan, 69, 191
Indochina, 178
Indonesia, 171
Inter-American Treaty of Reciprocal

Assistance. *See* Rio Treaty
International Atomic Energy Agency (IAEA), 110, 133–34
International Development Bank, 185
International law, 72, 194
International PEN Club, 52
International Red Cross, 71, 93
International Secretariat, 93
Iran, 12, 20, 31, 131–32, 139–40, 172, 205
  hostages in, 31
Iraq, 131–34, 139
Iron Curtain, 177
Islam, 135, 137
  Islamic fundamentalism, 73, 138–40
Islamic Conference, 83–84, 102
Isolationism, 11, 21, 182
Israel, 84–86, 95–96, 98, 103, 110–22, 124–25, 127–34, 136–37, 139–42, 144–51, 179
  Founding Fathers, 147
  Jewish voters, 10
  Proclamation of Independence, 147
  See also Begin, Menachem; Ben Gurion, David; Gaza; Golan Heights; Meir, Golda; West Bank
Italy, 3–5, 137, 179
Ivory Coast, 24

Japan, 4, 21, 84, 171–72
Jefferson, Thomas, 210
Jehovah's Witnesses, 69
Jerusalem, 135–36
Jihad, 141
Johnson, Samuel, 209
Jordan, 96, 114, 124, 128–29, 139, 142, 152
Jordan, Vernon, 17
Judeo-Christian civilization, 142, 212
Justice, 43, 146, 215
  social, 56

Kabul, 71, 73–74
Kampuchea (Cambodia), 13, 49, 81, 86, 110, 172, 195, 199, 201

Kant, Immanuel, 162
Karmal, Babrak, 72–73
Kaunda, Kenneth, 18
Kemp, Jack, 213
Kennedy, John F., 179
  administration, 179
Kennedy Years, The (Schlesinger), 29
Kenya, 24
Khalid, King, 138
Khmer Rouge, 214
Khomeini, Ayatollah, 20, 39, 138, 140, 142
Khrushchev, Nikita, 29
King, Martin Luther, Jr., 18
Kirghiz tribe, 74
Kissinger, Henry, 33
Kittani, President Ismat, 126
Korea, South, 24, 169, 171
Korean War, 180–81
Kristol, Irving, 10

La noche de los asesinos (Triana), 50
Labor Committee for Truman, 10
Laos, 13, 172, 199, 205
Latin America, 23, 48, 50, 56, 83–84, 100, 116, 175
Law, 46–48
  equal protection of, 49
Law of the sea treaty, 85
League of Nations, 93
Lebanon, 95, 131–32, 139, 150, 152, 156, 158
Legitimacy, 5, 12, 111, 116, 140
Lenin, Nikolai, 60
Liberalism, 6, 87
Liberation movements, national, 159, 178–79
Liberty, 5, 40–41, 43, 46, 181
Liberty Prize, 51
Libya, 27, 86, 131, 139–40, 158, 199
Linowitz, Sol, 149
Llopis, Rogelio, 50
Locke, John, 47
Love Life of the Elephant, The, 85
Loyola, Ignatius, 210

McGovern, George, 9
McHenry, Donald, 100
Machiavelli, Nicolo, 3–4, 31, 214
Macmillan, Harold, 179
Madagascar, 199
Madison, James, 214
Majority rule, 122, 217
Malawi, 24
Malaysia, 24, 171
Managua (Nicaragua), 186–87, 191
Market forces, 24
Market system, 6
Marshall, George C., 95
Marshall Plan, 29
Marsiglio of Padua, 3
Marti, Farabundo, 203–5
Martinez, Ana Guadalupe, 203
Martinez, Ana Maria de, 202
Marx, Karl, 80
Marxism-Leninism 4–7, 13–14, 36,
    59, 65, 160, 186, 203–4
    See also Soviet Union
Mecca, 146
Meir, Golda, 145
Memorias del subdesarrollo (Des-
    noes), 50
Mexico, 84, 191–92, 199, 204
    Mexican Communist party, 204
Middle East, 22–23, 32, 35, 96, 110–
    11, 114, 119, 122, 127, 131–32,
    134–35, 138–39, 143–44, 146–47,
    174
Military establishment, 11
Military rule, 56
Mill, John Stuart, 4, 214
Miskito Indians, 64–65, 67–68
    See also Nicaragua
Monde, Le, 51
Montesquieu, Baron, 47
Moral Man and Immoral Society
    (Niebuhr), 214
Morality, 41, 45
    private (personal), 40, 43, 213–15
    public (political) 40, 43, 213–15
Moranzanist Front for the Libera-
    tion of Honduras (FMLH), 189
Morocco, 27, 139, 143
Mosca, Gaetano, 4

Moscow, 60, 72–74, 204–5, 216
    See also Soviet Union
Moynihan, Daniel Patrick, 80, 87,
    97, 100
Mozambique, 199, 205
MPLA-PT (Liberation of Angola–
    Party of Labor), 159
Mubarak, Hosni, 137
Muller, Herbert, 36
Mussolini, Benito, 60
Myrdal, Gunnar, 18

Namibia (South West Territories),
    16, 25–26, 60, 85–86, 91, 97, 156–
    66
    Council on Namibia, UN, 160
    Council on Namibia Report, 156
Nasser, Gamal Abdul, 83, 86
National integrity, 69
National interest, 20, 105
National purpose, 103
National security, 21
National Urban League, 17, 19
NATO (North Atlantic Treaty Or-
    ganization), 28–30, 174–82
Nazi party, 63–64
Nazi Seizure of Power, The: The
    Experience of a Single German
    Town (Allen), 64
Nazi-Soviet Pact, 32
Nehru, Jawarhalal, 83, 86
Nepal, 171
Netherlands, the, 178
Neutralism 182
Neutrality, 16, 181
New International Economic Order,
    42, 88–90
New Left, 30
New World Information Order, 89–
    90
New York City, 48, 55, 116
New Zealand, 84, 170
Nicaragua, 13, 20, 60, 62–69, 84, 86,
    114, 141, 183–93, 195–96, 198–201,
    205–6
    Council of Elders, 67
    Council of State, 66
    CUS (Nicaraguan trade union), 66

MDN (Movimiento Democratic Nacional), 66, 204
National Guard, 64
See also Miskito Indians; Rio Coco; Sandinista; Sandino; Sandinismo; Somoza; Somozista party
Nicolson, Harold, 93
Niebuhr, Reinhold, 214
Nimeiry, President Mohammed Gaafar el-, 138
Non-Aligned Conference, 52
Non-Aligned Movement (NAM), 72, 83–87, 89, 102
Nonalignment, 16, 201
Nonintervention, principles of, 194–95, 198–99, 201
Non-Proliferation Treaty, 133
North Atlantic Treaty Organization. See NATO
North-South relations; conflict, 32, 90, 174
Novak, Michael, 118
Nuclear nonproliferation, 110, 133
Nuclear reactor, Iraqi, 131–33
Nuclear weapons, 131

OAS (Organization of American States), 179, 192–93, 203
OAS Charter, 193
OECD (Organization for Economic Cooperation and Development), 170
On Liberty (Mill), 214
OPEC (Organization of Petroleum Exporting Countries), 30
Organization of African Unity (OAU), 25, 27, 83–84, 102
Organization of American States. See OAS
Ortega Saavedra, Daniel, 20, 39, 64, 183–84, 190–91, 198, 200, 202, 205
Ortega, Humberto, 20, 39, 191–92, 203–4
Ortega y Gasset, Jose, 212
Orwell, George, 170, 173
Ovambo tribe, 158–59
Owen, Robert, 41

Padilla, Heberto, 50
Paine, Thomas, 44
Pakistan, 74, 171
Palestine, 126–27, 140, 146, 149
nationalism, 139–41
people, 86, 91, 122, 128, 140, 142, 150
Palestine Liberation Organization. See PLO
Panama, 84, 199
Paris, 50, 52
Partisan Review, 50
Pastora, Eden, 63
Penn, William, 93
Pérez de Cuellar, Javier, 215
Persian Gulf, 16, 70, 131
Philippines, 171
Pita, Juana Rosa, 50
Plato, 43
PLO (Palestine Liberation Organization), 85, 98–99, 112, 114, 141–43, 150
Point Four Program, 102
Poland, 14, 125, 158, 176–77, 205
Political parties, 8
Political philosophy, 3–4, 42–43, 215
Political pornography, 65
Political purism, 42–44, 91, 218
Political systems
American, 218
Latin, 11
Politics
practical, 5
primacy of, 4
Postwar era, 28, 30, 102
Pot, Pol, 49, 216
Poverty, 22–23, 41, 89–90
Power, 7, 14, 27, 36, 45, 49, 55, 57, 62–63, 67, 119, 139, 197–98, 215–16
arbitrary, 5–6, 65
imperial, 35
just, 5
Prensa, La, 65–66, 185, 196, 206
Present at the Creation (Acheson), 94
Press, free, 6, 20, 62, 155, 197

Prince, The (Machiavelli), 214
Prisoner of Castro (Valladares), 51
Prolegomenon to the Elephant, 85
Propaganda, 58, 175
Public force, 41
Public good, 4, 7, 213–16
Public opinion data, 10
Public opinion polls
  Gallup, Roper, Yankelovich, 11
Puerto Rico, 86

Qaddafi, Muammar, 138–39

Racial discrimination, 17
Racial equality, 18
Radical socialism, 23
Radio Catolica, 185
Radio Sandino, 64
Rama Indians, 67
Reagan, Ronald, 5, 7–11, 28, 30–31,
  89–90, 135–36, 150, 192
Reagan administration, 7–8, 12, 14–
  17, 19–20, 23, 25, 32, 45, 80, 100,
  121, 133, 158, 169, 172, 217–19
Reagan coalition, 9
Red Army. *See* Soviet Army
Religion, free, 6, 20, 62
Republican party (U.S.), 8–11, 100
Revolution, 27, 40, 50, 67, 140–41,
  217
Rhetoric, 41, 44, 92, 98
  Libyan, 87
Ricardo, David, 6
Right of
  free speech, 6, 20, 43, 62
  security of person, 41, 47, 54, 63
  See also Human rights; Right to;
    Rights
Right to
  development, 80
  education, 41, 49
  leisure, 41
  life, 41, 46, 49, 54
  privacy, 41
  property, 41
  pursuit of happiness, 46
  self-government, 41, 47, 92, 98,
    125, 166
  understand, 115

  See also Human rights; Right of;
    Rights
Rights, 5, 33, 39, 43–44, 46, 48, 129
  and goals, 39
  bills of, 6
  economic, 42
  maritime, 128
  minority, 122
  of Englishmen, 44
  universal declaration of, 41
  See also Human rights; Right of;
    Right to
Rio Coco (Nicaragua), 64–65
Rio Treaty (Inter-American Treaty
  of Reciprocal Assistance), 177,
  179
Ripoll, Carlos, 50–51
Robelo, Alfonso, 63, 66
Robespierre, 215
Rodriguez, Carlos Rafael, 52
Rome, 3, 16, 60, 212
Romero, Archbishop Oscar, 58
Romero, General Carlos Humberto,
  56
Roosevelt, Franklin D., 8, 176–77
Rousseau, Jean-Jacques, 47
Rule of law, 3, 6, 20–21, 49, 62, 181
Rusk, Dean, 179

Sadat, Anwar, 137–38, 142–44, 148–
  49
Sakharov, Andrei, 49
Salvadoran National Guard, 58
San José (Costa Rica), 188
Sandinismo, 195–96
  See also Nicaragua
Sandinista Defense Committees, 64,
  67
Sandinista party, 60, 63–68, 184–86,
  188, 198, 203, 205, 206
  See also Nicaragua
Sandino, Augusto Cesar, 204–5
Sartori, Giovanni, 4
Saudi Arabia, 85, 140, 142
Scammon, Richard, 101
Schifter, Richard, 118
Schlesinger, Arthur, 29
Schultz, George, 150
Security, international, 119, 124,

129, 132–33, 143, 148, 181–83, 190, 200
Self-determination, 25, 36, 41, 61, 92, 98, 101, 159, 194, 201
Seychelles, 199
Shah of Iran, 138–39
Shanghai communiqué, 172
Sharm el-Sheikh, 143
Sinai, 128, 143, 148
Singapore, 24, 171
Smith, Adam, 6, 214
Social contract, 3
Social Democratic party, 66, 204
Social hierarchy, 42
Social mobility, 90
Solidarity, 15, 98
Solzhenitsyn, Aleksandr, 30, 69
Somalia, 86
Somoza, Anastasio, 63, 66, 185–86, 196
  See also Nicaragua
Somozista party, 65, 67
  See also Nicaragua
South Africa, 26, 48, 83–86, 156, 159–60, 162, 165, 167, 168
  Afrikaaners, 158
  apartheid, 26, 48–49
  Horn of Africa, 16, 22
South America, 21, 32, 48
Sovereignty, 86, 93, 128, 183, 201–2, 204
Soviet Army, 74, 94, 177
Soviet bloc, 14, 23, 29, 35, 102, 141, 165, 217
Soviet Union, 4–5, 12–16, 27, 34, 49, 70–75, 81, 86–89, 96, 98–101, 112, 114, 116, 132, 139, 142–43, 159–60, 171–72, 174–75, 178, 182, 195, 199, 205–6
  Brezhnev Doctrine, 13
  military strength, 11, 32
  See also Marxism-Leninism; Moscow; Stalin, Joseph
Spanish Inquisition, 216
Sri Lanka, 24, 171
SS-20s, 35
Stalin, Joseph, 29, 32, 94, 177, 214
  See also Soviet Union
Sudan, 139

Suez, 179
Sumo Indians, 67
Sunni Moslems, 139
SWAPO, 159–61
Syria, 96, 99, 113–14, 116, 120, 132, 139–40, 199

Taiwan, 24, 171–72
Taiwan Relations Act, 172
Tehran, 12
Territorial integrity, 68, 72, 194, 198–99
Terrorism, 131, 143
Thailand, 171
Third World, 30, 35, 87, 103, 116
Thompson, John, 211
Time, 79
Tito, Joseph, 83, 86
Tocqueville, Alexis de, 84
Totalitarianism, 31, 64, 67, 69, 71, 178, 184, 202, 205
Toynbee, Arnold, 114
Trial and Error (Weizmann), 146
Triana, José, 50
Truman, Harry, 10, 102, 151
Truman Doctrine, 178
Turkey, 94, 177
Turtle Bay, 80, 92, 98–99, 109, 111
Tyranny, 22, 47, 63, 69

Uganda, 49, 199
UNEAC (Union de Escritores y Artistas de Cuba) prize, 50
Unheavenly City (Banfield), 175
UNITA (National Union for the Total Independence of Angola), 159
United Nations (UN), 23, 25, 33, 46, 48–49, 52–53, 72, 75, 79–81, 85–101, 116–25, 127–30, 147, 149, 155–58, 161–62, 164, 166–67, 175, 177, 179–80, 183, 193–95, 200–201, 215, 219
  Economic and Social Council, 79, 90
  General Assembly, 50, 82–84, 88, 96, 102–3, 110–12, 115, 119–20, 122, 126, 160, 167–68, 174, 191
  Human Rights Commission, 41–42, 50, 79, 118

Partition Plan of 1947, 147
Secretariat, 215
U.S. Mission to, 81, 109, 117
Special Committee to Investigate
    Israeli Practices in the Occupied
    Territories, 111
United Nations Charter, 70, 81, 94,
    95, 115, 120, 124–25, 129, 167–68,
    178, 183–84, 193–94, 198–200
    Article 51, 72–74
United Nations Security Council,
    82–83, 94–96, 112, 115–16, 119,
    124, 131, 133–34, 136, 160, 162–65,
    167–68, 174, 190, 193, 198, 200–
    201, 205
    Resolution 338, 113, 120, 125,
        127–28, 132, 150
    Resolution 242, 113, 120–21, 125,
        127–28, 132, 150
    Resolution 435, 156–57, 161
    Resolution 497, 120–21, 125
United States, 4–5, 18–23, 25, 27–29,
    32, 36, 46, 51, 57, 75, 80–81, 84–
    85, 88–89, 95–96, 98–99, 103, 111–
    12, 114, 117, 119–21, 124, 132–34,
    138, 140, 157, 159, 161–63, 169,
    172, 174–76, 178–86, 190–92, 194–
    99, 202, 206, 218
    Bill of Rights, 43
    Constitution, 43–44, 210
    Declaration of Independence, 46
    defense spending, 11–12
    and democratic tradition, 4, 14,
        20–22, 25, 98, 101, 206, 214–15
    Department of State, 79, 87
    Founding Fathers, 43–44, 80, 145,
        210
    government, democratic, 3, 5, 39
    House of Representatives, 8
    military and political power, 30
    Senate, 8, 104
    See also Washington, D.C.
Universal Declaration of Human
    Rights, 52, 125, 203, 205
Urcuyo, President Francisco Mali-
    nos, 63, 185
Urquhart, Brian, 94
Uruguay, 189
U.S.S.R. See Soviet Union

Utopianism, 35, 41–42, 49, 95, 176,
    216

Valladares, Armando, 51, 52
Vanuatu, 103
Venezuela, 52, 60
Vietnam, 13, 28, 86, 114, 172, 194,
    199, 205
Vietnam War, 11, 14, 30, 33, 169,
    180–81
Violence, 22, 47, 56–57, 64, 69, 123,
    135–36

Wakhan corridor, 74
Wall Street Journal, 202
Warsaw, 177
Washington, George, 93, 175, 210
Washington, D.C., 25, 104, 116, 135,
    151
Washington Post, 117
Weapons development and deploy-
    ment, 16
Weizmann, Chaim, 145–47, 151
Weizmann Institute of Science, 145
    See also Israel
West Bank, 48, 128–29, 152
    See also Golan Heights; Israel
Western civilization, 3–4, 212
Western Contact Group, 26, 159,
    161, 165–66
Western Hemisphere, 13, 56, 177
Western Sahara, 27
World Health Organization, 79
World War I, 131, 137, 146, 175
World War II, 34, 93, 101, 114, 169,
    175–76, 178, 181
World Zionist Organization, 146
Writers and Scholars International,
    52

Yalta, 94, 176–77
Yemen, 13, 35, 140
Yeselson and Gaglione, 97
Young, Andrew, 100

Zambia, 18
Zimbabwe, 26, 60, 199
Zionism, 42, 86, 110, 114, 141, 146
"Zionism Is Racism," 112

The Author

Jeane Jordan Kirkpatrick was appointed United States Permanent Representative to the United Nations by President Ronald Reagan in January 1981, the first woman ever to serve in this post. She is a member of the Cabinet and the National Security Council.

Ambassador Kirkpatrick is on leave as Leavey University Professor, Georgetown University, and as resident scholar at the American Enterprise Institute, both in Washington, D.C. Her academic career as a political scientist also includes associations with Trinity College, the University of Aix-Marseilles, France, the Georgetown Center for Strategic and International Studies, the Robert Taft Institute of Government (trustee), and the Twentieth Century Fund's Task Force on the Presidential Election Process (co-chairman). Her principal publications include *Dictatorships and Double Standards* (1982), *The New Presidential Elite* (1976), *Political Woman* (1974), *Leader and Vanguard in Mass Society* (1971), and numerous articles in *Commentary*, *The Journal of Politics*, *The American Political Science Review*, and *The New Republic*. She has lectured extensively throughout the United States and in Europe, Africa, Asia, and Latin America on political and international issues, frequently under the aegis of the U.S. Information Agency and the Department of State. During the 1980 presidential campaign she was a member of President Reagan's foreign policy advisory group.

Ambassador Kirkpatrick was born in Duncan, Oklahoma. She attended Stephens College (Missouri) and received her B.A. degree from Barnard College (1948), her M.A. (1950) and Ph.D. (1968) from Columbia University. She is married to Dr. Evron M. Kirkpatrick, longtime executive director of the American Political Science Association, now resident scholar at the American Enterprise Institute and president of the Helen Dwight Reid Educational Foundation. They have three sons and reside in Bethesda, Maryland.